BASIC DOCUMENTS

On

International Protection

Of Human Rights

Louis B. Sohn

Bemis Professor of International Law
Harvard University

and

Thomas Buergenthal

Professor of International Law
Faculty of Law and Jurisprudence
State University of New York at Buffalo

THE BOBBS-MERRILL COMPANY, INC.
A SUBSIDIARY OF HOWARD W. SAMS & CO., INC.
PUBLISHERS • INDIANAPOLIS • KANSAS CITY • NEW YORK

CONTEMPORARY LEGAL EDUCATION SERIES

ADVISORY COMMITTEE

ISBN-0-672-81890-6
Copyright © 1973
by The Bobbs-Merrill Company, Inc.
Printed in the United States of America
All Rights Reserved

Preface

This collection of documents is a companion volume to the coursebook published by the present Editors under the title *International Protection of Human Rights.* It was designed for classroom use in conjunction with that book as well as a separate reference work for basic international human rights texts.

The availability of various other collections of human rights documents, some more general and others limited to one category of documents, convinced the Editors that there was no need to duplicate these efforts and explains their decision to prepare this more specialized volume. It includes, in addition to the Charter of the United Nations, the major human rights conventions and declarations of the United Nations as well as the relevant instruments of the European and Inter-American regional systems for the protection of human rights. Also reproduced are the rules of procedure of the institutions that were established pursuant to the provisions of these instruments. The final section of the book contains selected historical documents of continuing scholarly interest.

Cambridge, Massachusetts
Buffalo, New York
March, 1973

Louis B. Sohn
Thomas Buergenthal

Table of Contents

PART I. UNITED NATIONS

SECTION A. DOCUMENTS OF GENERAL SCOPE

1. CHARTER OF THE UNITED NATIONS

Signed at San Francisco, 26 June 1945. Entered into force on 24 October 1945. US Department of State, Facsimile of the Charter of the United Nations 1-20 (US, DOS, Publ. 2368). Amendments to Articles 23, 27 and 61 of the Charter, adopted by the General Assembly on 17 December 1963, came into force on 31 August 1965. 16 UST 1134 (1965). An amendment to Article 109 of the Charter, adopted by the General Assembly on 20 December 1965, came into force on 12 June 1968. 20 GAOR, Suppl. No. 14(A/6014), at 90-91.

WE THE PEOPLES OF THE UNITED NATIONS

DETERMINED

to save succeeding generations from the scourge of war, which twice in our lifetime has brought untold sorrow to mankind, and

to reaffirm faith in fundamental human rights, in the dignity and worth of the human person, in the equal rights of men and women and of nations large and small, and

to establish conditions under which justice and respect for the obligations arising from treaties and other sources of international law can be maintained, and

to promote social progress and better standards of life in larger freedom,

AND FOR THESE ENDS

to practice tolerance and live together in peace with one another as good neighbors, and

to unite our strength to maintain international peace and security, and

to ensure, by the acceptance of principles and the institution of methods, that armed force shall not be used, save in the common interest, and

to employ international machinery for the promotion of the economic and social advancement of all peoples,

HAVE RESOLVED TO COMBINE OUR EFFORTS TO ACCOMPLISH THESE AIMS.

Accordingly, our respective Governments, through representatives assembled in the city of San Francisco, who have exhibited their full powers found to be in good and due form, have agreed to the present Charter of the United Nations and do hereby establish an international organization to be known as the United Nations.

Chapter I.   Purposes and Principles

Article 1

The Purposes of the United Nations are:

1.   To maintain international peace and security, and to that end: to take effective collective measures for the prevention and removal of threats to the peace, and for the suppression of acts of aggression or other breaches of the peace, and to bring about by peaceful means, and in conformity with the principles of justice and international law, adjustment or settlement of international disputes or situations which might lead to a breach of the peace;

2.   To develop friendly relations among nations based on respect for the principle of equal rights and self-determination of peoples, and to take other appropriate measures to strengthen universal peace;

3.   To achieve international cooperation in solving international problems of an economic, social, cultural, or humanitarian character, and in promoting and encouraging respect for human rights and for fundamental freedoms for all without distinction as to race, sex, language, or religion; and

4.   To be a center for harmonizing the actions of nations in the attainment of these common ends.

Article 2

The Organization and its Members, in pursuit of the Purposes stated in Article 1, shall act in accordance with the following Principles.

1.   The Organization is based on the principle of the sovereign equality of all its Members.

2.   All Members, in order to ensure to all of them the rights and benefits resulting from membership, shall fulfil in good faith the obligations assumed by them in accordance with the present Charter.

3.   All Members shall settle their international disputes by peaceful means in such a manner that international peace and security, and justice, are not endangered.

4.   All Members shall refrain in their international relations from the threat or use of force against the territorial integrity or political independence of any state, or in any other manner inconsistent with the Purposes of the United Nations.

5. All Members shall give the United Nations every assistance in any action it takes in accordance with the present Charter, and shall refrain from giving assistance to any state against which the United Nations is taking preventive or enforcement action.

6. The Organization shall ensure that states which are not Members of the United Nations act in accordance with these Principles so far as may be necessary for the maintenance of international peace and security.

7. Nothing contained in the present Charter shall authorize the United Nations to intervene in matters which are essentially within the domestic jurisdiction of any state or shall require the Members to submit such matters to settlement under the present Charter; but this principle shall not prejudice the application of enforcement measures under Chapter VII.

Chapter II. Membership
Article 3

The original Members of the United Nations shall be the states which, having participated in the United Nations Conference on International Organization at San Francisco, or having previously signed the Declaration by United Nations of January 1, 1942, sign the present Charter and ratify it in accordance with Article 110.

Article 4

1. Membership in the United Nations is open to all other peace-loving states which accept the obligations contained in the present Charter and, in the judgment of the Organization, are able and willing to carry out these obligations.

2. The admission of any such state to membership in the United Nations will be effected by a decision of the General Assembly upon the recommendation of the Security Council.

Article 5

A Member of the United Nations against which preventive or enforcement action has been taken by the Security Council may be suspended from the exercise of the rights and privileges of membership by the General Assembly upon the recommendation of the Security Council. The exercise of these rights and privileges may be restored by the Security Council.

Article 6

A Member of the United Nations which has persistently violated the Principles contained in the present Charter may be expelled from the Organization by the General Assembly upon the recommendation of the Security Council.

CHAPTER III. ORGANS

Article 7

1. There are established as the principal organs of the United Nations: a General Assembly, a Security Council, an Economic and Social Council, a Trusteeship Council, an International Court of Justice, and a Secretariat.

2. Such subsidiary organs as may be found necessary may be established in accordance with the present Charter.

Article 8

The United Nations shall place no restrictions on the eligibility of men and women to participate in any capacity and under conditions of equality in its principal and subsidiary organs.

CHAPTER IV. THE GENERAL ASSEMBLY

Composition

Article 9

1. The General Assembly shall consist of all the Members of the United Nations.

2. Each Member shall have not more than five representatives in the General Assembly.

Functions and Powers

Article 10

The General Assembly may discuss any questions or any matters within the scope of the present Charter or relating to the powers and functions of any organs provided for in the present Charter, and, except as provided in Article 12, may make recommendations to the Members of the United Nations or to the Security Council or to both on any such questions or matters.

Article 11

1. The General Assembly may consider the general principles of cooperation in the maintenance of international peace and security, including the principles governing disarmament and the regulation of armaments, and may make recommendations with regard to such principles to the Members or to the Security Council or to both.

2. The General Assembly may discuss any questions relating to the maintenance of international peace and security brought before it by any Member of the United Nations, or by the Security Council, or by a state which is not a Member of the United Nations in accordance with Article 35, paragraph 2, and, except as provided in Article 12, may make recommendations with regard to any such questions to the state or states concerned or to the Security Council or to both. Any such question on which action is necessary shall be referred to the Security Council by the General Assembly either before or after discussion.

3. The General Assembly may call the attention of the Security Council to situations which are likely to endanger international peace and security.

4. The powers of the General Assembly set forth in this Article shall not limit the general scope of Article 10.

Article 12

1. While the Security Council is exercising in respect of any dispute or situation the functions assigned to it in the present Charter, the General Assembly shall not make any recommendation with regard to that dispute or situation unless the Security Council so requests.

2. The Secretary-General, with the consent of the Security Council, shall notify the General Assembly at each session of any matters relative to the maintenance of international peace and security which are being dealt with by the Security Council and shall similarly notify the General Assembly, or the Members of the United Nations if the General Assembly is not in session, immediately the Security Council ceases to deal with such matters.

Article 13

1. The General Assembly shall initiate studies and make recommendations for the purpose of:

a. promoting international cooperation in the political field and encouraging the progressive development of international law and its codification;

b. promoting international cooperation in the economic, social, cultural, educational, and health fields, and assisting in the realization of human rights and fundamental freedoms for all without distinction as to race, sex, language, or religion.

2. The further responsibilities, functions, and powers of the General Assembly with respect to matters mentioned in paragraph 1 (b) above are set forth in Chapters IX and X.

Article 14

Subject to the provisions of Article 12, the General Assembly may recommend measures for the peaceful adjustment of any situation, regardless of origin, which it deems likely to impair the general welfare or friendly relations among nations, including situations resulting from a violation of the provisions of the present Charter setting forth the Purposes and Principles of the United Nations.

Article 15

1. The General Assembly shall receive and consider annual and special reports from the Security Council; these reports shall include an account of the measures that the Security Council has decided upon or taken to maintain international peace and security.

2. The General Assembly shall receive and consider reports from the other organs of the United Nations.

Article 16

The General Assembly shall perform such functions with respect to the international trusteeship system as are assigned to it under Chapters XII and XIII, including the approval of the trusteeship agreements for areas not designated as strategic.

Article 17

1. The General Assembly shall consider and approve the budget of the Organization.

2. The expenses of the Organization shall be borne by the Members as apportioned by the General Assembly.

3. The General Assembly shall consider and approve any financial and budgetary arrangements with specialized agencies referred to in Article 57 and shall examine the administrative budgets of such specialized agencies with a view to making recommendations to the agencies concerned.

Voting

Article 18

1. Each member of the General Assembly shall have one vote.

2. Decisions of the General Assembly on important questions shall be made by a two-thirds majority of the members present and voting. These questions shall include: recommendations with respect to the maintenance of international peace and security, the election of the non-permanent members of the Security Council, the election of the members of the Economic

and Social Council, the election of members of the Trusteeship Council in accordance with paragraph 1 (c) of Article 86, the admission of new Members to the United Nations, the suspension of the rights and privileges of membership, the expulsion of Members, questions relating to the operation of the trusteeship system, and budgetary questions.

3. Decisions on other questions, including the determination of additional categories of questions to be decided by a two-thirds majority, shall be made by a majority of the members present and voting.

Article 19

A Member of the United Nations which is in arrears in the payment of its financial contributions to the Organization shall have no vote in the General Assembly if the amount of its arrears equals or exceeds the amount of the contributions due from it for the preceding two full years. The General Assembly may, nevertheless, permit such a Member to vote if it is satisfied that the failure to pay is due to conditions beyond the control of the Member.

Procedure

Article 20

The General Assembly shall meet in regular annual sessions and in such special sessions as occasion may require. Special sessions shall be convoked by the Secretary-General at the request of the Security Council or of a majority of the Members of the United Nations.

Article 21

The General Assembly shall adopt its own rules of procedure. It shall elect its President for each session.

Article 22

The General Assembly may establish such subsidiary organs as it deems necessary for the performance of its functions.

Chapter V. The Security Council

Composition

Article 23

[1945 text]

1. The Security Council shall consist of eleven Members of the United Nations. The Republic of China, France, the

[1963 text]

1. The Security Council shall consist of fifteen Members of the United Nations. The Republic of China, France, the

Union of Soviet Socialist Republics, the United Kingdom of Great Britain and Northern Ireland, and the United States of America shall be permanent members of the Security Council. The General Assembly shall elect six other Members of the United Nations to be non-permanent members of the Security Council, due regard being specially paid, in the first instance to the contribution of Members of the United Nations to the maintenance of international peace and security and to the other purposes of the Organization, and also to equitable geographical distribution.

2. The non-permanent members of the Security Council shall be elected for a term of two years. In the first election of the non-permanent members, however, three shall be chosen for a term of one year. A retiring member shall not be eligible for immediate re-election.

Union of Soviet Socialist Republics, the United Kingdom of Great Britain and Northern Ireland, and the United States of America shall be permanent members of the Security Council. The General Assembly shall elect ten other Members of the United Nations to be non-permanent members of the Security Council, due regard being specially paid, in the first instance to the contribution of Members of the United Nations to the maintenance of international peace and security and to the other purposes of the Organization, and also to equitable geographical distribution.

2. The non-permanent members of the Security Council shall be elected for a term of two years. In the first election of the non-permanent members after the increase of the membership of the Security Council from eleven to fifteen, two of the four additional members shall be chosen for a term of one year. A retiring member shall not be eligible for immediate re-election.

3. Each member of the Security Council shall have one representative.

Functions and Powers

Article 24

1. In order to ensure prompt and effective action by the United Nations, its Members confer on the Security Council primary responsibility for the maintenance of international peace and security, and agree that in carrying out its duties under this responsibility the Security Council acts on their behalf.

2. In discharging these duties the Security Council shall act in accordance with the Purposes and Principles of the United

Nations. The specific powers granted to the Security Council for the discharge of these duties are laid down in Chapters VI, VII, VIII, and XII.

3. The Security Council shall submit annual and, when necessary, special reports to the General Assembly for its consideration.

Article 25

The Members of the United Nations agree to accept and carry out the decisions of the Security Council in accordance with the present Charter.

Article 26

In order to promote the establishment and maintenance of international peace and security with the least diversion for armaments of the world's human and economic resources, the Security Council shall be responsible for formulating, with the assistance of the Military Staff Committee referred to in Article 47, plans to be submitted to the Members of the United Nations for the establishment of a system for the regulation of armaments.

Voting

Article 27

1. Each member of the Security Council shall have one vote.

[1945 text]

2. Decisions of the Security Council on procedural matters shall be made by an affirmative vote of seven members.

3. Decisions of the Security Council on all other matters shall be made by an affirmative vote of seven members including the concurring votes of the permanent members; provided that, in decisions under Chapter VI, and under paragraph 3 of Article 52, a party to a dispute shall abstain from voting.

[1963 text]

2. Decisions of the Security Council on procedural matters shall be made by an affirmative vote of nine members.

3. Decisions of the Security Council on all other matters shall be made by an affirmative vote of nine members including the concurring votes of the permanent members; provided that, in decisions under Chapter VI, and under paragraph 3 of Article 52, a party to a dispute shall abstain from voting.

Procedure

Article 28

1. The Security Council shall be so organized as to be able to function continuously. Each member of the Security Council

shall for this purpose be represented at all times at the seat of the Organization.

2. The Security Council shall hold periodic meetings at which each of its members may, if it so desires, be represented by a member of the government or by some other specially designated representative.

3. The Security Council may hold meetings at such places other than the seat of the Organization as in its judgment will best facilitate its work.

Article 29

The Security Council may establish such subsidiary organs as it deems necessary for the performance of its functions.

Article 30

The Security Council shall adopt its own rules of procedure, including the method of selecting its President.

Article 31

Any Member of the United Nations which is not a member of the Security Council may participate, without vote, in the discussion of any question brought before the Security Council whenever the latter considers that the interests of that Member are specially affected.

Article 32

Any Member of the United Nations which is not a member of the Security Council or any state which is not a Member of the United Nations, if it is a party to a dispute under consideration by the Security Council, shall be invited to participate, without vote, in the discussion relating to the dispute. The Security Council shall lay down such conditions as it deems just for the participation of a state which is not a Member of the United Nations.

CHAPTER VI.   PACIFIC SETTLEMENT OF DISPUTES

Article 33

1. The parties to any dispute, the continuance of which is likely to endanger the maintenance of international peace and security, shall, first of all, seek a solution by negotiation, enquiry, mediation, conciliation, arbitration, judicial settlement, resort to regional agencies or arrangements, or other peaceful means of their own choice.

2. The Security Council shall, when it deems necessary, call upon the parties to settle their dispute by such means.

Article 34

The Security Council may investigate any dispute, or any situation which might lead to international friction or give rise to a dispute, in order to determine whether the continuance of the dispute or situation is likely to endanger the maintenance of international peace and security.

Article 35

1. Any Member of the United Nations may bring any dispute, or any situation of the nature referred to in Article 34, to the attention of the Security Council or of the General Assembly.

2. A state which is not a Member of the United Nations may bring to the attention of the Security Council or of the General Assembly any dispute to which it is a party if it accepts in advance, for the purposes of the dispute, the obligations of pacific settlement provided in the present Charter.

3. The proceedings of the General Assembly in respect of matters brought to its attention under this Article will be subject to the provisions of Articles 11 and 12.

Article 36

1. The Security Council may, at any stage of a dispute of the nature referred to in Article 33 or of a situation of like nature, recommend appropriate procedures or methods of adjustment.

2. The Security Council should take into consideration any procedures for the settlement of the dispute which have already been adopted by the parties.

3. In making recommendations under this Article the Security Council should also take into consideration that legal disputes should as a general rule be referred by the parties to the International Court of Justice in accordance with the provisions of the Statute of the Court.

Article 37

1. Should the parties to a dispute of the nature referred to in Article 33 fail to settle it by the means indicated in that Article, they shall refer it to the Security Council.

2. If the Security Council deems that the continuance of the dispute is in fact likely to endanger the maintenance of international peace and security, it shall decide whether to take action

under Article 36 or to recommend such terms of settlement as it may consider appropriate.

Article 38

Without prejudice to the provisions of Articles 33 to 37, the Security Council may, if all the parties to any dispute so request, make recommendations to the parties with a view to a pacific settlement of the dispute.

CHAPTER VII. ACTION WITH RESPECT TO THREATS TO THE PEACE, BREACHES OF THE PEACE, AND ACTS OF AGGRESSION

Article 39

The Security Council shall determine the existence of any threat to the peace, breach of the peace, or act of aggression and shall make recommendations, or decide what measures shall be taken in accordance with Articles 41 and 42, to maintain or restore international peace and security.

Article 40

In order to prevent an aggravation of the situation, the Security Council may, before making the recommendations or deciding upon the measures provided for in Article 39, call upon the parties concerned to comply with such provisional measures as it deems necessary or desirable. Such provisional measures shall be without prejudice to the rights, claims, or position of the parties concerned. The Security Council shall duly take account of failure to comply with such provisional measures.

Article 41

The Security Council may decide what measures not involving the use of armed force are to be employed to give effect to its decisions, and it may call upon the Members of the United Nations to apply such measures. These may include complete or partial interruption of economic relations and of rail, sea, air, postal, telegraphic, radio, and other means of communication, and the severance of diplomatic relations.

Article 42

Should the Security Council consider that measures provided for in Article 41 would be inadequate or have proved to be inadequate, it may take such action by air, sea, or land forces as may be necessary to maintain or restore international peace and security. Such action may include demonstrations, blockade, and other operations by air, sea, or land forces of Members of the United Nations.

Article 43

1. All Members of the United Nations, in order to contribute to the maintenance of international peace and security, undertake to make available to the Security Council, on its call and in accordance with a special agreement or agreements, armed forces, assistance, and facilities, including rights of passage, necessary for the purpose of maintaining international peace and security.

2. Such agreement or agreements shall govern the numbers and types of forces, their degree of readiness and general location, and the nature of the facilities and assistance to be provided.

3. The agreement or agreements shall be negotiated as soon as possible on the initiative of the Security Council. They shall be concluded between the Security Council and Members or between the Security Council and groups of Members and shall be subject to ratification by the signatory states in accordance with their respective constitutional processes.

Article 44

When the Security Council has decided to use force it shall, before calling upon a Member not represented on it to provide armed forces in fulfillment of the obligations assumed under Article 43, invite that Member, if the Member so desires, to participate in the decisions of the Security Council concerning the employment of contingents of that Member's armed forces.

Article 45

In order to enable the United Nations to take urgent military measures, Members shall hold immediately available national air-force contingents for combined international enforcement action. The strength and degree of readiness of these contingents and plans for their combined action shall be determined, within the limits laid down in the special agreement or agreements referred to in Article 43, by the Security Council with the assistance of the Military Staff Committee.

Article 46

Plans for the application of armed force shall be made by the Security Council with the assistance of the Military Staff Committee.

Article 47

1. There shall be established a Military Staff Committee to advise and assist the Security Council on all questions relating

to the Security Council's military requirements for the maintenance of international peace and security, the employment and command of forces placed at its disposal, the regulation of armaments, and possible disarmament.

2.   The Military Staff Committee shall consist of the Chiefs of Staff of the permanent members of the Security Council or their representatives. Any Member of the United Nations not permanently represented on the Committee shall be invited by the Committee to be associated with it when the efficient discharge of the Committtee's responsibilities requires the participation of that Member in its work.

3.   The Military Staff Committee shall be responsible under the Security Council for the strategic direction of any armed forces placed at the disposal of the Security Council. Questions relating to the command of such forces shall be worked out subsequently.

4.   The Military Staff Committee, with the authorization of the Security Council and after consultation with appropriate regional agencies, may establish regional subcommittees.

Article 48

1.   The action required to carry out the decisions of the Security Council for the maintenance of international peace and security shall be taken by all the Members of the United Nations or by some of them, as the Security Council may determine.

2.   Such decisions shall be carried out by the Members of the United Nations directly and through their action in the appropriate international agencies of which they are members.

Article 49

The Members of the United Nations shall join in affording mutual assistance in carrying out the measures decided upon by the Security Council.

Article 50

If preventive or enforcement measures against any state are taken by the Security Council, any other state, whether a Member of the United Nations or not, which finds itself confronted with special economic problems arising from the carrying out of those measures shall have the right to consult the Security Council with regard to a solution of those problems.

Article 51

Nothing in the present Charter shall impair the inherent right of individual or collective self-defense if an armed attack occurs against a Member of the United Nations, until the Security Council has taken the measures necessary to maintain international peace and security. Measures taken by Members in the exercise of this right of self-defense shall be immediately reported to the Security Council and shall not in any way affect the authority and responsibility of the Security Council under the present Charter to take at any time such action as it deems necessary in order to maintain or restore international peace and security.

CHAPTER VIII. REGIONAL ARRANGEMENTS

Article 52

1.   Nothing in the present Charter precludes the existence of regional arrangements or agencies for dealing with such matters relating to the maintenance of international peace and security as are appropriate for regional action, provided that such arrangements or agencies and their activities are consistent with the Purposes and Principles of the United Nations.

2.   The Members of the United Nations entering into such arrangements or constituting such agencies shall make every effort to achieve pacific settlement of local disputes through such regional arrangements or by such regional agencies before referring them to the Security Council.

3.   The Security Council shall encourage the development of pacific settlement of local disputes through such regional arrangements or by such regional agencies either on the initiative of the states concerned or by reference from the Security Council.

4.   This Article in no way impairs the application of Articles 34 and 35.

Article 53

1.   The Security Council shall, where appropriate, utilize such regional arrangements or agencies for enforcement action under its authority. But no enforcement action shall be taken under regional arrangements or by regional agencies without the authorization of the Security Council, with the exception of measures against any enemy state, as defined in paragraph 2 of this Article, provided for pursuant to Article 107 or in regional arrangements directed against renewal of aggressive policy on the part of any such state, until such time as the Organization may, on request of the Governments concerned, be charged with the responsibility for preventing further aggression by such a state.

2.   The term enemy state as used in paragraph 1 of this Article applies to any state which during the Second World War has been an enemy of any signatory of the present Charter.

Article 54

The Security Council shall at all times be kept fully informed of activities undertaken or in contemplation under regional arrangements or by regional agencies for the maintenance of international peace and security.

CHAPTER IX. INTERNATIONAL ECONOMIC AND SOCIAL COOPERATION

Article 55

With a view to the creation of conditions of stability and well-being which are necessary for peaceful and friendly relations among nations based on respect for the principle of equal rights and self-determination of peoples, the United Nations shall promote:

a. higher standards of living, full employment, and conditions of economic and social progress and development;

b. solutions of international economic, social, health, and related problems; and international cultural and educational cooperation; and

c. universal respect for, and observance of, human rights and fundamental freedoms for all without distinction as to race, sex, language or religion.

Article 56

All Members pledge themselves to take joint and separate action in cooperation with the Organization for the achievement of the purposes set forth in Article 55.

Article 57

1. The various specialized agencies, established by intergovernmental agreement and having wide international responsibilities, as defined in their basic instruments, in economic, social, cultural, educational, health, and related fields, shall be brought into relationship with the United Nations in accordance with the provisions of Article 63.

2. Such agencies thus brought into relationship with the United Nations are hereinafter referred to as specialized agencies.

Article 58

The Organization shall make recommendations for the coordination of the policies and activities of the specialized agencies.

Article 59

The Organization shall, where appropriate, initiate negotiations among the states concerned for the creation of any new specialized agencies required for the accomplishment of the purposes set forth in Article 55.

Article 60

Responsibility for the discharge of the functions of the Organization set forth in this Chapter shall be vested in the General Assembly and, under the authority of the General Assembly, in the Economic and Social Council, which shall have for this purpose the powers set forth in Chapter X.

CHAPTER X. THE ECONOMIC AND SOCIAL COUNCIL

Composition

Article 61

[1945 text]

1. The Economic and Social Council shall consist of eighteen Members of the United Nations elected by the General Assembly.

2. Subject to the provisions of paragraph 3, six members of the Economic and Social Council shall be elected each year for a term of three years. A retiring member shall be eligible for immediate re-election.

3. At the first election, eighteen members of the Economic and Social Council shall be chosen. The term of office of six members so chosen shall expire at the end of one year, and of six other members at the end of two years, in accordance with arrangements made by the General Assembly.

[1963 text]

1. The Economic and Social Council shall consist of twenty-seven* Members of the United Nations elected by the General Assembly.

2. Subject to the provisions of paragraph 3, nine members of the Economic and Social Council shall be elected each year for a term of three years. A retiring member shall be eligible for immediate re-election.

3. At the first election after the increase in the membership of the Economic and Social Council from eighteen to twenty-seven members, in addition to the members elected in place of the six members whose term of office expires at the end of that year, nine additional members shall be elected. Of these nine additional

---

* In 1971, the General Assembly adopted another amendment increasing the number to fifty-four. GA Resolution 2847 (XXVI), 20 December 1971; 26 GAOR, Suppl. No. 29 (A/8429), at 67-68.

members, the term of office of
three members so elected shall
expire at the end of one year,
and of three other members at
the end of two years, in accordance with arrangements
made by the General Assembly.

4. Each member of the Economic and Social Council shall
have one representative.

Functions and Powers

Article 62

1. The Economic and Social Council may make or initiate
studies and reports with respect to international economic, social,
cultural, educational, health, and related matters and may make
recommendations with respect to any such matters to the General Assembly, to the Members of the United Nations, and to
the specialized agencies concerned.

2. It may make recommendations for the purpose of promoting respect for, and observance of, human rights and fundamental freedoms for all.

3. It may prepare draft conventions for submission to the
General Assembly, with respect to matters falling within its
competence.

4. It may call, in accordance with the rules prescribed by the
United Nations, international conferences on matters falling
within its competence.

Article 63

1. The Economic and Social Council may enter into agreements with any of the agencies referred to in Article 57, defining
the terms on which the agency concerned shall be brought into
relationship with the United Nations. Such agreements shall be
subject to approval by the General Assembly.

2. It may coordinate the activities of the specialized agencies
through consultation with and recommendations to such agencies
and through recommendations to the General Assembly and to
the Members of the United Nations.

Article 64

1. The Economic and Social Council may take appropriate
steps to obtain regular reports from the specialized agencies. It
may make arrangements with the Members of the United Nations and with the specialized agencies to obtain reports on the

steps taken to give effect to its own recommendations and to recommendations on matters falling within its competence made by the General Assembly.

2. It may communicate its observations on these reports to the General Assembly.

Article 65

The Economic and Social Council may furnish information to the Security Council and shall assist the Security Council upon its request.

Article 66

1. The Economic and Social Council shall perform such functions as fall within its competence in connection with the carrying out of the recommendations of the General Assembly.

2. It may, with the approval of the General Assembly, perform services at the request of Members of the United Nations and at the request of specialized agencies.

3. It shall perform such other functions as are specified elsewhere in the present Charter or as may be assigned to it by the General Assembly.

Voting

Article 67

1. Each member of the Economic and Social Council shall have one vote.

2. Decisions of the Economic and Social Council shall be made by a majority of the members present and voting.

Procedure

Article 68

The Economic and Social Council shall set up commissions in economic and social fields and for the promotion of human rights, and such other commissions as may be required for the performance of its functions.

Article 69

The Economic and Social Council shall invite any Member of the United Nations to participate, without vote, in its deliberations on any matter of particular concern to that Member.

Article 70

The Economic and Social Council may make arrangements for representatives of the specialized agencies to participate without vote, in its deliberations and in those of the commissions established by it, and for its representatives to participate in the deliberations of the specialized agencies.

Article 71

The Economic and Social Council may make suitable arrangements for consultation with non-governmental organizations which are concerned with matters within its competence. Such arrangements may be made with international organizations and, where appropriate, with national organizations after consultation with the Member of the United Nations concerned.

Article 72

1. The Economic and Social Council shall adopt its own rules of procedure, including the method of selecting its President.

2. The Economic and Social Council shall meet as required in accordance with its rules, which shall include provision for the convening of meetings on the request of a majority of its members.

CHAPTER XI. DECLARATION REGARDING NON-SELF-GOVERNING TERRITORIES

Article 73

Members of the United Nations which have or assume responsibilities for the administration of territories whose peoples have not yet attained a full measure of self-government recognize the principle that the interests of the inhabitants of these territories are paramount, and accept as a sacred trust the obligation to promote to the utmost, within the system of international peace and security established by the present Charter, the well-being of the inhabitants of these territories, and, to this end:

a.   to ensure, with due respect for the culture of the peoples concerned, their political, economic, social, and educational advancement, their just treatment, and their protection against abuses;

b.   to develop self-government to take due account of the political aspirations of the peoples, and to assist them in the progressive development of their free political institutions, according to the particular circumstances of each territory and its peoples and their varying stages of advancement;

c.   to further international peace and security;

d.   to promote constructive measures of development, to encourage research, and to cooperate with one another and, when and where appropriate, with specialized international bodies with a view to the practical achievement of the social, economic, and scientific purposes set forth in this Article; and

e. to transmit regularly to the Secretary-General for information purposes, subject to such limitation as security and constitutional considerations may require, statistical and other information of a technical nature relating to economic, social, and educational conditions in the territories for which they are respectively responsible other than those territories to which Chapters XII and XIII apply.

Article 74

Members of the United Nations also agree that their policy in respect of the territories to which this Chapter applies, no less than in respect of their metropolitan areas, must be based on the general principle of good-neighborliness, due account being taken of the interests and well-being of the rest of the world, in social, economic, and commercial matters.

CHAPTER XII. INTERNATIONAL TRUSTEESHIP SYSTEM

Article 75

The United Nations shall establish under its authority an international trusteeship system for the administration and supervision of such territories as may be placed thereunder by subsequent individual agreements. These territories are hereinafter referred to as trust territories.

Article 76

The basic objectives of the trusteeship system, in accordance with the Purposes of the United Nations laid down in Article 1 of the present Charter, shall be:

a. to further international peace and security;

b. to promote the political, economic, social, and educational advancement of the inhabitants of the trust territories, and their progressive development towards self-government or independence as may be appropriate to the particular circumstances of each territory and its peoples and the freely expressed wishes of the peoples concerned, and as may be provided by the terms of each trusteeship agreement;

c. to encourage respect for human rights and for fundamental freedoms for all without distinction as to race, sex, language, or religion, and to encourage recognition of the interdependence of the peoples of the world; and

d.   to ensure equal treatment in social, economic, and commercial matters for all Members of the United Nations and their nationals, and also equal treatment for the latter in the administration of justice, without prejudice to the attainment of the foregoing objectives and subject to the provisions of Article 80.

Article 77

1.   The trusteeship system shall apply to such territories in the following categories as may be placed thereunder by means of trusteeship agreements:

     a.   territories now held under mandate;

     b.   territories which may be detached from enemy states as a result of the Second World War; and

     c.   territories voluntarily placed under the system by states responsible for their administration.

2.   It will be a matter for subsequent agreement as to which territories in the foregoing categories will be brought under the trusteeship system and upon what terms.

Article 78

The trusteeship system shall not apply to territories which have become Members of the United Nations, relationship among which shall be based on respect for the principle of sovereign equality.

Article 79

The terms of trusteeship for each territory to be placed under the trusteeship system, including any alteration or amendment, shall be agreed upon by the states directly concerned, including the mandatory power in the case of territories held under mandate by a Member of the United Nations, and shall be approved as provided for in Articles 83 and 85.

Article 80

1.   Except as may be agreed upon in individual trusteeship agreements, made under Articles 77, 79, and 81, placing each territory under the trusteeship system, and until such agreements have been concluded, nothing in this Chapter shall be construed in or of itself to alter in any manner the rights whatsoever of any states or any peoples or the terms of existing international instruments to which Members of the United Nations may respectively be parties.

2.   Paragraph 1 of this Article shall not be interpreted as giving grounds for delay or postponement of the negotiation and

conclusion of agreements for placing mandated and other territories under the trusteeship system as provided for in Article 77.

Article 81

The trusteeship agreement shall in each case include the terms under which the trust territory will be administered and designate the authority which will exercise the administration of the trust territory. Such authority, hereinafter called the administering authority, may be one or more states or the Organization itself.

Article 82

There may be designated, in any trusteeship agreement, a strategic area or areas which may include part or all of the trust territory to which the agreement applies, without prejudice to any special agreement or agreements made under Article 43.

Article 83

1. All functions of the United Nations relating to strategic areas, including the approval of the terms of the trusteeship agreements and of their alteration or amendment, shall be exercised by the Security Council.

2. The basic objectives set forth in Article 76 shall be applicable to the people of each strategic area.

3. The Security Council shall, subject to the provisions of the trusteeship agreements and without prejudice to security considerations, avail itself of the assistance of the Trusteeship Council to perform those functions of the United Nations under the trusteeship system relating to political, economic, social, and educational matters in the strategic areas.

Article 84

It shall be the duty of the administering authority to ensure that the trust territory shall play its part in the maintenance of international peace and security. To this end the administering authority may make use of volunteer forces, facilities, and assistance from the trust territory in carrying out the obligations towards the Security Council undertaken in this regard by the administering authority, as well as for local defense and the maintenance of law and order within the trust territory.

Article 85

1. The functions of the United Nations with regard to trusteeship agreements for all areas not designated as strategic, including the approval of the terms of the trusteeship agreements and

of their alteration or amendment, shall be exercised by the General Assembly.

2. The Trusteeship Council, operating under the authority of the General Assembly, shall assist the General Assembly in carrying out these functions.

CHAPTER XIII. THE TRUSTEESHIP COUNCIL

Composition

Article 86

1. The Trusteeship Council shall consist of the following Members of the United Nations:

   a.   those Members administering trust territories;

   b.   such of those Members mentioned by name in Article 23 as are not administering trust territories; and

   c.   as many other Members elected for three-year terms by the General Assembly as may be necessary to ensure that the total number of members of the Trusteeship Council is equally divided between those Members of the United Nations which administer trust territories and those which do not.

2. Each member of the Trusteeship Council shall designate one specially qualified person to represent it therein.

Functions and Powers

Article 87

The General Assembly and, under its authority, the Trusteeship Council, in carrying out their functions, may:

   a.   consider reports submitted by the administering authority;

   b.   accept petitions and examine them in consultation with the administering authority;

   c.   provide for periodic visits to the respective trust territories at times agreed upon with the administering authority; and

   d.   take these and other actions in conformity with the terms of the trusteeship agreements.

Article 88

The Trusteeship Council shall formulate a questionnaire on the political, economic, social, and educational advancement of the inhabitants of each trust territory, and the administering authority for each trust territory within the competence of the General Assembly shall make an annual report to the General Assembly upon the basis of such questionnaire.

Voting

Article 89

1. Each member of the Trusteeship Council shall have one vote.

2. Decisions of the Trusteeship Council shall be made by a majority of the members present and voting.

Procedure

Article 90

1. The Trusteeship Council shall adopt its own rules of procedure including the method of selecting its President.

2. The Trusteeship Council shall meet as required in accordance with its rules, which shall include provision for the convening of meetings on the request of a majority of its members.

Article 91

The Trusteeship Council shall, when appropriate, avail itself of the assistance of the Economic and Social Council and of the specialized agencies in regard to matters with which they are respectively concerned.

CHAPTER XIV. THE INTERNATIONAL COURT OF JUSTICE

Article 92

The International Court of Justice shall be the principal judicial organ of the United Nations. It shall function in accordance with the annexed Statute, which is based upon the Statute of the Permanent Court of International Justice and forms an integral part of the present Charter.

Article 93

1. All Members of the United Nations are *ipso facto* parties to the Statute of the International Court of Justice.

2. A state which is not a Member of the United Nations may become a party to the Statute of the International Court of Justice on conditions to be determined in each case by the General Assembly upon the recommendation of the Security Council.

Article 94

1. Each Member of the United Nations undertakes to comply with the decision of the International Court of Justice in any case to which it is a party.

2. If any party to a case fails to perform the obligations incumbent upon it under a judgment rendered by the Court, the

other party may have recourse to the Security Council, which may, if it deems necessary, make recommendations or decide upon measures to be taken to give effect to the judgment.

Article 95

Nothing in the present Charter shall prevent Members of the United Nations from entrusting the solution of their differences to other tribunals by virtue of agreements already in existence or which may be concluded in the future.

Article 96

1. The General Assembly or the Security Council may request the International Court of Justice to give an advisory opinion on any legal question.

2. Other organs of the United Nations and specialized agencies, which may at any time be so authorized by the General Assembly, may also request advisory opinions of the Court on legal questions arising within the scope of their activities.

Chapter XV. The Secretariat

Article 97

The Secretariat shall comprise a Secretary-General and such staff as the Organization may require. The Secretary-General shall be appointed by the General Assembly upon the recommendation of the Security Council. He shall be the chief administrative officer of the Organization.

Article 98

The Secretary-General shall act in that capacity in all meetings of the General Assembly, of the Security Council, of the Economic and Social Council, and of the Trusteeship Council, and shall perform such other functions as are entrusted to him by these organs. The Secretary-General shall make an annual report to the General Assembly on the work of the Organization.

Article 99

The Secretary-General may bring to the attention of the Security Council any matter which in his opinion may threaten the maintenance of international peace and security.

Article 100

1. In the performance of their duties the Secretary-General and the staff shall not seek or receive instructions from any gov-

ernment or from any other authority external to the Organization. They shall refrain from any action which might reflect on their position as international officials responsible only to the Organization.

2. Each Member of the United Nations undertakes to respect the exclusively international character of the responsibilities of the Secretary-General and the staff and not to seek to influence them in the discharge of their responsibilities.

Article 101

1. The staff shall be appointed by the Secretary-General under regulations established by the General Assembly.

2. Appropriate staffs shall be permanently assigned to the Economic and Social Council, the Trusteeship Council, and, as required, to other organs of the United Nations. These staffs shall form a part of the Secretariat.

3. The paramount consideration in the employment of the staff and in the determination of the conditions of service shall be the necessity of securing the highest standards of efficiency, competence, and integrity. Due regard shall be paid to the importance of recruiting the staff on as wide a geographical basis as possible.

CHAPTER XVI. MISCELLANEOUS PROVISIONS

Article 102

1. Every treaty and every international agreement entered into by any Member of the United Nations after the present Charter comes into force shall as soon as possible be registered with the Secretariat and published by it.

2. No party to any such treaty or international agreement which has not been registered in accordance with the provisions of paragraph 1 of this Article may invoke that treaty or agreement before any organ of the United Nations.

Article 103

In the event of a conflict between the obligations of the Members of the United Nations under the present Charter and their obligations under any other international agreement, their obligations under the present Charter shall prevail.

Article 104

The Organization shall enjoy in the territory of each of its Members such legal capacity as may be necessary for the exercise of its functions and the fulfillment of its purposes.

Article 105

1. The Organization shall enjoy in the territory of each of its Members such privileges and immunities as are necessary for the fulfillment of its purposes.

2. Representatives of the Members of the United Nations and officials of the Organization shall similarly enjoy such privileges and immunities as are necessary for the independent exercise of their functions in connection with the Organization.

3. The General Assembly may make recommendations with a view to determining the details of the application of paragraphs 1 and 2 of this Article or may propose conventions to the Members of the United Nations for this purpose.

CHAPTER XVII.   TRANSITIONAL SECURITY ARRANGEMENTS

Article 106

Pending the coming into force of such special agreements referred to in Article 43 as in the opinion of the Security Council enable it to begin the exercise of its responsibilities under Article 42, the parties to the Four-Nation Declaration, signed at Moscow, October 30, 1943, and France, shall, in accordance with the provisions of paragraph 5 of that Declaration, consult with one another and as occasion requires with other Members of the United Nations with a view to such joint action on behalf of the Organization as may be necessary for the purpose of maintaining international peace and security.

Article 107

Nothing in the present Charter shall invalidate or preclude action, in relation to any state which during the Second World War has been an enemy of any signatory to the present Charter, taken or authorized as a result of that war by the Governments having responsibility for such action.

CHAPTER XVIII.   AMENDMENTS

Article 108

Amendments to the present charter shall come into force for all Members of the United Nations when they have been adopted by a vote of two thirds of the members of the General Assembly and ratified in accordance with their respective constitutional processes by two thirds of the Members of the United Nations, including all the permanent members of the Security Council.

Article 109

[1945 text]	[1965 text]
1. A General Conference of the Members of the United Nations for the purpose of reviewing the present Charter may be held at a date and place to be fixed by a two-thirds vote of the members of the General Assembly and by a vote of any seven members of the Security Council. Each Member of the United Nations shall have one vote in the conference.	1. A General Conference of the Members of the United Nations for the purpose of reviewing the present Charter may be held at a date and place to be fixed by a two-thirds vote of the members of the General Assembly and by a vote of any nine members of the Security Council. Each Member of the United Nations shall have one vote in the conference.

2. Any alteration of the present Charter recommended by a two-thirds vote of the conference shall take effect when ratified in accordance with their respective constitutional processes by two thirds of the Members of the United Nations including all the permanent members of the Security Council.

3. If such a conference has not been held before the tenth annual session of the General Assembly following the coming into force of the present Charter, the proposal to call such a conference shall be placed on the agenda of that session of the General Assembly, and the conference shall be held if so decided by a majority vote of the members of the General Assembly and by a vote of any seven members of the Security Council.

CHAPTER XIX.   RATIFICATION AND SIGNATURE

Article 110

1. The present Charter shall be ratified by the signatory states in accordance with their respective constitutional processes.

2. The ratifications shall be deposited with the Government of the United States of America, which shall notify all the signatory states of each deposit as well as the Secretary-General of the Organization when he has been appointed.

3. The present Charter shall come into force upon the deposit of ratifications by the Republic of China, France, the Union of Soviet Socialist Republics, the United Kingdom of Great Britain and Northern Ireland, and the United States of America, and by a majority of the other signatory states. A protocol of the ratifications deposited shall thereupon be drawn up by the Government of the United States of America which shall communicate copies thereof to all the signatory states.

4. The states signatory to the present Charter which ratify it after it has come into force will become original Members of the United Nations on the date of the deposit of their respective ratifications.

Article 111

The present Charter, of which the Chinese, French, Russian, English, and Spanish texts are equally authentic, shall remain deposited in the archives of the Government of the United States of America. Duly certified copies thereof shall be transmitted by that Government to the Governments of the other signatory states.

IN FAITH WHEREOF the representatives of the Governments of the United Nations have signed the present Charter.

DONE at the city of San Francisco the twenty-sixth day of June, one thousand nine hundred and forty-five.

2. UNIVERSAL DECLARATION OF HUMAN RIGHTS
Approved by Resolution 217A (III) of the General Assembly, 10 December 1948. 3 (pt. 1) GAOR, Resolutions (A/810), at 71-77.

Whereas recognition of the inherent dignity and of the equal and inalienable rights of all members of the human family is the foundation of freedom, justice and peace in the world,

Whereas disregard and contempt for human rights have resulted in barbarous acts which have outraged the conscience of mankind, and the advent of a world in which human beings shall enjoy freedom of speech and belief and freedom from fear and want has been proclaimed as the highest aspiration of the common people,

Whereas it is essential, if man is not to be compelled to have recourse, as a last resort, to rebellion against tyranny and oppression, that human rights should be protected by the rule of law,

Whereas it is essential to promote the development of friendly relations between nations,

Whereas the peoples of the United Nations have in the Charter reaffirmed their faith in fundamental human rights, in the dignity and worth of the human person and in the equal rights of men and women and have determined to promote social progress and better standards of life in larger freedom,

Whereas Member States have pledged themselves to achieve, in co-operation with the United Nations, the promotion of universal respect for and observance of human rights and fundamental freedoms,

Whereas a common understanding of these rights and freedoms is of the greatest importance for the full realization of this pledge,

Now, therefore,

The General Assembly

Proclaims this Universal Declaration of Human Rights as a common standard of achievement for all peoples and all nations, to the end that every individual and every organ of society, keeping this Declaration constantly in mind, shall strive by teaching and education to promote respect for these rights and freedoms and by progressive measures, national and international, to secure their universal and effective recognition and observance, both among the peoples of Member States themselves and among the peoples of territories under their jurisdiction.

Article 1.   All human beings are born free and equal in dignity and rights. They are endowed with reason and conscience and should act towards one another in a spirit of brotherhood.

Article 2.   Everyone is entitled to all the rights and freedoms set forth in this Declaration, without distinction of any kind, such as race, colour, sex, language, religion, political or other opinion, national or social origin, property, birth or other status.

Furthermore, no distinction shall be made on the basis of the political, jurisdictional or international status of the country or territory to which a person belongs, whether it be independent, trust, non-self-governing or under any other limitation of sovereignty.

Article 3.   Everyone has the right to life, liberty and the security of person.

Article 4.   No one shall be held in slavery or servitude; slavery and the slave trade shall be prohibited in all their forms.

Article 5.   No one shall be subjected to torture or to cruel, inhuman or degrading treatment or punishment. which nelson was.

Article 6.   Everyone has the right to recognition everywhere as a person before the law.

Article 7.   All are equal before the law and are entitled without any discrimination to equal protection of the law. All are entitled to equal protection against any discrimination in violation of this Declaration and against any incitement to such discrimination.

Article 8.   Everyone has the right to an effective remedy by the competent national tribunals for acts violating the fundamental rights granted him by the constitution or by law.

Article 9.   No one shall be subjected to arbitrary arrest, detention or exile. which nelson was

Article 10.   Everyone is entitled to full equality to a fair and public hearing by an independent and impartial tribunal, in the determination of his rights and obligations and of any criminal charge against him.

Article 11.—1. Everyone charged with a penal offence has the right to be presumed innocent until proved guilty according to law in a public trial at which he has had all the guarantees necessary for his defence.

2. No one shall be held guilty of any penal offence on account of any act or omission which did not constitute a penal offence, under national or international law, at the time when it was committed. Nor shall a heavier penalty be imposed than the one that was applicable at the time the penal offence was committed.

Article 12. No one shall be subjected to arbitrary interference with his privacy, family, home or correspondence, nor to attacks upon his honour and reputation. Everyone has the right to the protection of the law against such interference or attacks.

Article 13.—1. Everyone has the right to freedom of movement and residence within the borders of each state.

2. Everyone has the right to leave any country, including his own, and to return to his country.

Article 14.—1. Everyone has the right to seek and to enjoy in other countries asylum from persecution.

2. This right may not be invoked in the case of prosecutions genuinely arising from non-political crimes or from acts contrary to the purposes and principles of the United Nations.

Article 15.—1. Everyone has the right to a nationality.

2. No one shall be arbitrarily deprived of his nationality nor denied the right to change his nationality.

Article 16.—1. Men and women of full age, without any limitation due to race, nationality or religion, have the right to marry and to found a family. They are entitled to equal rights as to marriage, during marriage and at its dissolution.

2. Marriage shall be entered into only with the free and full consent of the intending spouses.

3. The family is the natural and fundamental group unit of society and is entitled to protection by society and the State.

Article 17.—1. Everyone has the right to own property alone as well as in association with others.

2. No one shall be arbitrarily deprived of his property.

Article 18. Every one has the right to freedom of thought, conscience and religion; this right includes freedom to change his religion or belief, and freedom, either alone or in community with others and in public or private, to manifest his religion or belief in teaching, practice, worship and observance.

Article 19. Everyone has the right to freedom of opinion and expression; this right includes freedom to hold opinions without interference and to seek, receive and impart information and ideas through any media and regardless of frontiers.

Article 20.—1. Everyone has the right to freedom of peaceful assembly and association.

2. No one may be compelled to belong to an association.

Article 21.—1. Everyone has the right to take part in the Government of his country, directly or through freely chosen representatives.

2. Everyone has the right of equal access to public service in his country.

3. The will of the people shall be the basis of the authority of government; this will shall be expressed in periodic and genuine elections which shall be by universal and equal suffrage and shall be held by secret vote or by equivalent free voting procedures.

Article 22. Everyone, as a member of society, has the right to social security and is entitled to realization, through national effort and international co-operation and in accordance with the organization and resources of each State, of the economic, social and cultural rights indispensable for his dignity and the free development of his personality.

Article 23.—1. Everyone has the right to work, to free choice of employment, to just and favourable conditions of work and to protection against unemployment.

2. Everyone, without any discrimination, has the right to equal pay for equal work.

3. Everyone who works has the right to just and favourable remuneration insuring for himself and his family an existence worthy of human dignity, and supplemented, if necessary, by other means of social protection.

4. Everyone has the right to form and to join trade unions for the protection of his interests.

Article 24. Everyone has the right to rest and leisure, including reasonable limitation of working hours and periodic holidays with pay.

Article 25.—1. Everyone has the right to a standard of living adequate for the health and well-being of himself and of his family, including food, clothing, housing and medical care and necessary social services, and the right to security in the event of unemployment, sickness, disability, widowhood, old age or other lack of livelihood in circumstances beyond his control.

2.   Motherhood and childhood are entitled to special care and assistance. All children, whether born in or out of wedlock, shall enjoy the same social protection.

Article 26.—1.   Everyone has the right to education. Education shall be free, at least in the elementary and fundamental stages. Elementary education shall be compulsory. Technical and professional education shall be made generally available and higher education shall be equally accessible to all on the basis of merit.

2.   Education shall be directed to the full development of the human personality and to the strengthening of respect for human rights and fundamental freedoms. It shall promote understanding, tolerance and friendship among all nations, racial or religious groups, and shall further the activities of the United Nations for the maintenance of peace.

3.   Parents have a prior right to choose the kind of education that shall be given to their children.

Article 27.—1.   Everyone has the right freely to participate in the cultural life of the community, to enjoy the arts and to share in scientific advancement and its benefits.

2.   Everyone has the right to the protection of the moral and material interests resulting from any scientific, literary or artistic production of which he is the author.

Article 28.   Everyone is entitled to a social and international order in which the rights and freedoms set forth in this Declaration can be fully realized.

Article 29.—1.   Everyone has duties to the community in which alone the free and full development of his personality is possible.

2.   In the exercise of his rights and freedoms, everyone shall be subject only to such limitations as are determined by law solely for the purpose of securing due recognition and respect for the rights and freedoms of others and of meeting the just requirements of morality, public order and the general welfare in a democratic society.

3.   These rights and freedoms may in no case be exercised contrary to the purposes and principles of the United Nations.

Article 30.   Nothing in this Declaration may be interpreted as implying for any State, group or person any right to engage in any activity or to perform any act aimed at the destruction of any of the rights and freedoms set forth herein.

3. INTERNATIONAL COVENANT ON ECONOMIC, SOCIAL AND CULTURAL RIGHTS

Adopted by Resolution 2200 (XXI) of the General Assembly, 16 December 1966. 21 GAOR, Suppl. No. 16 (A/6316), at 49-52.

PREAMBLE

The States Parties to the present Covenant,

Considering that, in accordance with the principles proclaimed in the Charter of the United Nations, recognition of the inherent dignity and of the equal and inalienable rights of all members of the human family is the foundation of freedom, justice and peace in the world,

Recognizing that these rights derive from the inherent dignity of the human person,

Recognizing that, in accordance with the Universal Declaration of Human Rights, the ideal of free human beings enjoying freedom from fear and want can only be achieved if conditions are created whereby everyone may enjoy his economic, social and cultural rights, as well as his civil and political rights,

Considering the obligation of States under the Charter of the United Nations to promote universal respect for, and observance of, human rights and freedoms,

Realizing that the individual, having duties to other individuals and to the community to which he belongs, is under a responsibility to strive for the promotion and observance of the rights recognized in the present Covenant,

Agree upon the following articles:

PART I

Article 1.—1. All peoples have the right of self-determination. By virtue of the right they freely determine their political status and freely pursue their economic, social and cultural development.

2. All peoples may, for their own ends, freely dispose of their natural wealth and resources without prejudice to any obligations arising out of international economic co-operation, based upon the principle of mutual benefit, and international law. In no case may a people be deprived of its own means of subsistence.

3. The States Parties to the present Covenant, including those having responsibility for the administration of Non-Self-Governing and Trust Territories, shall promote the realization of the right of self-determination, and shall respect that right, in conformity with the provisions of the United Nations Charter.

PART II

Article 2.—1. Each State Party to the present Covenant undertakes to take steps, individually and through international assistance and co-operation especially economic and technical, to the maximum of its available resources, with a view to achieving progressively the full realization of the rights recognized in the present Covenant by all appropriate means, including particularly the adoption of legislative measures.

2. The States Parties to the present Covenant undertake to guarantee that the rights enunciated in the present Covenant will be exercised without discrimination of any kind as to race, colour, sex, religion, political or other opinion, national or social origin, property, birth or other status.

3. Developing countries, with due regard to human rights and their national economy, may determine to what extent they would guarantee the economic rights recognized in the present Covenant to non-nationals.

Article 3. The States Parties to the present Covenant undertake to ensure the equal right of men and women to the enjoyment of all economic, social and cultural rights set forth in this Covenant.

Article 4. The States Parties to the present Covenant recognize that in the enjoyment of those rights provided by the State in conformity with the present Covenant, the State may subject such rights only to such limitations as are determined by law only in so far as this may be compatible with the nature of these rights and solely for the purpose of promoting the general welfare in a democratic society.

Article 5.—1. Nothing in the present Covenant may be interpreted as implying for any State, group or person, any right to engage in any activity or to perform any act aimed at the destruction of any of the rights or freedoms recognized herein, or at their limitation to a greater extent than is provided for in the present Covenant.

2. No restriction upon or derogation from any of the fundamental human rights recognized or existing in any country in virtue of law, conventions, regulations or custom shall be admitted on the pretext that the present Covenant does not recognize such rights or that it recognizes them to a lesser extent.

PART III

Article 6.—1. The States Parties to the present Covenant recognize the right to work, which includes the right of everyone to the opportunity to gain his living by work which he freely chooses or accepts, and will take appropriate steps to safeguard this right.

2. The steps to be taken by a State Party to the present Covenant to achieve the full realization of this right shall include technical and vocational guidance and training programmes, policies and techniques to achieve steady economic, social and cultural development and full and productive employment under conditions safeguarding fundamental political and economic freedoms to the individual.

Article 7. The States Parties to the present Covenant recognize the right of everyone to the enjoyment of just and favourable conditions of work, which ensure, in particular:

(a) Remuneration which provides all workers as a minimum with:

(i) Fair wages and equal remuneration for work of equal value without distinction of any kind, in particular women being guaranteed conditions of work not inferior to those enjoyed by men, with equal pay for equal work; and

(ii) A decent living for themselves and their families in accordance with the provisions of the present Covenant;

(b) Safe and healthy working conditions;

(c) Equal opportunity for everyone to be promoted in his employment to an appropriate higher level, subject to no considerations other than those of seniority and competence;

(d) Rest, leisure and reasonable limitation of working hours and periodic holidays with pay, as well as remuneration for public holidays.

Article 8.—1. The States Parties to the present Covenant undertake to ensure:

(a) The right of everyone to form trade unions and join the trade union of his choice subject only to the rules of the organization concerned, for the promotion and protection of his economic and social interests. No restrictions may be placed on the exercise of this right other than those prescribed by law and which are necessary in a democratic society in the interests of national security or public order or for the protection of the rights and freedoms of others;

(b) The right of trade unions to establish national federations or confederations and the right of the latter to form or join international trade-union organizations;

(c) The right of trade unions to function freely subject to no limitations other than those prescribed by law and which are necessary in a democratic society in the interests of national security or public order or for the protection of the rights and freedoms of others;

(d) The right to strike, provided that it is exercised in conformity with the laws of the particular country.

2. This article shall not prevent the imposition of lawful restrictions on the exercise of these rights by members of the armed forces, or of the police, or of the administration of the State.

3. Nothing in this article shall authorize State Parties to the International Labour Convention of 1948 on Freedom of Association and Protection of the Right to Organize to take legislative measures which would prejudice, or apply the law in such a manner as would prejudice, the guarantees provided for in that Convention.

Article 9. The States Parties to the present Covenant recognize the right of everyone to social security including social insurance.

Article 10. The States Parties to the present Covenant recognize that:

1. The widest possible protection and assistance should be accorded to the family, which is the natural and fundamental group unit of society, particularly for its establishment and while it is responsible for the care and education of dependent children. Marriage must be entered into with the free consent of the intending spouses;

2. Special protection should be accorded to mothers during a reasonable period before and after childbirth. During such period working mothers should be accorded paid leave or leave with adequate social security benefits;

3. Special measures of protection and assistance should be taken on behalf of all children and young persons without any discrimination for reasons of parentage or other conditions. Children and young persons should be protected from economic and social exploitation. Their employment in work harmful to their morals or health or dangerous to life or likely to hamper their normal development should be punishable by law. States should also set age limits below which the paid employment of child labour should be prohibited and punishable by law.

Article 11.—1. The States Parties to the present Covenant recognize the right of everyone to an adequate standard of living for himself and his family, including adequate food, clothing and housing, and to the continuous improvement of living conditions. The States Parties will take appropriate steps to ensure the realization of this right, recognizing to this effect the essential importance of international co-operation based on free consent.

2. The States Parties to the present Covenant, recognizing the fundamental right of everyone to be free from hunger, shall take, individually and through international co-operation, the measures, including specific programmes, which are needed:

(a) To improve methods of production, conservation and distribution of food by making full use of technical and scientific knowledge, by disseminating knowledge of the principles of nutrition and by developing or reforming agrarian systems in such a way as to achieve the most efficient development and utilization of natural resources; and

(b) Take into account the problems of both food-importing and food-exporting countries, to ensure an equitable distribution of world food supplies in relation to need.

Article 12.—1. The States Parties to the present Covenant recognize the right of everyone to the enjoyment of the highest attainable standard of physical and mental health.

2. The steps to be taken by the States Parties to the present Covenant to achieve the full realization of this right shall include those necessary for:

(a) The provision for the reduction of the still-birth-rate and of infant mortality and for the healthy development of the child;

(b) The improvement of all aspects of environmental and industrial hygiene;

(c) The prevention, treatment and control of epidemic, endemic, occupational and other diseases;

(d) The creation of conditions which would assure to all medical service and medical attention in the event of sickness.

Article 13.—1. The States Parties to the present Covenant recognize the right of everyone to education. They agree that education shall be directed to the full development of the human personality and the sense of its dignity, and shall strengthen the respect for human rights and fundamental freedoms. They further agree that education shall enable all persons to participate effectively in a free society, promote understanding, tolerance and friendship among all nations and all racial, ethnic or religious groups, and further the activities of the United Nations for the maintenance of peace.

2. The States Parties to the present Covenant recognize that, with a view to achieving the full realization of this right:

(a) Primary education shall be compulsory and available free to all;

(b) Secondary education in its different forms, including technical and vocational secondary education, shall be made generally available and accessible to all by every appropriate means, and in particular by the progressive introduction of free education;

(c) Higher education shall be made equally accessible to all, on the basis of capacity, by every appropriate means, and in particular by the progressive introduction of free education;

(d) Fundamental education shall be encouraged or intensified as far as possible for those persons who have not received or completed the whole period of their primary education;

(e) The development of a system of schools at all levels shall be actively pursued, an adequate fellowship system shall be established, and the material conditions of teaching staff shall be continuously improved.

3. The States Parties to the present Covenant undertake to have respect for the liberty of parents and, when applicable, legal guardians, to choose for their children schools other than those established by the public authorities which conform to such minimum educational standards as may be laid down or approved by the State and to ensure the religious and moral education of their children in conformity with their own convictions.

4. No part of this article shall be construed so as to interfere with the liberty of individuals and bodies to establish and direct educational institutions, subject always to the observance of the principles set forth in paragraph 1 and to the requirement that the education given in such institutions shall conform to such minimum standards as may be laid down by the State.

Article 14. Each State Party to the present Covenant which, at the time of becoming a Party, has not been able to secure in its metropolitan territory or other territories under its jurisdiction compulsory primary education, free of charge, undertakes, within two years, to work out and adopt a detailed plan of action for the progressive implementation, within a reasonable number of years, to be fixed in the plan, of the principle of compulsory education free of charge for all.

Article 15.—1. The States Parties to the present Covenant recognize the right of everyone:

(a) To take part in cultural life;

(b) To enjoy the benefits of scientific progress and its applications;

(c) To benefit from the protection of the moral and material interests resulting from any scientific, literary or artistic production of which he is the author.

2. The steps to be taken by the States Parties to the present Covenant to achieve the full realization of this right shall include those necessary for the conservation, the development and the diffusion of science and culture.

3. The States Parties to the present Covenant undertake to respect the freedom indispensable for scientific research and creative activity.

4. The States Parties to the present Covenant recognize the benefits to be derived from the encouragement and development of international contracts and co-operation in the scientific and cultural fields.

PART IV

Article 16.—1. The States Parties to the present Covenant undertake to submit in conformity with this part of the Covenant reports on the measures which they have adopted and the progress made in achieving the observance of the rights recognized herein.

2. (a) All reports shall be submitted to the Secretary-General of the United Nations who shall transmit copies to the Economic and Social Council for consideration in accordance with the provisions of the present Covenant.

(b) The Secretary-General of the United Nations shall also transmit to the specialized agencies copies of the reports, or any relevant parts therefrom, from States Parties to the present Covenant which are also members of these specialized agencies in so far as these reports, or parts therefrom, relate to any matters which fall within the responsibilities of the said agencies in accordance with their constitutional instruments.

Article 17.—1. The States Parties to the present Covenant shall furnish their reports in stages, in accordance with a programme to be established by the Economic and Social Council within one year of the entry into force of the present Covenant after consultation with the States Parties and the specialized agencies concerned.

2. Reports may indicate factors and difficulties affecting the degree of fulfilment of obligations under the present Covenant.

3. Where relevant information has previously been furnished to the United Nations or to any specialized agency by any State Party to the present Covenant it will not be necessary to reproduce that information but a precise reference to the information so furnished will suffice.

Article 18. Pursuant to its responsibilities under the Charter in the field of human rights and fundamental freedoms, the Economic and Social Council may make arrangements with the specialized agencies in respect of their reporting to it on the progress made in achieving the observance of the provisions of the present Covenant falling within the scope of their activities. These reports may include particulars of decisions and recommendations on such implementation adopted by their competent organs.

Article 19. The Economic and Social Council may transmit to the Commission on Human Rights for study and general recommendation or as appropriate for information the reports concerning human rights submitted by States in accordance with articles 16 and 17, and those concerning human rights submitted by the specialized agencies in accordance with article 18.

Article 20. The States Parties to the present Covenant and the specialized agencies concerned may submit comments to the Economic and Social Council on any general recommendation under article 19 or reference to such general recommendation in any report of the Commission or any documentation referred to therein.

Article 21. The Economic and Social Council may submit from time to time to the General Assembly reports with recommendations of a general nature and a summary of the information received from the States Parties to the present Covenant and the specialized agencies on the measures taken and the progress made in achieving general observance of the rights recognized in the present Covenant.

Article 22. The Economic and Social Council may bring to the attention of other organs of the United Nations, their subsidiary organs and specialized agencies concerned with furnishing technical assistance, any matters arising out of the reports referred to in this part of the present Covenant which may assist such bodies in deciding each within its field of competence, on the advisability of international measures likely to contribute to the effective progressive implementation of the present Covenant.

Article 23. The States Parties to the present Covenant agree that international action for the achievement of the rights recognized in the present Covenant includes such methods as the conclusion of conventions, the adoption of recommendations, the furnishing of technical assistance and the holding of regional meetings and technical meetings for the purpose of consultation and study organized in conjunction with the Governments concerned.

Article 24. Nothing in the present Covenant shall be interpreted as impairing the provisions of the Charter of the United Nations and of the constitutions of the specialized agencies which define the respective responsibilities of the various organs of the United Nations and of the specialized agencies in regard to the matters dealt with in the present Covenant.

Article 25. Nothing in the present Covenant shall be interpreted as impairing the inherent right of all peoples to enjoy and utilize fully and freely their natural wealth and resources.

PART V

Article 26.—1. The present Covenant is open for signature by any State Member of the United Nations or member of any of its specialized agencies, by any State Party to the Statute of the International Court of Justice, and by any other State which has been invited by the General Assembly of the United Nations to become a party to the present Covenant.

2. The present Covenant is subject to ratification. Instruments of ratification shall be deposited with the Secretary-General of the United Nations.

3. The present Covenant shall be open to accession by any State referred to in paragraph 1 of this article.

4. Accession shall be effected by the deposit of an instrument of accession with the Secretary-General of the United Nations.

5. The Secretary-General of the United Nations shall inform all States which have signed the present Covenant or acceded to it of the deposit of each instrument of ratification or accession.

Article 27.—1. The present Covenant shall enter into force three months after the date of the deposit with the Secretary-General of the United Nations of the thirty-fifth instrument of ratification or instrument of accession.

2. For each State ratifying the present Covenant or acceding to it after the deposit of the thirty-fifth instrument of ratification or instrument of accession, the present Covenant shall enter into force three months after the date of the deposit of its own instrument of ratification or instrument of accession.

Article 28. The provisions of the present Covenant shall extend to all parts of federal States without any limitations or exceptions.

Article 29.—1. Any State Party to the present Covenant may propose an amendment and file it with the Secretary-General of the United Nations. The Secretary-General of the United Nations shall thereupon communicate any proposed amendments to the States Parties to the present Covenant with a request that they notify him whether they favour a conference of States Parties for the purpose of considering and voting upon the proposal. In the event that at least one third of the States Parties favours such a conference the Secretary-General of the United Nations shall convene the conference under the auspices of the United Nations. Any amendment adopted by a majority of the States Parties present and voting at the conference shall be submitted to the General Assembly of the United Nations for approval.

2. Amendments shall come into force when they have been approved by the General Assembly and accepted by a two-thirds majority of the States Parties to the present Covenant in accordance with their respective constitutional processes.

3. When amendments come into force they shall be binding on those States Parties which have accepted them, other States Parties being still bound by the provisions of the present Covenant and any earlier amendment which they have accepted.

Article 30. Irrespective of the notifications made under article 26, paragraph 5, the Secretary-General of the United Nations shall inform all States referred to in paragraph 1 of the same article of the following particulars:

(a) Signatures, ratifications and accessions under article 26;

(b) The date of the entry into force of the present Covenant under article 27 and the date of the entry into force of any amendments under article 29.

Article 31.—1. The present Covenant, of which the Chinese, English, French, Russian and Spanish texts are equally authentic, shall be deposited in the archives of the United Nations.

2. The Secretary-General of the United Nations shall transmit certified copies of the present Covenant to all States referred to in article 26.

4. INTERNATIONAL COVENANT ON CIVIL AND POLITICAL RIGHTS
Adopted by Resolution 2200 (XXI) of the General Assembly, 16 December 1966. GAOR, XXI, Suppl. No. 16 (A/6316), pp. 52-58.

PREAMBLE

The States Parties to the present Covenant,

Considering that, in accordance with the principles proclaimed in the Charter of the United Nations, recognition of the inherent dignity and of the equal and inalienable rights of all members of the human family is the foundation of freedom, justice and peace in the world,

Recognizing that these rights derive from the inherent dignity of the human person,

Recognizing that, in accordance with the Universal Declaration of Human Rights, the ideal of free human beings enjoying civil and political freedom and freedom from fear and want can only be achieved if conditions are created whereby everyone may enjoy his civil and political rights, as well as his economic, social and cultural rights,

Considering the obligation of States under the Charter of the United Nations to promote universal respect for, and observance of, human rights and freedoms,

Realizing that the individual, having duties to other individuals and to the community to which he belongs, is under a responsibility to strive for the promotion and observance of the rights recognized in the present Covenant,

Agree upon the following articles:

PART I

Article 1.—1. All peoples have the right of self-determination. By virtue of the right they freely determine their political status and freely pursue their economic, social and cultural development.

2. All peoples may, for their own ends, freely dispose of their natural wealth and resources without prejudice to any obligations arising out of international economic co-operation, based upon the principle of mutual benefit, and international law. In no case may a people be deprived of its own means of subsistence.

3. The States Parties to the present Covenant, including those having responsibility for the administration of Non-Self-Governing and Trust Territories, shall promote the realization of the right of self-determination, and shall respect that right, in conformity with the provisions of the United Nations Charter.

PART II

Article 2.—1. Each State Party to the present Covenant undertakes to respect and to ensure to all individuals within its territory and subject to its jurisdiction the rights recognized in the present Covenant, without distinction of any kind, such as race, colour, sex, language, religion, political or other opinion, national or social origin, property, birth or other status.

2. Where not already provided for by existing legislative or other measures, each State Party to the present Covenant undertakes to take the necessary steps, in accordance with its constitutional processes and with the provisions of the present Covenant, to adopt such legislative or other measures as may be necessary to give effect to the rights recognized in the present Covenant.

3. Each State Party to the present Covenant undertakes:

(a) To ensure that any person whose rights or freedoms as herein recognized are violated shall have an effective remedy notwithstanding that the violation has been committed by persons acting in an official capacity;

(b) To ensure that any person claiming such a remedy shall have his right thereto determined by competent judicial, administrative or legislative authorities, or by any other competent authority provided for by the legal system of the State, and to develop the possibilities of judicial remedy;

(c) To ensure that the competent authorities shall enforce such remedies when granted.

Article 3. The States Parties to the present Covenant undertake to ensure the equal right of men and women to the enjoyment of all civil and political rights set forth in the present Covenant.

Article 4.—1. In time of public emergency which threatens the life of the nation and the existence of which is officially proclaimed, the States Parties to the present Covenant may take measures derogating from their obligations under the present Covenant to the extent strictly required by the exigencies of the situation, provided that such measures are not inconsistent with their other obligations under international law and do not involve discrimination solely on the ground of race, colour, sex, language, religion or social origin.

2. No derogation from articles 6, 7, 8 (paragraphs 1 and 2), 11, 15, 16 and 18 may be made under this provision.

3. Any State Party to the present Covenant availing itself of the right of derogation shall inform immediately the other States Parties to the present Covenant, through the intermediary of the Secretary-General of the United Nations of the provisions from which it has derogated and of the reasons by which it was actuated. A further communication shall be made, through the same intermediary, on the date on which it terminates such derogation.

Article 5.—1. Nothing in the present Covenant may be interpreted as implying for any State, group or person any right to engage in any activity or perform any act aimed at the destruction of any of the rights and freedoms recognized herein or at their limitation to a greater extent than is provided for in the present Covenant.

2. There shall be no restriction upon or derogation from any of the fundamental human rights recognized or existing in any State Party to the present Covenant pursuant to law, conventions, regulations or custom on the pretext that the present Covenant

does not recognize such rights or that it recognizes them to a lesser extent.

PART III

Article 6.—1. Every human being has the inherent right to life. This right shall be protected by law. No one shall be arbitrarily deprived of his life.

2. In countries which have not abolished the death penalty, sentence of death may be imposed only for the most serious crimes in accordance with law in force at the time of the commission of the crime and not contrary to the provisions of the present Covenant and to the Convention on the Prevention and Punishment of the Crime of Genocide. This penalty can only be carried out pursuant to a final judgment rendered by a competent court.

3. When deprivation of life constitutes the crime of genocide, it is understood that nothing in this article shall authorize any State Party to the present Covenant to derogate in any way from any obligation assumed under the provisions of the Convention on the Prevention and Punishment of the Crime of Genocide.

4. Anyone sentenced to death shall have the right to seek pardon or commutation of the sentence. Amnesty, pardon or commutation of the sentence of death may be granted in all cases.

5. Sentence of death shall not be imposed for crimes committed by persons below eighteen years of age and shall not be carried out on pregnant women.

6. Nothing in this article shall be invoked to delay or to prevent the abolition of capital punishment by any State Party to the present Covenant.

Article 7. No one shall be subjected to torture or to cruel, inhuman or degrading treatment or punishment. In particular, no one shall be subjected without his free consent to medical or scientific experimentation.

Article 8.—1. No one shall be held in slavery; slavery and the slave-trade in all their forms shall be prohibited.

2. No one shall be held in servitude.

3. (a) No one shall be required to perform forced or compulsory labour;

(b) The preceding sub-paragraph shall not be held to preclude in countries where imprisonment with hard labour may be imposed as a punishment for a crime, the performance of hard labour in pursuance of a sentence to such punishment by a competent court;

(c) For the purpose of this paragraph the term "forced or compulsory labour" shall not include:

(i) Any work or service, not referred to in subparagraph (b), normally required of a person who is under detention in consequence of a lawful order of a court, or of a person during conditional release from such detention;

(ii) Any service of a military character and, in countries where conscientious objection is recognized, any national service required by law of conscientious objectors;

(iii) Any service exacted in cases of emergency or calamity threatening the life or well-being of the community;

(iv) Any work or service which forms part of normal civil obligations.

Article 9.—1. Everyone has the right to liberty and security of person. No one shall be subjected to arbitrary arrest or detention. No one shall be deprived of his liberty except on such grounds and in accordance with such procedures as are established by law.

2. Anyone who is arrested shall be informed, at the time of arrest, of the reasons for his arrest and shall be promptly informed of any charges against him.

3. Anyone arrested or detained on a criminal charge shall be brought promptly before a judge or other officer authorized by law to exercise judicial power and shall be entitled to trial within a reasonable time or to release. It shall not be the general rule that persons awaiting trial shall be detained in custody, but release may be subject to guarantees to appear for trial, at any other stage of the judicial proceedings, and, should occasion arise, for execution of the judgment.

4. Anyone who is deprived of his liberty by arrest or detention shall be entitled to take proceedings before a court, in order that such court may decide without delay on the lawfulness of his detention and order his release if the detention is not lawful.

5. Anyone who has been the victim of unlawful arrest or detention shall have an enforceable right to compensation.

Article 10.—1. All persons deprived of their liberty shall be treated with humanity and with respect for the inherent dignity of the human person.

2. (a) Accused persons shall, save in exceptional circumstances, be segregated from convicted persons, and shall be subject to separate treatment appropriate to their status as unconvicted persons;

(b) Accused juvenile persons shall be separated from adults and brought as speedily as possible for adjudication.

3. The penitentiary system shall comprise treatment of prisoners the essential aim of which shall be their reformation and social rehabilitation. Juvenile offenders shall be segregated from adults and be accorded treatment appropriate to their age and legal status.

Article 11. No one shall be imprisoned merely on the ground of inability to fulfil a contractual obligation.

Article 12.—1. Everyone lawfully within the territory of a State shall, within that territory, have the right to liberty of movement and freedom to choose his residence.

2. Everyone shall be free to leave any country, including his own.

3. The above-mentioned rights shall not be subject to any restrictions except those which are provided by law, are necessary to protect national security, public order (*"ordre public"*), public health or morals or the rights and freedoms of others, and are consistent with the other rights recognized in the present Covenant.

4. No one shall be arbitrarily deprived of the right to enter his own country.

Article 13. An alien lawfully in the territory of a State Party to the present Covenant may be expelled therefrom only in pursuance of a decision reached in accordance with law and shall, except where compelling reasons of national security otherwise require, be allowed to submit the reasons against his expulsion and to have his case reviewed by, and be represented for the purpose before, the competent authority or a person or persons especially designated by the competent authority.

Article 14.—1. All persons shall be equal before the courts and tribunals. In the determination of any criminal charge against him, or of his rights and obligations in a suit at law, everyone shall be entitled to a fair and public hearing by a competent, independent and impartial tribunal established by law. The Press and the public may be excluded from all or part of a trial for reasons of morals, public order (*"ordre public"*) or national security in a democratic society, or when the interest of the private lives of the parties so requires, or to the extent strictly necessary in the opinion of the court in special circumstances where publicity would prejudice the interests of justice; but any judgment rendered in a criminal case or in a suit at law shall be made public except where the interest of juveniles otherwise requires or the proceedings concern matrimonial disputes or the guardianship of children.

2. Everyone charged with a criminal offence shall have the right to be presumed innocent until proved guilty according to law.

3. In the determination of any criminal charge against him, everyone shall be entitled to the following minimum guarantees, in full equality:

(a) To be informed promptly and in detail in a language which he understands of the nature and cause of the charge against him;

(b) To have adequate time and facilities for the preparation of his defence and to communicate with counsel of his own choosing;

(c) To be tried without undue delay;

(d) To be tried in his presence, and to defend himself in person or through legal assistance of his own choosing; to be informed, if he does not have legal assistance, of this right; and to have legal assistance assigned to him, in any case where the interests of justice so require, and without payment by him in any such case if he does not have sufficient means to pay for it;

(e) To examine, or have examined, the witnesses against him and to obtain the attendance and examination of witnesses on his behalf under the same conditions as witnesses against him;

(f) To have the free assistance of an interpreter if he cannot understand or speak the language used in court;

(g) Not to be compelled to testify against himself, or to confess guilt.

4. In the case of juveniles, the procedure shall be such as will take account of their age and the desirability of promoting their rehabilitation.

5. Everyone convicted of a crime shall have the right to his conviction and sentence being reviewed by a higher tribunal according to law.

6. When a person has by a final decision been convicted of a criminal offence and when subsequently his conviction has been reversed or he has been pardoned on the ground that a new or newly discovered fact shows conclusively that there has been a miscarriage of justice, the person who has suffered punishment as a result of such conviction shall be compensated according to law, unless it is proved that the non-disclosure of the unknown fact in time is wholly or partly attributable to him.

7. No one shall be liable to be tried or punished again for an offence for which he has already been finally convicted or acquitted in accordance with the law and penal procedure of each country.

Article 15.—1. No one shall be held guilty of any criminal offence on account of any act or omission which did not constitute a criminal offence, under national or international law, at the time when it was committed. Nor shall a heavier penalty be imposed than the one that was applicable at the time when the criminal offence was committed. If, subsequently to the commission of the offence, provision is made by law for the imposition of a lighter penalty, the offender shall benefit thereby.

2. Nothing in this article shall prejudice the trial and punishment of any person for any act or omission which, at the time when it was committed, was criminal according to the general principles of law recognized by the community of nations.

Article 16. Everyone shall have the right to recognition everywhere as a person before the law.

Article 17.—1. No one shall be subjected to arbitrary or unlawful interference with his privacy, family, home or correspondence, nor to unlawful attacks on his honour and reputation.

2. Everyone has the right to the protection of the law against such interference or attacks.

Article 18.—1. Everyone shall have the right to freedom of thought, conscience and religion. This right shall include freedom to have or to adopt a religion or belief of his choice, and freedom either individually or in community with others and in public or private, to manifest his religion or belief in worship, observance, practice and teaching.

2. No one shall be subject to coercion which would impair his freedom to have or to adopt a religion or belief of his choice.

3. Freedom to manifest one's religion or beliefs may be subject only to such limitations as are prescribed by law and are necessary to protect public safety, order, health, or morals or the fundamental rights and freedoms of others.

4. The States Parties to the present Covenant undertake to have respect for the liberty of parents and, when applicable, legal guardians, to ensure the religious and moral education of their children in conformity with their own convictions.

Article 19.—1. Everyone shall have the right to hold opinions without interference.

2. Everyone shall have the right to freedom of expression; this right shall include freedom to seek, receive and impart information and ideas of all kinds, regardless of frontiers, either orally, in writing or in print, in the form of art, or through any other media of his choice.

3. The exercise of the rights provided for in the foregoing paragraph carries with it special duties and responsibilities. It may therefore be subject to certain restrictions, but these shall be such only as are provided by law and are necessary, (1) for respect of the rights or reputations of others, (2) for the protection of national security or of public order (*"ordre public"*), or of public health or morals.

Article 20.—1. Any propaganda for war shall be prohibited by law.

2. Any advocacy of national, racial, or religious hatred that constitutes incitement to discrimination, hostility or violence shall be prohibited by law.

Article 21. The right of peaceful assembly shall be recognized. No restrictions may be placed on the exercise of this right other than those imposed in conformity with the law and which are necessary in a democratic society in the interests of national security or public safety, public order (*"ordre public"*), the protection of public health or morals or the protection of the rights and freedoms of others.

Article 22.—1. Everyone shall have the right to freedom of association with others, including the right to form and join trade unions for the protection of his interests.

2. No restrictions may be placed on the exercise of this right other than those prescribed by law and which are necessary in a democratic society in the interests of national security or public safety, public order (*"ordre public"*), the protection of public health or morals or the protection of the rights and freedoms of others. This article shall not prevent the imposition of lawful restrictions on members of the armed forces and of the police in their exercise of this right.

3. Nothing in this article shall authorize States Parties to the International Labour Convention of 1948 on Freedom of Association and Protection of the Right to Organise to take legislative measures which would prejudice, or to apply the law in such a manner as to prejudice, the guarantees provided for in the Convention.

Article 23.—1. The family is the natural and fundamental group unit of society and is entitled to protection by society and the State.

2. The right of men and women of marriageable age to marry and to found a family shall be recognized.

3. No marriage shall be entered into without the free and full consent of the intending spouses.

4. States Parties to the present Covenant shall take appropriate steps to ensure equality of rights and responsibilities of spouses as to marriage, during marriage and at its dissolution. In the case of dissolution, provision shall be made for the necessary protection of any children.

Article 24.—1. Every child shall have, without any discrimination as to race, colour, sex, language, religion, national or social origin, property or birth, the right to such measures of protection as required by his status as a minor, on the part of his family, the society and the State.

2. Every child shall be registered immediately after birth and shall have a name.

3. Every child has the right to acquire a nationality.

Article 25. Every citizen shall have the right and the opportunity, without any of the distinctions mentioned in article 2 and without unreasonable restrictions:

(a) To take part in the conduct of public affairs, directly or through freely chosen representatives;

(b) To vote and to be elected at genuine periodic elections which shall be by universal and equal suffrage and shall be held by secret ballot, guaranteeing the free expression of the will of the electors;

(c) To have access, on general terms of equality, to public service in his country.

Article 26. All persons are equal before the law and are entitled without any discrimination to equal protection of the law. In this respect the law shall prohibit any discrimination and guarantee to all persons equal and effective protection against discrimination on any ground such as race, colour, sex, language, religion, political or other opinion, national or social origin, property, birth or other status.

Article 27. In those States in which ethnic, religious or linguistic minorities exist, persons belonging to such minorities shall not be denied the right, in community with the other members of their group, to enjoy their own culture, to profess and practise their own religion, or to use their own language.

PART IV

Article 28.—1. There shall be established a Human Rights Committee (hereafter referred to in the present Covenant as "the Committee"). It shall consist of eighteen members and shall carry out the functions hereinafter provided.

2. The Committee shall be composed of nationals of the State Parties to the present Covenant who shall be persons of

high moral character and recognized competence in the field of human rights, consideration being given to the usefulness of the participation of some persons having legal experience.

3.   The members of the Committee shall be elected and shall serve in their personal capacity.

Article 29.—1.   The members of the Committee shall be elected by secret ballot from a list of persons possessing the qualifications prescribed in article 28 and nominated for the purpose by the States Parties to the present Covenant.

2.   Each State Party to the present Covenant may nominate not more than two persons. These persons shall be nationals of the nominating State.

3.   A person shall be eligible for renomination.

Article 30.—1.   The initial election shall be held no later than six months after the date of the entry into force of the present Covenant.

2.   At least four months before the date of each election of the Committee, other than an election to fill a vacancy declared in accordance with article 34, the Secretary-General of the United Nations shall address a written invitation to the States Parties to the present Covenant to submit their nominations for membership of the Committee within three months.

3.   The Secretary-General of the United Nations shall prepare a list in alphabetical order of all the persons thus nominated, with an indication of the States Parties which have nominated them, and shall submit it to the States Parties to the present Covenant no later than one month before the date of each election.

4.   Elections of the members of the Committee shall be held at a meeting of the States Parties to the present Covenant convened by the Secretary-General of the United Nations at the Headquarters of the United Nations. At that meeting, for which two thirds of the States Parties to the present Covenant shall constitute a quorum, the persons elected to the Committee shall be those nominees who obtain the largest number of votes and an absolute majority of the votes of the representatives of States Parties present and voting.

Article 31.—1.   The Committee may not include more than one national of the same State.

2.   In the election of the Committee consideration shall be given to equitable geographical distribution of membership and to the representation of the different forms of civilization as well as of the principal legal systems.

Article 32.—1. The members of the Committee shall be elected for a term of four years. They shall be eligible for re-election if renominated. However, the terms of nine of the members elected at the first election shall expire at the end of two years; immediately after the first election the names of these nine members shall be chosen by lot by the Chairman of the meeting referred to in paragraph 4 of article 30.

2. Elections at the expiry of office shall be held in accordance with the preceding articles of this part of the present Covenant.

Article 33.—1. If, in the unanimous opinion of the other members, a member of the Committee has ceased to carry out his functions for any cause other than absence of a temporary character, the Chairman of the Committee shall notify the Secretary-General of the United Nations who shall then declare the seat of that member to be vacant.

2. In the event of the death or the resignation of a member of the Committee, the Chairman shall immediately notify the Secretary-General of the United Nations who shall declare the seat vacant from the date of death or the date on which the resignation takes effect.

Article 34.—1. When a vacancy is declared in accordance with article 33 and if the term of office of the member to be replaced does not expire within six months of the declaration of the vacancy, the Secretary-General of the United Nations shall notify each of the States Parties to the present Covenant which may within two months submit nominations in accordance with article 29 for the purpose of filling the vacancy.

2. The Secretary-General of the United Nations shall prepare a list in alphabetical order of the persons thus nominated and shall submit it to the States Parties to the present Covenant. The election to fill the vacancy shall then take place in accordance with the relevant provisions of this part of the present Covenant.

3. A member of the Committee elected to fill a vacancy declared in accordance with article 33 shall hold office for the remainder of the term of the member who vacated the seat on the Committee under the provisions of that article.

Article 35. The members of the Committee shall, with the approval of the General Assembly of the United Nations, receive emoluments from United Nations resources on such terms and conditions as the General Assembly may decide having regard to the importance of the Committee's responsibilities.

Article 36. The Secretary-General of the United Nations shall provide the necessary staff and facilities for the effective performance of the functions of the Committee under this Covenant.

Article 37.—1. The Secretary-General of the United Nations shall convene the initial meeting of the Committee at the Headquarters of the United Nations.

2. After its initial meeting, the Committee shall meet at such times as shall be provided in its rules of procedure.

3. The Committee shall normally meet at the Headquarters of the United Nations or at the United Nations Office at Geneva.

Article 38. Every member of the Committee shall, before taking up his duties, make a solemn declaration in open committee that he will perform his functions impartially and conscientiously.

Article 39.—1. The Committee shall elect its officers for a term of two years. They may be re-elected.

2. The Committee shall establish its own rules of procedure, but these rules shall provide, *inter alia,* that:

(a) Twelve members shall constitute a quorum;

(b) Decisions of the Committee shall be made by a majority vote of the members present.

Article 40.—1. The States Parties to the present Covenant undertake to submit reports on the measures they have adopted which give effect to the rights recognized herein and on the progress made in the enjoyment of those rights; (a) within one year of the entry into force of the present Covenant for the States Parties concerned and (b) thereafter whenever the Committee so requests.

2. All reports shall be submitted to the Secretary-General of the United Nations who shall transmit them to the Committee for consideration. Reports shall indicate the factors and difficulties, if any, affecting the implementation of the present Covenant.

3. The Secretary-General of the United Nations may after consultation with the Committee transmit to the specialized agencies concerned copies of such parts of the reports as may fall within their field of competence.

4. The Committee shall study the reports submitted by the States Parties to the present Covenant. It shall transmit its reports and such general comments as it may consider appropriate to the States Parties. The Committee may also transmit to the Economic and Social Council these comments along with the copies of the reports it has received from States Parties to the present Covenant.

5. The States Parties to the present Covenant may submit to the Committee observations on any comments that may be made in accordance with paragraph 4 of this article.

Article 41.—1. A State Party to the present Covenant may at any time declare under this article that it recognizes the competence of the Committee to receive and consider communications to the effect that a State Party claims that another State Party is not fulfilling its obligations under the present Covenant. Communications under this article may be received and considered only if submitted by a State Party which has made a declaration recognizing in regard to itself the competence of the Committee. No communication shall be received by the Committee if it concerns a State Party which has not made such a declaration. Communications received under this article shall be dealt with in accordance with the following procedure:

(a) If a State Party to the present Covenant considers that another State Party is not giving effect to the provisions of the present Covenant, it may, by written communication, bring the matter to the attention of that State Party. Within three months after the receipt of the communication, the receiving State shall afford the State which sent the communication an explanation or any other statement in writing clarifying the matter, which should include, to the extent possible and pertinent, reference to domestic procedures and remedies taken, pending, or available in the matter.

(b) If the matter is not adjusted to the satisfaction of both States Parties concerned within six months after the receipt by the receiving State of the initial communication, either State shall have the right to refer the matter to the Committee, by notice given to the Committee and to the other State.

(c) The Committee shall deal with a matter referred to it only after it has ascertained that all available domestic remedies have been invoked and exhausted in the matter, in conformity with the generally recognized principles of international law. This shall not be the rule where the application of the remedies is unreasonably prolonged.

(d) The Committee shall hold closed meetings when examining communications under this article.

(e) Subject to the provisions of sub-paragraph (c), the Committee shall make available its good offices to the States Parties concerned with a view to a friendly solution of the matter on the basis of respect for human rights and fundamental freedoms as recognized in this Covenant.

(f) In any matter referred to it, the Committee may call upon the States Parties concerned, referred to in sub-paragraph (b), to supply any relevant information.

(g) The States Parties concerned, referred to in sub-paragraph (b), shall have the right to be represented when the matter is being considered in the Committee and to make submissions orally and/or in writing.

(h) The Committee shall, within twelve months after the date of receipt of notice under sub-paragraph (b), submit a report:

(i) If a solution within the terms of sub-paragraph (e) is reached, the Committee shall confine its report to a brief statement of the facts and of the solution reached;

(ii) If a solution is not reached, within the terms of sub-paragraph (e), the Committee shall confine its report to a brief statement of the facts; the written submissions and record of the oral submissions made by the States Parties concerned shall be attached to the report.

In every matter the report shall be communicated to the States Parties concerned.

2. The provisions of this article shall come into force when ten States Parties to the present Covenant have made declarations under paragraph 1 of this article. Such declarations shall be deposited by the States Parties with the Secretary-General of the United Nations who shall transmit copies thereof to the other States Parties. A declaration may be withdrawn at any time by notification to the Secretary-General. Such a withdrawal shall not prejudice the consideration of any matter which is the subject of a communication already transmitted under this article; no further communication by any State Party shall be received after the notification of withdrawal of the declaration has been received by the Secretary-General of the United Nations unless the State Party concerned had made a new declaration.

Article 42.—1. (a) If a matter referred to the Committee in accordance with article 41 is not resolved to the satisfaction of the States Parties concerned, the Committee may, with the prior consent of the States Parties concerned, appoint an *ad hoc* Conciliation Commission (hereinafter referred to as "the Commission"). The good offices of the Commission shall be made available to the States Parties concerned with a view to an amicable solution of the matter on the basis of respect for the present Covenant;

(b) The Commission shall consist of five persons acceptable to the States Parties concerned. If the States Parties concerned fail to reach agreement within three months on all or part of the composition of the Commission the members of the Commission concerning whom no agreement was reached shall be elected by secret ballot by a two-thirds majority vote of the Committee from among its members.

2. The members of the Commission shall serve in their personal capacity. They shall not be nationals of the States Parties concerned, or of a State not party to the present Covenant, or of a State Party which has not made a declaration under article 41.

3. The Commission shall elect its own Chairman and adopt its own rules of procedure.

4. The meetings of the Commission shall normally be held at the Headquarters of the United Nations or at the United Nations Office at Geneva. However, they may be held at such other convenient places as the Commission may determine in consultation with the Secretary-General of the United Nations and the States Parties concerned.

5. The secretariat provided in accordance with article 36 shall also service the Commissions appointed under this article.

6. The information received and collated by the Committee shall be made available to the Commission and the Commission may call upon the States Parties concerned to supply any other relevant information.

7. When the Commission has fully considered the matter, but in any event not later than twelve months after having been seized of the matter, it shall submit to the Chairman of the Committee a report for communication to the States Parties concerned.

(a) If the Commission is unable to complete its consideration of the matter within twelve months, it shall confine its report to a brief statement of the status of its consideration of the matter.

(b) If an amicable solution to the matter on the basis of respect for human rights as recognized in the present Covenant is reached, the Commission shall confine its report to a brief statement of the facts and of the solution reached.

(c) If a solution within the terms of sub-paragraph (b) is not reached, the Commission's report shall embody its findings on all questions of fact relevant to the issues between the States Parties concerned, as well as its views on the possibilities of amicable solution of the matter. This report shall also contain the written submissions and a record of the oral submissions made by the States Parties concerned.

(d) If the Commission's report is submitted under sub-paragraph (c), the States Parties concerned shall, within three months of the receipt of the report, inform the Chairman of the Committee whether or not they accept the contents of the report of the Commission.

8. The provisions of this article are without prejudice to the responsibilities of the Committee under article 41.

9. The States Parties concerned shall share equally all the expenses of the members of the Commission in accordance with estimates to be provided by the Secretary-General of the United Nations.

10. The Secretary-General of the United Nations shall be empowered to pay the expenses of the members of the Commission, if necessary, before reimbursement by the States Parties concerned in accordance with paragraph 9 of this article.

Article 43. The members of the Committee and of the *ad hoc* conciliation commissions which may be appointed under article 41, shall be entitled to the facilities, privileges and immunities of experts on mission for the United Nations as laid down in the relevant sections of the Convention on the Privileges and Immunities of the United Nations.

Article 44. The provisions for the implementation of the present Covenant shall apply without prejudice to the procedures prescribed in the field of human rights by or under the constituent instruments and the conventions of the United Nations and of the specialized agencies and shall not prevent the States Parties to the present Covenant from having recourse to other procedures for settling a dispute in accordance with general or special international agreements in force between them.

Article 45. The Committee shall submit to the General Assembly, through the Economic and Social Council, an annual report on its activities.

PART V

Article 46. Nothing in the present Covenant shall be interpreted as impairing the provisions of the Charter of the United Nations and of the constitutions of the specialized agencies which define the respective responsibilities of the various organs of the United Nations and of the specialized agencies in regard to the matters dealt with in the present Covenant.

Article 47. Nothing in the Covenant shall be interpreted as impairing the inherent right of all peoples to enjoy and utilize fully and freely their natural wealth and resources.

PART VI

Article 48.—1. The present Covenant is open for signature by any State Member of the United Nations or member of any of its specialized agencies, by any State Party to the Statute of the International Court of Justice, and by any other State which has been invited by the General Assembly of the United Nations to become a party to the present Covenant.

2. The present Covenant is subject to ratification. Instruments of ratification shall be deposited with the Secretary-General of the United Nations.

3. The present Covenant shall be open to accession by any State referred to in paragraph 1 of this article.

4. Accession shall be effected by the deposit of an instrument of accession with the Secretary-General of the United Nations.

5. The Secretary-General of the United Nations shall inform all States which have signed this Covenant or acceded to it of the deposit of each instrument of ratification or accession.

Article 49.—1. The present Covenant shall enter into force three months after the date of the deposit with the Secretary-General of the United Nations of the thirty-fifth instrument of ratification or instrument of accession.

2. For each State ratifying the present Covenant or acceding to it after the deposit of the thirty-fifth instrument of ratification or instrument of accession, the present Covenant shall enter into force three months after the date of the deposit of its own instrument of ratification or instrument of accession.

Article 50. The provisions of the present Covenant shall extend to all parts of federal States without any limitations or exceptions.

Article 51.—1. Any State Party to the present Covenant may propose an amendment and file it with the Secretary-General of the United Nations. The Secretary-General of the United Nations shall thereupon communicate any proposed amendments to the States Parties to the present Covenant with a request that they notify him whether they favour a conference of States Parties for the purpose of considering and voting upon the proposal. In the event that at least one third of the States Parties favours such a conference the Secretary-General of the United Nations shall convene the conference under the auspices of the United Nations. Any amendment adopted by a majority of the States Parties present and voting at the conference shall be submitted to the General Assembly of the United Nations for approval.

2. Amendments shall come into force when they have been approved by the General Assembly and accepted by a two-thirds majority of the States Parties to the present Covenant in accordance with their respective constitutional processes.

3. When amendments come into force they shall be binding on those States Parties which have accepted them, other States Parties being still bound by the provisions of the present Covenant and any earlier amendment which they have accepted.

Article 52. Irrespective of the notifications made under article 48, paragraph 5, the Secretary-General of the United Nations shall inform all States referred to in paragraph 1 of the same article of the following particulars:

(a) Signatures, ratifications and accessions under article 48;

(b) The date of the entry into force of the present Covenant under article 49 and the date of the entry into force of any amendments under article 51.

Article 53.—1. The present Covenant, of which the Chinese, English, French, Russian and Spanish texts are equally authentic, shall be deposited in the archives of the United Nations.

2. The Secretary-General of the United Nations shall transmit certified copies of the present Covenant to all States referred to in article 48.

5. OPTIONAL PROTOCOL TO THE INTERNATIONAL COVENANT ON CIVIL AND POLITICAL RIGHTS

Adopted by Resolution 2200 (XXI) of the General Assembly, 16 December 1966. 21 GAOR, Suppl. No. 16 (A/6316), at 59-60.

The States Parties to the present Protocol,

Considering that in order further to achieve the purposes of the Covenant on Civil and Political Rights (hereinafter referred to as "the Covenant") and the implementation of its provisions it would be appropriate to enable the Human Rights Committee set up in part IV of the Covenant (hereinafter referred to as "the Committee") to receive and consider, as provided in the present Protocol, communications from individuals claiming to be victims of violations of any of the rights set forth in the Covenant,

Have agreed as follows:

Article 1. A State Party to the Covenant that becomes a party to the present Protocol recognizes the competence of the Committee to receive and consider communications from individuals, subject to its jurisdiction, claiming to be victims of a violation by that State Party of any of the rights set forth in the Covenant. No communication shall be received by the Committee if it concerns a State Party to the Covenant which is not a Party to the present Protocol.

Article 2. Subject to the provision of article 1, individuals claiming that any of their rights enumerated in the Covenant have been violated and who have exhausted all available domestic remedies may submit a written communication to the Committee for consideration.

Article 3. The Committee shall consider inadmissible any communication under this Protocol which is anonymous, or which it considers to be an abuse of the right of submission of such communications or to be incompatible with the provisions of the Covenant.

Article 4.—1. Subject to the provisions of article 3, the Committee shall bring any communications submitted to it under the present Protocol to the attention of the State Party to the present Protocol alleged to be violating any provision of the Covenant.

2. Within six months, the receiving State shall submit to the Committee written explanations or statements clarifying the matter and the remedy, if any, that may have been taken by that State.

Article 5.—1. The Committee shall consider communications received under the present Protocol in the light of all written information made available to it by the individual and by the State Party concerned.

2. The Committee shall not consider any communication from an individual unless it has ascertained that:

(a) the same matter is not being examined under another procedure of international investigation or settlement;

(b) the individual has exhausted all available domestic remedies. This shall not be the rule where the application of the remedies is unreasonably prolonged.

3. The Committee shall hold closed meetings when examining communications under the present Protocol.

4. The Committee shall forward its views to the State Party concerned and to the individual.

Article 6. The Committee shall include in its annual report under article 45 of the Covenant a summary of its activities under the present Protocol.

Article 7. Pending the achievement of the objectives of General Assembly resolution 1514 (XV) of 14 December 1960 concerning the Declaration on the Granting of Independence to Colonial Countries and Peoples, the provisions of the present Protocol shall in no way limit the right of petition granted to these peoples by the Charter of the United Nations and other international conventions and instruments under the United Nations and its specialized agencies.

Article 8.—1. The present Protocol is open for signature by any State which has signed the Covenant.

2. The present Protocol is subject to ratification by any State which has ratified or acceded to the Covenant. Instruments of ratification shall be deposited with the Secretary-General of the United Nations.

3. The present Protocol shall be open to accession by any State which has ratified or acceded to the Covenant.

4. Accession shall be effected by the deposit of an instrument of accession with the Secretary-General of the United Nations.

5. The Secretary-General of the United Nations shall inform all States which have signed the present Protocol or acceded to it of the deposit of each instrument of ratification or accession.

Article 9.—1. Subject to the entry into force of the Covenant, the present Protocol shall enter into force three months after the date of the deposit with the Secretary-General of the United Nations of the tenth instrument of ratification or instrument of accession.

2. For each State ratifying the present Protocol or acceding to it after the deposit of the tenth instrument of ratification or instrument of accession, the present Protocol shall enter into force three months after the date of the deposit of its own instrument of ratification or instrument of accession.

Article 10. The provision of the present Protocol shall extend to all parts of federal States without any limitations or exceptions.

Article 11.—1. Any State Party to the present Protocol may propose an amendment and file it with the Secretary-General of the United Nations. The Secretary-General of the United Nations shall thereupon communicate any proposed amendments to the States Parties to the present Protocol with a request that they notify him whether they favour a conference of States Parties for the purpose of considering and voting upon the proposal. In the event that at least one third of the State Parties favours such a conference the Secretary-General of the United Nations shall convene the conference under the auspices of the United Nations. Any amendment adopted by a majority of the States Parties present and voting at the conference shall be submitted to the General Assembly of the United Nations for approval.

2. Amendments shall come into force when they have been approved by the General Assembly and accepted by a two-thirds majority of the States Parties to the present Protocol in accordance with their respective constitutional processes.

3. When amendments come into force they shall be binding on those States Parties which have accepted them, other States Parties being still bound by the provisions of the present Protocol and any earlier amendment which they have accepted.

Article 12.—1. Any State Party may denounce the present Protocol at any time by written notification addressed to the Secretary-General of the United Nations. Denunciation shall take effect three months after the date of receipt of the notification by the Secretary-General of the United Nations.

2. Denunciation shall be without prejudice to the continued application of the provisions of the present Protocol to any communication submitted under article 2 before the effective date of denunciation.

Article 13. Irrespective of the notifications made under article 8, paragraph 5, of the present Protocol, the Secretary-General of the United Nations shall inform all States referred to in article 48, paragraph 1, of the Covenant of the following particulars:

(a) Signatures, ratifications and accessions under article 8;

(b) The date of the entry into force of the present Protocol under article 9 and the date of the entry into force of any amendments under article 11;

(c) Denunciations under article 12.

Article 14.—1. The present Protocol, of which the Chinese, English, French, Russian and Spanish texts are equally authentic, shall be deposited in the archives of the United Nations.

2. The Secretary-General of the United Nations shall transmit certified copies of the present Protocol to all States referred to in article 48 of the Covenant.

6. PROCLAMATION OF TEHERAN

Adopted at the International Conference on Human Rights, Teheran, 13 May 1968. United Nations, Final Act of the International Conference on Human Rights, Teheran, 22 April to 13 May 1968, at 3-5 (UN Doc. A/CONF. 32/41, UN Publ. E.68.XIV.2). Endorsed by the General Assembly of the United Nations "as an important and timely reaffirmation of the principles embodied in the Universal Declaration of Human Rights and in other international instruments in the field of human rights." GA Resolution 2442 (XXIII), 19 December 1968, para. 5; 23 GAOR, Suppl. No. 18 (A/7218), at 49-50.

The International Conference on Human Rights,

Having met at Teheran from April 22 to May 13, 1968 to review the progress made in the twenty years since the adoption of the Universal Declaration of Human Rights and to formulate a programme for the future,

Having considered the problems relating to the activities of the United Nations for the promotion and encouragement of respect for human rights and fundamental freedoms,

Bearing in mind the resolutions adopted by the Conference,

Noting that the observance of the International Year for Human Rights takes place at a time when the world is undergoing a process of unprecedented change,

Having regard to the new opportunities made available by the rapid progress of science and technology,

Believing that, in an age when conflict and violence prevail in many parts of the world, the fact of human interdependence and the need for human solidarity are more evident than ever before,

Recognizing that peace is the universal aspiration of mankind and that peace and justice are indispensable to the full realization of human rights and fundamental freedoms,

Solemnly proclaims that:

1. It is imperative that the members of the international community fulfil their solemn obligations to promote and encourage respect for human rights and fundamental freedoms for all without distinctions of any kind such as race, colour, sex, language, religion, political or other opinions;

2. The Universal Declaration of Human Rights states a common understanding of the peoples of the world concerning the inalienable and inviolable rights of all members of the human family and constitutes an obligation for the members of the international community;

3. The International Covenant on Civil and Political Rights, the International Covenant on Economic, Social and Cultural Rights, the Declaration on the Granting of Independence to Colonial Countries and Peoples, the International Convention on the Elimination of All Forms of Racial Discrimination, as well as other conventions and declarations in the field of human rights adopted under the auspices of the United Nations, the specialized agencies and the regional inter-governmental organizations, have created new standards and obligations to which States should conform;

4. Since the adoption of the Universal Declaration of Human Rights the United Nations has made substantial progress in defining standards for the enjoyment and protection of human rights and fundamental freedoms. During this period many important international instruments were adopted but much remains to be done in regard to the implementation of those rights and freedoms;

5. The primary aim of the United Nations in the sphere of human rights is the achievement by each individual of the maximum freedom and dignity. For the realization of this objective, the laws of every country should grant each individual, irrespective of race, language, religion or political belief, freedom of expression, of information, of conscience and of religion, as well as the right to participate in the political, economic, cultural and social life of his country;

6. States should reaffirm their determination effectively to enforce the principles enshrined in the Charter of the United Nations and in other international instruments that concern human rights and fundamental freedoms;

7. Gross denials of human rights under the repugnant policy of *apartheid* is a matter of the gravest concern to the international community. This policy of *apartheid,* condemned as a crime against humanity, continues seriously to disturb international peace and security. It is therefore imperative for the international community to use every possible means to eradicate this evil. The struggle against *apartheid* is recognized as legitimate;

8. The peoples of the world must be made fully aware of the evils of racial discrimination and must join in combating them. The implementation of this principle of non-discrimination, embodied in the Charter of the United Nations, the Universal Declaration of Human Rights, and other international instruments in the field of human rights, constitutes a most urgent task of mankind, at the international as well as at the national level. All ideologies based on racial superiority and intolerance must be condemned and resisted;

9. Eight years after the General Assembly's Declaration on the Granting of Independence to Colonial Countries and Peoples the problems of colonialism continue to preoccupy the international community. It is a matter of urgency that all Member States should co-operate with the appropriate organs of the United Nations so that effective measures can be taken to ensure that the Declaration is fully implemented;

10. Massive denials of human rights, arising out of aggression or any armed conflict with their tragic consequences, and resulting in untold human misery, engender reactions which could engulf the world in ever growing hostilities. It is the obligation of the international community to co-operate in eradicating such scourges;

11. Gross denials of human rights arising from discrimination on grounds of race, religion, belief or expressions of opinion outrage the conscience of mankind and endanger the foundations of freedom, justice and peace in the world;

12. The widening gap between the economically developed and developing countries impedes the realization of human rights in the international community. The failure of the Development Decade to reach its modest objectives makes it all the more imperative for every nation, according to its capacities, to make the maximum possible effort to close this gap;

13. Since human rights and fundamental freedoms are indivisible, the full realization of civil and political rights without the enjoyment of economic, social and cultural rights, is impossible. The achievement of lasting progress in the implementation of human rights is dependent upon sound and effective national and international policies of economic and social development;

14. The existence of over seven hundred million illiterates throughout the world is an enormous obstacle to all efforts at realizing the aims and purposes of the Charter of the United Nations and the provisions of the Universal Declaration of Human Rights. International action aimed at eradicating illiteracy from the face of the earth and promoting education at all levels requires urgent attention;

15. The discrimination of which women are still victims in various regions of the world must be eliminated. An inferior status for women is contrary to the Charter of the United Nations as well as the provisions of the Universal Declaration of Human Rights. The full implementation of the Declaration on the Elimination of All Forms of Discrimination Against Women is a necessity for the progress of mankind;

16. The protection of the family and of the child remains the concern of the international community. Parents have a basic human right to determine freely and responsibly the number and the spacing of their children;

17. The aspirations of the younger generation for a better world, in which human rights and fundamental freedoms are fully implemented, must be given the highest encouragement. It is imperative that youth participate in shaping the future of mankind;

18. While recent scientific discoveries and technological advances have opened vast prospects for economic, social and cultural progress, such developments may nevertheless endanger the rights and freedoms of individuals and will require continuing attention;

19. Disarmament would release immense human and material resources now devoted to military purposes. These resources should be used for the promotion of human rights and fundamental freedoms. General and complete disarmament is one of the highest aspirations of all peoples;

Therefore,

The International Conference on Human Rights,

1. *Affirming* its faith in the principles of the Universal Declaration of Human Rights and other international instruments in this field,

2. *Urges* all peoples and governments to dedicate themselves to the principles enshrined in the Universal Declaration of Human Rights and to redouble their efforts to provide for all human beings a life consonant with freedom and dignity and conducive to physical, mental, social and spiritual welfare.

SECTION B.   DOCUMENTS RELATING TO SPECIAL QUESTIONS

1.   CONVENTION ON THE PREVENTION AND PUNISHMENT OF THE CRIME OF GENOCIDE

Approved by Resolution 260A (III) of the General Assembly, 9 December 1948; entered into force on 12 January 1951. 78 UNTS 277 (1951).

The Contracting Parties,

Having considered the declaration made by the General Assembly of the United Nations in its resolution 96 (I) dated 11 December 1946 that genocide is a crime under international law, contrary to the spirit and aims of the United Nations and condemned by the civilized world;

Recognizing that at all periods of history genocide has inflicted great losses on humanity; and

Being convinced that, in order to liberate mankind from such an odious scourge, international co-operation is required:

Hereby agree as hereinafter provided.

Article I. The Contracting Parties confirm that genocide, whether committed in time of peace or in time of war, is a crime under international law which they undertake to prevent and to punish.

Article II. In the present Convention, genocide means any of the following acts committed with intent to destroy, in whole or in part, a national, ethnical, racial or religious group as such:

(a) Killing members of the group;

(b) Causing serious bodily or mental harm to members of the group;

(c) Deliberately inflicting on the group conditions of life calculated to bring about its physical destruction in whole or in part;

(d) Imposing measures intended to prevent births within the group;

(e) Forcibly transferring children of the group to another group.

Article III. The following acts shall be punishable:

(a) Genocide;
(b) Conspiracy to commit genocide;
(c) Direct and public incitement to commit genocide;
(d) Attempt to commit genocide;
(e) Complicity in genocide.

Article IV. Persons committing genocide or any of the other acts enumerated in article III shall be punished, whether they are constitutionally responsible rulers, public officials or private individuals.

Article V. The Contracting Parties undertake to enact, in accordance with their respective Constitutions, the necessary legislation to give effect to the provisions of the present Convention and, in particular, to provide effective penalties for persons guilty of genocide or any of the other acts enumerated in article III.

Article VI. Persons charged with genocide or any of the other acts enumerated in article III shall be tried by a competent tribunal of the State in the territory of which the act was committed, or by such international penal tribunal as may have jurisdiction with respect to those Contracting Parties which shall have accepted its jurisdiction.

Article VII. Genocide and the other acts enumerated in article III shall not be considered as political crimes for the purpose of extradition.

The Contracting Parties pledge themselves in such cases to grant extradition in accordance with their laws and treaties in force.

Article VIII. Any Contracting Party may call upon the competent organs of the United Nations to take such action under the Charter of the United Nations as they consider appropriate for the prevention and suppression of acts of genocide or any of the other acts enumerated in article III.

Article IX. Disputes between the Contracting Parties relating to the interpretation, application or fulfilment of the present Convention, including those relating to the responsibility of a State for genocide or any of the other acts enumerated in article III, shall be submitted to the International Court of Justice at the request of any of the parties to the dispute.

Article X. The present Convention of which the Chinese, English, French, Russian and Spanish texts are equally authentic, shall bear the date of 9 December 1948.

Article XI. The present Convention shall be open until 31 December 1949 for signature on behalf of any Member of the United Nations and of any non-member State to which an invitation to sign has been addressed by the General Assembly.

The present Convention shall be ratified, and the instruments of ratification shall be deposited with the Secretary-General of the United Nations.

After 1 January 1950, the present Convention may be acceded to on behalf of any Member of the United Nations and of any non-member State which has received an invitation as aforesaid.

Instruments of accession shall be deposited with the Secretary-General of the United Nations.

Article XII. Any Contracting Party may at any time, by notification addressed to the Secretary-General of the United Nations, extend the application of the present Convention to all or any of the territories for the conduct of whose foreign relations that Contracting Party is responsible.

Article XIII. On the day when the first twenty instruments of ratification or accession have been deposited, the Secretary-General shall draw up a *procès-verbal* and transmit a copy of it to each Member of the United Nations and to each of the non-member States contemplated in article XI.

The present Convention shall come into force on the ninetieth day following the date of deposit of the twentieth instrument of ratification or accession.

Any ratification or accession effected subsequent to the latter date shall become effective on the ninetieth day following the deposit of the instrument of ratification or accession.

Article XIV. The present Convention shall remain in effect for a period of ten years as from the date of its coming into force.

It shall thereafter remain in force for successive periods of five years for such Contracting Parties as have not denounced it at least six months before the expiration of the current period.

Denunciation shall be affected by a written notification addressed to the Secretary-General of the United Nations.

Article XV. If, as a result of denunciations, the number of Parties to the present Convention should become less than sixteen, the Convention shall cease to be in force as from the date on which the last of these denunciations shall become effective.

Article XVI. A request for the revision of the present Convention may be made at any time by any Contracting Party by means of a notification in writing addressed to the Secretary-General.

The General Assembly shall decide upon the steps, if any, to be taken in respect of such request.

Article XVII. The Secretary-General of the United Nations shall notify all Members of the United Nations and the non-member States contemplated in article XI of the following:

(a) Signatures, ratifications and accessions received in accordance with article XI;

(b) Notifications received in accordance with article XII;

(c) The date upon which the present Convention comes into force in accordance with article XIII;

(d) Denunciations received in accordance with article XIV;

(e) The abrogation of the Convention in accordance with Article XV;

(f) Notifications received in accordance with article XVI.

Article XVIII. The original of the present Convention shall be deposited in the archives of the United Nations.

A certified copy of the Convention shall be transmitted to all Members of the United Nations and to the non-member States contemplated in article XI.

Article XIX. The present Convention shall be registered by the Secretary-General of the United Nations on the date of its coming into force.

2. CONVENTION ON THE POLITICAL RIGHTS OF WOMEN
Approved by Resolution 640 (VII) of the General Assembly, 20 December 1952; entered into force on 7 July 1954. 193 UNTS 135 (1954).

The Contracting Parties

Desiring to implement the principle of equality of rights for men and women contained in the Charter of the United Nations,

Recognizing that everyone has the right to take part in the government of his country, directly or indirectly through freely chosen representatives, and has the right to equal access to public service in his country, and desiring to equalize the status of men and women in the enjoyment and exercise of political rights, in accordance with the provisions of the Charter of the United Nations and of the Universal Declaration of Human Rights,

Having resolved to conclude a Convention for this purpose,

Hereby agree as hereinafter provided:

Article I

Women shall be entitled to vote in all elections on equal terms with men, without any discrimination.

Article II

Women shall be eligible for election to all publicly elected bodies, established by national law, on equal terms with men, without any discrimination.

Article III

Women shall be entitled to hold public office and to exercise all public functions, established by national law, on equal terms with men, without any discrimination.

Article IV

1. This Convention shall be open for signature on behalf of any Member of the United Nations and also on behalf of any other State to which an invitation has been addressed by the General Assembly.

2. This Convention shall be ratified and the instruments of ratification shall be deposited with the Secretary-General of the United Nations.

Article V

1. This Convention shall be open for accession to all States referred to in paragraph 1 of article IV.

2. Accession shall be effected by the deposit of an instrument of accession with the Secretary-General of the United Nations.

Article VI

1. This Convention shall come into force on the ninetieth day following the date of deposit of the sixth instrument of ratification or accession.

2. For each State ratifying or acceding to the Convention after the deposit of the sixth instrument of ratification or accession the Convention shall enter into force on the ninetieth day after deposit by such State of its instrument of ratification or accession.

Article VII

In the event that any State submits a reservation to any of the articles of this Convention at the time of signature, ratification or accession, the Secretary-General shall communicate the text of the reservation to all States which are or may become parties to this Convention. Any State which objects to the reservation may, within a period of ninety days from the date of the said communication (or upon the date of its becoming a party to the Convention), notify the Secretary-General that it does not accept it. In such case, the Convention shall not enter into force as between such State and the State making the reservation.

Article VIII

1. Any State may denounce this Convention by written notification to the Secretary-General of the United Nations. Denunciation shall take effect one year after the date of receipt of the notification by the Secretary-General.

2. This Convention shall cease to be in force as from the date when the denunciation which reduces the number of parties to less than six becomes effective.

Article IX

Any dispute which may arise between any two or more Contracting States concerning the interpretation or application of this Convention which is not settled by negotiation, shall at the request of any one of the parties to the dispute be referred to the International Court of Justice for decision, unless they agree to another mode of settlement.

Article X

The Secretary-General of the United Nations shall notify all Members of the United Nations and the non-member States contemplated in paragraph 1 of article IV of this Convention of the following:

(a) Signatures and instruments of ratifications received in accordance with article IV;

(b) Instruments of accession received in accordance with article V;

(c) The date upon which this Convention enters into force in accordance with article VI;

(d) Communications and notifications received in accordance with article VII;

(e) Notifications of denunciation received in accordance with paragraph 1 of article VIII;

(f) Abrogation in accordance with paragraph 2 of article VIII.

Article XI

1. This Convention, of which the Chinese, English, French, Russian and Spanish texts shall be equally authentic, shall be deposited in the archives of the United Nations.

2. The Secretary-General of the United Nations shall transmit a certified copy to all Members of the United Nations and to the non-member States contemplated in paragraph 1 of article IV.

3. DECLARATION ON THE ELIMINATION OF ALL FORMS OF RACIAL DISCRIMINATION

Approved by Resolution 1904 (XVIII) of the General Assembly, 20 November 1963. 18 GAOR, Suppl. No. 15 (A/5515), at 35-37.

The General Assembly,

Considering that the Charter of the United Nations is based on the principles of the dignity and equality of all human beings and seeks, among other basic objectives, to achieve international co-operation in promoting and encouraging respect for human rights and fundamental freedoms for all without distinction as to race, sex, language or religion,

Considering that the Universal Declaration of Human Rights proclaims that all human beings are born free and equal in dignity and rights and that everyone is entitled to all the rights and freedoms set out in the Declaration, without distinction of any kind, in particular as to race, colour or national origin,

Considering that the Universal Declaration of Human Rights proclaims further that all are equal before the law and are entitled without any discrimination to equal protection of the law and that all are entitled to equal protection against any discrimination and against any incitement to such discrimination,

Considering that the United Nations has condemned colonialism and all practices of segregation and discrimination associated therewith, and that the Declaration on the granting of independence to colonial countries and peoples proclaims in particular the necessity of bringing colonialism to a speedy and unconditional end,

Considering that any doctrine of racial differentiation or superiority is scientifically false, morally condemnable, socially unjust and dangerous, and that there is no justification for racial discrimination either in theory or in practice,

Taking into account the other resolutions adopted by the General Assembly and the international instruments adopted by the specialized agencies, in particular the International Labour Organisation and the United Nations Educational, Scientific and Cultural Organization, in the field of discrimination,

Taking into account the fact that, although international action and efforts in a number of countries have made it possible to achieve progress in that field, discrimination based on race, colour or ethnic origin in certain areas of the world none the less continues to give cause for serious concern,

Alarmed by the manifestations of racial discrimination still in evidence in some areas of the world, some of which are imposed by certain Governments by means of legislative, administrative or other measures, in the form, *inter alia,* of *apartheid,* segregation and separation, as well as by the promotion and dissemination of doctrines of racial superiority and expansionism in certain areas,

Convinced that all forms of racial discrimination and, still more so, governmental policies based on the prejudice of racial superiority or on racial hatred, besides constituting a violation of fundamental human rights, tend to jeopardize friendly relations among peoples, co-operation between nations and international peace and security,

Convinced also that racial discrimination harms not only those who are its objects but also those who practice it,

Convinced further that the building of a world society free from all forms of racial segregation and discrimination, factors which create hatred and division among men, is one of the fundamental objectives of the United Nations,

1. *Solemnly affirms* the necessity of speedily eliminating racial discrimination throughout the world, in all its forms and manifestations, and of securing understanding of and respect for the dignity of the human person;

2. *Solemnly affirms* the necessity of adopting national and international measures to that end, including teaching, education and information, in order to secure the universal and effective recognition and observance of the principles set forth below;

3. *Proclaims* this Declaration:

Article 1

Discrimination between human beings on the grounds of race, colour or ethnic origin is an offence to human dignity and shall be condemned as a denial of the principles of the Charter of the United Nations, as a violation of the human rights and fundamental freedoms proclaimed in the Universal Declaration of Human Rights, as an obstacle to friendly and peaceful relations among nations and as a fact capable of disturbing peace and security among peoples.

Article 2

1. No State, institution, group or individual shall make any discrimination whatsoever in matters of human rights and fundamental freedoms in the treatment of persons, groups of persons or institutions on the grounds of race, colour or ethnic origin.

2. No State shall encourage, advocate or lend its support through police action or otherwise, to any discrimination based on race, colour or ethnic origin by any group, institution or individual.

3. Special concrete measures shall be taken in appropriate circumstances in order to secure adequate development or protection of individuals belonging to certain racial groups with the object of ensuring the full enjoyment by such individuals of human rights and fundamental freedoms. These measures shall in no circumstances have as a consequence the maintenance of unequal or separate rights for different racial groups.

Article 3

1. Particular efforts shall be made to prevent discrimination based on race, colour or ethnic origin, especially in the fields of civil rights, access to citizenship, education, religion, employment, occupation and housing.
2. Everyone shall have equal access to any place or facility intended for use by the general public, without distinction as to race, colour or ethnic origin.

Article 4

All States shall take effective measures to revise governmental and other public policies and to rescind laws and regulations which have the effect of creating and perpetuating racial discrimination wherever it still exists. They should pass legislation for prohibiting such discrimination and should take all appropriate measures to combat those prejudices which lead to racial discrimination.

Article 5

An end shall be put without delay to governmental and other public policies of racial segregation and especially policies of *apartheid,* as well as all forms of racial discrimination and separation resulting from such policies.

Article 6

No discrimination by reason of race, colour or ethnic origin shall be admitted in the enjoyment by any person of political and citizenship rights in his country, in particular the right to participate in elections through universal and equal suffrage and to take part in the government. Everyone has the right of equal access to public service in his country.

Article 7

1. Everyone has the right to equality before the law and to equal justice under the law. Everyone, without distinction as to race, colour or ethnic origin, has the right to security of person

and protection by the State against violence or bodily harm, whether inflicted by government officials or by any individual, group or institution.

2. Everyone shall have the right to an effective remedy and protection against any discrimination he may suffer on the ground of race, colour or ethnic origin with respect to his fundamental rights and freedoms through independent national tribunals competent to deal with such matters.

Article 8

All effective steps shall be taken immediately in the fields of teaching, education and information, with a view to eliminating racial discrimination and prejudice and promoting understanding, tolerance and friendship among nations and racial groups, as well as to propagating the purposes and principles of the Charter of the United Nations, of the Universal Declaration of Human Rights, and of the Declaration on the granting of independence to colonial countries and peoples.

Article 9

1. All propaganda and organizations based on ideas or theories of the superiority of one race or group of persons of one colour or ethnic origin with a view to justifying or promoting racial discrimination in any form shall be severely condemned.

2. All incitement to or acts of violence, whether by individuals or organizations, against any race or group of persons of another colour or ethnic origin shall be considered an offence against society and punishable under law.

3. In order to put into effect the purposes and principles of the present Declaration, all States shall take immediate and positive measures, including legislative and other measures, to prosecute and/or outlaw organizations which promote or incite to racial discrimination, or incite to or use violence for purposes of discrimination based on race, colour or ethnic origin.

Article 10

The United Nations, the specialized agencies, State and non-governmental organizations shall do all in their power to promote energetic action which, by combining legal and other practical measures, will make possible the abolition of all forms of racial discrimination. They shall, in particular, study the causes of such discrimination with a view to recommending appropriate and effective measures to combat and eliminate it.

Article 11

Every State shall promote respect for and observance of human rights and fundamental freedoms in accordance with the Charter of the United Nations, and shall fully and faithfully observe the provisions of the present Declaration, the Universal Declaration of Human Rights and the Declaration on the granting of independence to colonial countries and peoples.

4. INTERNATIONAL CONVENTION ON THE ELIMINATION OF ALL FORMS OF RACIAL DISCRIMINATION

Adopted by Resolution 2106A (XX) of the General Assembly, 21 December 1965; entered into force on 4 January 1969. GAOR, XX, Suppl. No. 14 (A/6014), pp. 47-51.

The States Parties to This Convention,

Considering that the Charter of the United Nations is based on the principles of the dignity and equality inherent in all human beings, and that all Member States have pledged themselves to take joint and separate action in co-operation with the Organization for the achievement of one of the purposes of the United Nations which is to promote and encourage universal respect for and observance of human rights and fundamental freedoms for all without distinction as to race, sex, language or religion,

Considering that the Universal Declaration of Human Rights proclaims that all human beings are born free and equal in dignity and rights and that everyone is entitled to all the rights and freedoms set out therein, without distinctions of any kind, in particular as to race, colour or national origin,

Considering that all human beings are equal before the law and are entitled to equal protection of the law against any discrimination and against any incitement to discrimination,

Considering that the United Nations has condemned colonialism and all practices of segregation and discrimination associated therewith, in whatever form and wherever they exist, and that the Declaration on the Granting of Independence to Colonial Countries and Peoples of 14 December 1960 (General Assembly resolution 1514 (XV)) has affirmed and solemnly proclaimed the necessity of bringing them to a speedy and unconditional end,

Considering that the United Nations Declaration on the Elimination of All Forms of Racial Discrimination of 20 November 1963 (General Assembly resolution 1904 (XVIII)) solemnly affirms the necessity of speedily eliminating racial discrimination throughout the world in all its forms and manifestations and of securing understanding of and respect for the dignity of the human person,

Convinced that any doctrine of superiority based on racial differentiation is scientifically false, morally condemnable, socially unjust and dangerous, and that there is no justification for racial discrimination, in theory or in practice, anywhere,

Reaffirming that discrimination between human beings on the grounds of race, colour or ethnic origin is an obstacle to friendly and peaceful relations among nations and is capable of disturbing peace and security among peoples and the harmony of persons living side by side even within one and the same State,

Convinced that the existence of racial barriers is repugnant to the ideals of any human society,

Alarmed by manifestations of racial discrimination still in evidence in some areas of the world and by governmental policies based on racial superiority or hatred, such as policies of *apartheid,* segregation or separation,

Resolved to adopt all necessary measures for speedily eliminating racial discrimination in all its forms and manifestations and to prevent and combat racist doctrines and practices in order to promote understanding between races and to build an international community free from all forms of racial segregation and racial discrimination,

Bearing in mind the Convention on Discrimination in Respect of Employment and Occupation adopted by the International Labour Organisation in 1958, and the Convention Against Discrimination in Education adopted by the United Nations Educational, Scientific and Cultural Organization in 1960,

Desiring to implement the principles embodied in the United Nations Declaration on the Elimination of All Forms of Racial Discrimination and to secure the earliest adoption of practical measures to that end,

Have agreed as follows:

PART I

Article 1

1.   In this Convention the term "racial discrimination" shall mean any distinction, exclusion, restriction or preference based on race, colour, descent, or national or ethnic origin which has the purpose or effect of nullifying or impairing the recognition, enjoyment or exercise, on an equal footing, of human rights and fundamental freedoms in the political, economic, social, cultural or any other field of public life.

2.   This Convention shall not apply to distinctions, exclusions, restrictions or preferences made by a State Party to this Convention between citizens and non-citizens.

3. Nothing in this Convention may be interpreted as affecting in any way the legal provisions of States Parties concerning nationality, citizenship or naturalization, provided that such provisions do not discriminate against any particular nationality.

4. Special measures taken for the sole purpose of securing adequate advancement of certain racial or ethnic groups or individuals requiring such protection as may be necessary in order to ensure to such groups or individuals equal enjoyment or exercise of human rights and fundamental freedoms shall not be deemed racial discrimination, provided, however, that such measures do not, as a consequence, lead to the maintenance of separate rights for different racial groups and that they shall not be continued after the objectives for which they were taken have been achieved.

Article 2

1. States Parties condemn racial discrimination and undertake to pursue by all appropriate means and without delay a policy of eliminating racial discrimination in all its forms, and promoting understanding among all races, and to this end:

(a) Each State Party undertakes to engage in no act or practice of racial discrimination against persons, groups of persons or institutions and to ensure that all public authorities and public institutions, national and local, shall act in conformity with this obligation;

(b) Each State Party undertakes not to sponsor, defend or support racial discrimination by any persons or organizations;

(c) Each State Party shall take effective measures to review governmental, national and local policies, and to amend, rescind or nullify any laws and regulations which have the effect of creating or perpetuating racial discrimination wherever it exists;

(d) Each State Party shall prohibit and bring to an end, by all appropriate means, including legislation as required by circumstances, racial discrimination by any persons, group or organization;

(e) Each State Party undertakes to encourage, where appropriate, integrationist multi-racial organizations and movements and other means of eliminating barriers between races, and to discourage anything which tends to strengthen racial division.

2. States Parties shall, when the circumstances so warrant, take, in the social, economic, cultural and other fields, special and concrete measures to ensure the adequate development and protection of certain racial groups or individuals belonging to them for

the purpose of guaranteeing them the full and equal enjoyment of human rights and fundamental freedoms. These measures shall in no case entail as a consequence the maintenance of unequal or separate rights for different racial groups after the objectives for which they were taken have been achieved.

Article 3

States Parties particularly condemn racial segregation and *apartheid* and undertake to prevent, prohibit and eradicate, in territories under their jurisdiction, all practices of this nature.

Article 4

States Parties condemn all propaganda and all organizations which are based on ideas or theories of superiority of one race or group of persons of one colour or ethnic origin, or which attempt to justify or promote racial hatred and discrimination in any form, and undertake to adopt immediate and positive measures designed to eradicate all incitement to, or acts of, such discrimination, and to this end, with due regard to the principles embodied in the Universal Declaration of Human Rights and the rights expressly set forth in article 5 of this Convention, *inter alia:*

(a)   Shall declare an offence punishable by law all dissemination of ideas based on racial superiority or hatred, incitement to racial discrimination, as well as all acts of violence or incitement to such acts against any race or group of persons of another colour or ethnic origin, and also the provision of any assistance to racist activities, including the financing thereof;

(b)   Shall declare illegal and prohibit organizations, and also organized and all other propaganda activities, which promote and incite racial discrimination, and shall recognize participation in such organizations or activities as an offence punishable by law;

(c)   Shall not permit public authorities or public institutions, national or local, to promote or incite racial discrimination.

Article 5

In compliance with the fundamental obligations laid down in article 2, States Parties undertake to prohibit and to eliminate racial discrimination in all its forms and to guarantee the right of everyone, without distinction as to race, colour, or national or ethnic origin, to equality before the law, notably in the enjoyment of the following rights:

(a)   The right to equal treatment before the tribunals and all other organs administering justice;

(b)   The right to security of person and protection by the State against violence or bodily harm, whether inflicted by Government officials or by any individual, group or institution;

(c)   Political rights, in particular the rights to participate in elections, to vote and to stand for election—on the basis of universal and equal suffrage, to take part in the Government as well as in the conduct of public affairs at any level and to have equal access to public service;

(d)   Other civil rights, in particular:

(i)   the right to freedom of movement and residence within the border of the State;

(ii)   the right to leave any country, including his own, and to return to his country;

(iii)   the right to nationality;

(iv)   the right to marriage and choice of spouse;

(v)   the right to own property alone as well as in association with others;

(vi)   the right to inherit;

(vii)   the right to freedom of thought, conscience and religion;

(viii)   the right to freedom of opinion and expression;

(ix)   the right to freedom of peaceful assembly and association;

(e)   Economic, social and cultural rights, in particular:

(i)   the rights to work, free choice of employment, just and favourable conditions of work, protection against unemployment, equal pay for equal work, just and favourable remuneration;

(ii)   the right to form and join trade unions;

(iii)   the right to housing;

(iv)   the right to public health, medical care and social security and social services;

(v)   the right to education and training;

(vi)   the right to equal participation in cultural activities;

(f)   The right of access to any place or service intended for use by the general public such as transport, hotels, restaurants, cafés, theatres, parks.

Article 6

States Parties shall assure to everyone within their jurisdiction effective protection and remedies through the competent national tribunals and other State institutions against any acts of racial discrimination which violate his human rights and fundamental freedoms contrary to this Convention, as well as the right to seek from such tribunals just and adequate reparation or satisfaction for any damage suffered as a result of such discrimination.

Article 7

States Parties undertake to adopt immediate and effective measures, particularly in the fields of teaching, education, culture and information, with a view to combating prejudices which lead to racial discrimination and to promoting understanding, tolerance and friendship among nations and racial or ethnical groups, as well as to propagating the purposes and principles of the Charter of the United Nations, the Universal Declaration of Human Rights, the United Nations Declaration on the Elimination of All Forms of Racial Discrimination, and this Convention.

PART II
Article 8

1.   There shall be established a Committee on the Elimination of Racial Discrimination (hereinafter referred to as the Committee) consisting of eighteen experts of high moral standing and acknowledged impartiality elected by States Parties from amongst their nationals who shall serve in their personal capacity, consideration being given to equitable geographical distribution and to the representation of the different forms of civilizations as well as of the principal legal systems.

2.   The members of the Committee shall be elected by secret ballot from a list of persons nominated by the States Parties. Each State Party may nominate one person from among its own nationals.

3.   The initial election shall be held six months after the date of the entry into force of this Convention. At least three months before the date of each election the Secretary-General of the United Nations shall address a letter to the States Parties inviting them to submit their nominations within two months. The Secretary-General shall prepare a list in alphabetical order of all persons thus nominated indicating the States Parties which have nominated them and shall submit it to the States Parties.

4.   Elections of the members of the Committee shall be held at a meeting of States Parties convened by the Secretary-General at the Headquarters of the United Nations. At that meeting, for which two-thirds of the States Parties shall constitute a quorum, the persons elected to the Committee shall be those nominees who obtain the largest number of votes and an absolute majority of the votes of the representatives of States Parties present and voting.

5. (a) The members of the Committee shall be elected for a term of four years. However, the terms of nine of the members elected at the first election shall expire at the end of two years; immediately after the first election the names of these nine members shall be chosen by lot by the Chairman of the Committee.

(b) For the filling of casual vacancies, the State Party whose expert has ceased to function as a member of the Committee shall appoint another expert from among its nationals subject to the approval of the Committee.

6. The States Parties shall be responsible for the expenses of the members of the Committee while they are in performance of Committee duties.

Article 9

1. The States Parties undertake to submit to the Secretary-General for consideration by the Committee a report on the legislative, judicial, administrative, or other measures that they have adopted and that give effect to the provisions of this Convention: (a) within one year after the entry into force of the Convention for the State concerned; and (b) thereafter every two years and whenever the Committee so requests. The Committee may request further information from the States Parties.

2. The Committee shall report annually through the Secretary-General to the General Assembly on its activities and may make suggestions and general recommendations based on the examination of the reports and information received from the States Parties. Such suggestions and general recommendations shall be reported to the General Assembly together with comments, if any, from States Parties.

Article 10

1. The Committee shall adopt its own rules of procedure.

2. The Committee shall elect its officers for a term of two years.

3. The secretariat of the Committee shall be provided by the Secretary-General of the United Nations.

4. The meetings of the Committee shall normally be held at the Headquarters of the United Nations.

Article 11

1. If a State Party considers that another State Party is not giving effect to the provisions of this Convention, it may bring the matter to the attention of the Committee. The Committee shall then transmit the communication to the State Party concerned.

Within three months, the receiving State shall submit to the Committee written explanations or statements clarifying the matter and the remedy, if any, that may have been taken by that State.

2. If the matter is not adjusted to the satisfaction of both parties, either by bilateral negotiations or by any other procedure open to them, within six months after the receipt by the receiving State of the initial communication, either State shall have the right to refer the matter again to the Committee by notice given to the Committee and also to the other State.

3. The Committee shall deal with a matter referred to it in accordance with paragraph 2 of this article after it has ascertained that all available domestic remedies have been invoked and exhausted in the case, in conformity with the generally recognized principles of international law. This shall not be the rule where the application of the remedies is unreasonably prolonged.

4. In any matter referred to it, the Committee may call upon the States Parties concerned to supply any other relevant information.

5. When any matter arising out of this article is being considered by the Committee, the States Parties concerned shall be entitled to send a representative to take part in the proceedings of the Committee, without voting rights, while the matter is under consideration.

Article 12

1. (a) After the Committee has obtained and collated all the information it thinks necessary, the Chairman shall appoint an *ad hoc* Conciliation Commission (hereinafter referred to as "the Commission") comprising five persons who may or may not be members of the Committee. The members of the Commission shall be appointed with the unanimous consent of the parties to the dispute, and its good offices shall be made available to the States concerned with a view to an amicable solution to the matter on the basis of respect for this Convention.

(b) If the States Parties to the dispute fail to reach agreement on all or part of the composition of the Commission within three months, the members of the Commission not agreed upon by the States Parties to the dispute shall be elected by two-thirds majority vote by secret ballot of the Committee from among its own members.

2. The members of the Commission shall serve in their personal capacity. They shall not be nationals of the States Parties to the dispute or of a State not Party to this Convention.

3. The Commission shall elect its own Chairman and adopt its own rules of procedure.

4. The meetings of the Commission shall normally be held at the Headquarters of the United Nations, or at any other convenient place as determined by the Commission.

5. The secretariat provided in accordance with article 10, paragraph 3, shall also service the Commission whenever a dispute among States Parties brings the Commission into being.

6. The States Parties to the dispute shall share equally all the expenses of the members of the Commission in accordance with estimates to be provided by the Secretary-General.

7. The Secretary-General shall be empowered to pay the expenses of the members of the Commission, if necessary, before reimbursement by the States Parties to the dispute in accordance with paragraph 6 of this article.

8. The information obtained and collated by the Committee shall be made available to the Commission and the Commission may call upon the States concerned to supply any other relevant information.

Article 13

1. When the Commission has fully considered the matter, it shall prepare and submit to the Chairman of the Committee a report embodying its findings on all questions of fact relevant to the issue between the parties and containing such recommendations as it may think proper for the amicable solution of the dispute.

2. The Chairman of the Committee shall communicate the report of the Commission to each of the States Parties to the dispute. These States shall within three months inform the Chairman of the Committee whether or not they accept the recommendations contained in the report of the Commission.

3. After the period provided for in paragraph 2 of this article, the Chairman of the Committee shall communicate the report of the Commission and the declarations of States Parties concerned to the other States Parties to this Convention.

Article 14

1. A State Party may at any time declare that it recognizes the competence of the Committee to receive and consider communications from individuals or groups of individuals within its jurisdiction claiming to be victims of a violation by that State Party of any of the rights set forth in this Convention. No communication shall be received by the Committee if it concerns a State Party which has not made such a declaration.

2. Any State Party which makes a declaration as provided for in paragraph 1 of this article may establish or indicate a body

within its national legal order which shall be competent to receive and consider petitions from individuals and groups of individuals within its jurisdiction who claim to be victims of a violation of any of the rights set forth in this Convention and who have exhausted other available local remedies.

3. A declaration made in accordance with paragraph 1 of this article and the name of any body established or indicated in accordance with paragraph 2 of this article, shall be deposited by the State Party concerned with the Secretary-General of the United Nations, who shall transmit copies thereof to the other States Parties. A declaration may be withdrawn at any time by notification to the Secretary-General, but such a withdrawal shall not affect communications pending before the Committee.

4. A register of petitions shall be kept by the body established or indicated in accordance with paragraph 2 of this article, and certified copies of the register shall be filed annually through appropriate channels with the Secretary-General on the understanding that the contents shall not be publicly disclosed.

5. In the event of failure to obtain satisfaction from the body established or indicated in accordance with paragraph 2 of this article, the petitioner shall have the right to communicate the matter to the Committee within six months.

6. (a) The Committee shall confidentially bring any communication referred to it to the attention of the State Party alleged to be violating any provision of this Convention, but the identity of the individual or groups of individuals concerned shall not be revealed without his or their express consent. The Committee shall not receive anonymous communications.

(b) Within three months, the receiving State shall submit to the Committee written explanations or statements clarifying the matter and the remedy, if any, that may have been taken by that State.

7. (a) The Committee shall consider communications in the light of all information made available to it by the State Party concerned and by the petitioner. The Committee shall not consider any communication from a petitioner unless it has ascertained that the petitioner has exhausted all available domestic remedies. However, this shall not be the rule where the application of the remedies is unreasonably prolonged.

(b) The Committee shall forward its suggestions and recommendations, if any, to the State Party concerned and to the petitioner.

8. The Committee shall include in its annual report a summary of such communications and, where appropriate, a summary

of the explanations and statements of the States Parties concerned and of its own suggestions and recommendations.

9. The Committee shall be competent to exercise the functions provided for in this article only when at least ten States Parties to this Convention are bound by declarations in accordance with paragraph 1 of this article.

Article 15

1. Pending the achievement of the objectives of General Assembly resolution 1514 (XV) of December 1960 concerning the Declaration on the Granting of Independence to Colonial Countries and Peoples, the provisions of this Convention shall in no way limit the right of petition granted to these peoples by other international instruments or by the United Nations and its specialized agencies.

2. (a) The Committee established under article 8, paragraph 1, shall receive copies of the petitions from, and submit expressions of opinion and recommendations on these petitions to, the bodies of the United Nations which deal with matters directly related to the principles and objectives of this Convention in their consideration of petitions from the inhabitants of Trust and Non-Self-Governing Territories, and all other territories to which General Assembly resolution 1514 (XV) applies, relating to matters covered by this Convention which are before these bodies.

(b) The Committee shall receive from the competent bodies of the United Nations copies of the reports concerning the legislative, judicial, administrative or other measures directly related to the principles and objectives of this Convention applied by the Administering Powers within the territories mentioned in sub-paragraph (a) of this paragraph and shall express opinions and make recommendations to these bodies.

3. The Committee shall include in its report to the General Assembly a summary of the petitions and reports it has received from United Nations bodies, and the expressions of opinion and recommendations of the Committee related to the said petitions and reports.

4. The Committee shall request from the Secretary-General of the United Nations all information relevant to the objectives of this Convention and available to him regarding the territories mentioned in paragraph 2 (a) of this article.

Article 16

The provisions of this Convention concerning the settlement of disputes or complaints shall be applied without prejudice to other procedures for settling disputes or complaints in the field of discrimination laid down in the constituent instruments of, or in conventions adopted by, the United Nations and its specialized agencies, and shall not prevent the States Parties from having recourse to other procedures for settling a dispute in accordance with general or special international agreements in force between them.

PART III

Article 17

1. This Convention is open for signature by any State Member of the United Nations or member of any of its specialized agencies, by any State Party to the Statute of the International Court of Justice, and by any other State which has been invited by the General Assembly of the United Nations to become a party to this Convention.

2. This Convention is subject to ratification. Instruments of ratification shall be deposited with the Secretary-General of the United Nations.

Article 18

1. This Convention shall be open to accession by any State referred to in article 17, paragraph 1.

2. Accession shall be effected by the deposit of an instrument of accession with the Secretary-General of the United Nations.

Article 19

1. This Convention shall enter into force on the thirtieth day after the date of the deposit with the Secretary-General of the United Nations of the twenty-seventh instrument of ratification or instrument of accession.

2. For each State ratifying this Convention or acceding to it after the deposit of the twenty-seventh instrument of ratification or instrument of accession, the Convention shall enter into force on the thirtieth day after the date of the deposit of its own instrument of ratification or instrument of accession.

Article 20

1. The Secretary-General of the United Nations shall receive and circulate to all States which are or may become parties to this Convention reservations made by States at the time of ratification or accession. Any State which objects to the reservation shall, within a period of ninety days from the date of the said communication, notify the Secretary-General that it does not accept it.

2. A reservation incompatible with the object and purpose of this Convention shall not be permitted, nor shall a reservation the effect of which would inhibit the operation of any of the bodies established by the Convention be allowed. A reservation shall be considered incompatible or inhibitive if at least two-thirds of the States Parties to this Convention object to it.

3. Reservations may be withdrawn at any time by notification to this effect addressed to the Secretary-General. Such notification shall take effect on the date on which it is received.

Article 21

A State Party may denounce this Convention by written notification to the Secretary-General of the United Nations. Denunciation shall take effect one year after the date of receipt of the notification by the Secretary-General.

Article 22

Any dispute between two or more States Parties over the interpretation or application of this Convention, which is not settled by negotiation or by the procedures expressly provided for in this Convention, shall at the request of any of the parties to the dispute be referred to the International Court of Justice for decision, unless the disputants agree to another mode of settlement.

Article 23

1. A request for the revision of this Convention may be made at any time by any State Party by means of a notification in writing addressed to the Secretary-General.

2. The General Assembly shall decide upon the steps, if any, to be taken in respect of such a request.

Article 24

The Secretary-General of the United Nations shall inform all States referred to in article 17, paragraph 1, of the following particulars:

(a) Signatures, ratifications and accessions under articles 17 and 18;

(b) The date of entry into force of this Convention under article 19;

(c) Communications and declarations received under articles 14, 20 and 23;

(d) Denunciations under article 21.

Article 25

1.   This Convention, of which the Chinese, English, French, Russian and Spanish texts are equally authentic, shall be deposited in the archives of the United Nations.

2.   The Secretary-General of the United Nations shall transmit certified copies of this Convention to all States belonging to any of the categories mentioned in article 17, paragraph 1, of the Convention.

5.   PROVISIONAL RULES OF PROCEDURE OF THE COMMITTEE ON THE ELIMINATION OF RACIAL DISCRIMINATION

Adopted by the Committee at the first and second sessions, with amendments adopted at its fourth and fifth sessions. 25 GAOR, Suppl. No. 27 (A/8027), at 17-31 (1970); 26 *idem*, Suppl. No. 18 (A/8418), at 33 (1971); 27 *idem*, Suppl. No. 18 (A/8718), at 37 (1972).

PART I.   GENERAL RULES

I.   SESSIONS

Rule 1

The Committee on the Elimination of Racial Discrimination (hereinafter referred to as "the Committee"), established under the International Convention on the Elimination of All Forms of Racial Discrimination (hereinafter referred to as "the Convention"), shall hold two regular sessions each year.

Rule 2

Regular sessions of the Committee shall be convened at dates decided by the Committee in consultation with the Secretary-General of the United Nations (hereinafter referred to as "the Secretary-General"), taking into account the calendar of conferences as approved by the General Assembly.

Rule 3

1.   Special sessions of the Committee shall be convened by decision of the Committee. When the Committee is not in session, the Chairman may convene special sessions of the Committee in consultation with the other officers of the Committee. The Chairman of the Committee shall also convene special sessions:

(a)   at the request of a majority of the members of the Committee;

(b)   at the request of a State Party to the Convention.

2.   Special sessions shall be convened as soon as possible at a date fixed by the Chairman in consultation with the Secretary-General and with the other officers of the Committee, taking into

account the calendar of conferences as approved by the General Assembly.

Rule 4

The Secretary-General shall notify the members of the Committee of the date and place of the first meeting of each session. Such notifications shall be sent, in the case of regular sessions, at least thirty days in advance, and in the case of a special session, at least eighteen days in advance, of the first meeting.

Rule 5

Sessions of the Committee shall normally be held at the Headquarters of the United Nations. Another place for a session may be designated by the Committee in consultation with the Secretary-General, taking into account the relevant rules of the United Nations on the subject.

II. AGENDA

Rule 6

The provisional agenda of each regular session shall be prepared by the Secretary-General in consultation with the Chairman of the Committee, in conformity with the relevant provisions of articles 9, 11, 12, 13, 14 and 15 of the Convention, and shall include:

(a) Any item decided upon by the Committee at a previous session;

(b) Any item proposed by the Chairman of the Committee;

(c) Any item proposed by a State Party to the Convention;

(d) Any item proposed by a member of the Committee;

(e) Any item proposed by the Secretary-General.

Rule 7

The provisional agenda for a special session of the Committee shall consist only of those items which are proposed for its consideration at that special session.

Rule 8

The first item on the provisional agenda of any session shall be the adoption of the agenda, except for the election of the officers when required under rule 15.

Rule 9

During a session, the Committee may revise the agenda and may, as appropriate, add, defer or delete items.

Rule 10

The provisional agenda and basic documents relating to items appearing thereon shall be transmitted to the members of the Committee by the Secretary-General as early as possible. The provisional agenda of a special session shall be transmitted to the members of the Committee by the Secretary-General simultaneously with the notification of the meeting under rule 4.

III.   MEMBERS OF THE COMMITTEE

Rule 11

Members of the Committee shall be the eighteen experts designated in accordance with article 8 of the Convention.

Rule 12

The members of the Committee elected at the first election shall begin their term of office on the date of the first meeting of the Committee. In the case of members of the Committee elected at subsequent elections, their term of office shall begin on the day following the date of the expiration of the term of office of the members of the Committee whom they replace.

Rule 13

1.   When a casual vacancy occurs in the Committee, the Secretary-General shall immediately request the State Party whose expert has ceased to function as a member of the Committee to appoint another expert from among its nationals within two months to serve for the remainder of his predecessor's term. The name of the expert so appointed shall be submitted by the Secretary-General to the Committee for approval.

2.   After the approval of the expert by the Committee, the Secretary-General shall notify the States Parties to the Convention of the name of the member of the Committee filling a casual vacancy.

Rule 14

Upon assuming his duties, each member of the Committee shall make the following solemn declaration in open Committee:

"I solemnly declare that I will perform my duties and exercise my powers as a member of the Committee on the Elimination of Racial Discrimination honourably, faithfully, impartially and conscientiously."

IV. OFFICERS
Rule 15

The Committee shall elect from among its own members a Chairman, three Vice-Chairmen and a Rapporteur.

Rule 16

The officers of the Committee shall be elected for a term of two years. They shall be eligible for re-election. None of them, however, may hold office if he ceases to be a member of the Committee.

Rule 17

In exercising his functions as Chairman, the Chairman shall remain under the authority of the Committee.

Rule 18

If the Chairman is unable to be present at a meeting or any part thereof, he shall designate one of the Vice-Chairmen to act in his place.

Rule 19

A Vice-Chairman acting as Chairman shall have the same powers and duties as the Chairman.

Rule 20

If any of the officers of the Committee ceases or declares his inability to function as a member of the Committee or, for any reason, is no longer able to act as an officer, a new officer shall be elected for the unexpired term of his predecessor.

V. SECRETARIAT
Rule 21

The secretariat of the Committee and of such subsidiary bodies as may be established by the Committee (hereinafter referred to as "the Secretariat") shall be provided by the Secretary-General.

Rule 22

The Secretary-General or his representative shall be present at all meetings of the Committee. He or his representative may, subject to rule 36, make either oral or written statements to the meetings of the Committee or its subsidiary bodies.

Rule 23

The Secretary-General shall be responsible for all the necessary arrangements for meetings of the Committee and its subsidiary bodies.

Rule 24

The Secretary-General shall be responsible for keeping the members of the Committee informed of any questions which may be brought before it for consideration.

Rule 25

Before any proposal which involves expenditures is approved by the Committee or by any of its subsidiary bodies, the Secretary-General shall prepare and circulate to its members, as early as possible, an estimate of the cost involved in the proposal. It shall be the duty of the Chairman to draw the attention of members to this estimate and to invite discussions on it when the proposal is considered by the Committee or by a subsidiary body.

VI. LANGUAGES

Rule 26

Chinese, English, French, Russian and Spanish shall be the official languages and English, French, Russian and Spanish shall be the working languages of the Committee.

Rule 27

Speeches made in any of the working languages shall be interpreted into the other working languages.

Rule 28

Any person appearing before the Committee, may make a speech in a language other than the official languages. In this case, he shall himself provide for interpretation into one of the working languages. Interpretation into the other working languages by the interpreters of the Secretariat may be based on the interpretation in the first working language.

Rule 29

Summary records of meetings of the Committee shall be drawn up in the working languages.

Rule 30

All formal decisions of the Committee shall be made available in the official languages. All official documents of the Committee shall be issued in the working languages, and any of them may be issued in the other official language upon the decision of the Committee.

VII. Public and Private Meetings
Rule 31

The meetings of the Committee and its subsidiary bodies shall be held in public, unless the Committee decides otherwise, or it appears from the relevant provisions of the Convention that the meeting should be held in private.

Rule 32

At the close of each private meeting the Committee or its subsidiary body may issue a communiqué through the Secretary-General.

VIII. Records
Rule 33

Summary records of the public and private meetings of the Committee and its subsidiary bodies shall be prepared by the Secretariat. They shall be distributed in provisional form as soon as possible to the members of the Committee, and to any others participating in the meetings. All such participants may, within three working days of the receipt of the provisional records of the meetings, submit corrections to the Secretariat. Any disagreement concerning such corrections shall be decided by the Chairman of the Committee or the Chairman of the subsidiary body to which the record relates or, in case of continued disagreement, by decision of the Committee or of the subsidiary body.

Rule 34

1.   The records of public meetings in their final form shall be distributed to the members of the Committee and to the States Parties to the Convention and made available to other persons and bodies as may be determined by the Committee.

2.   The records of private meetings shall be distributed to the members of the Committee and may be made available to others upon decision of the Committee at such time and under such conditions as the Committee may decide.

3.   The Committee shall also determine when and under what conditions the records may be consulted by the public.

IX. Conduct of Business
Rule 35

A majority of the members of the Committee shall constitute a quorum. The presence of two-thirds of the members of the Committee is, however, required for a decision to be taken.

Rule 36

In addition to exercising the powers conferred upon him by the Convention and elsewhere by these rules, the Chairman shall declare the opening and closing of each meeting of the Committee, shall direct the discussion, ensure observance of these rules, accord the right to speak, put questions to the vote and announce decisions. The Chairman, subject to these rules, shall have control of the proceedings of the Committee and over the maintenance of order at its meetings. The Chairman may, in the course of the discussion of an item, propose to the Committee the limitation of the time to be allowed to speakers, the limitation of the number of times each speaker may speak on any question and the closure of the list of speakers. He shall rule on points of order. He may also propose the adjournment or the closure of the debate or the adjournment or the suspension of a meeting. Debate shall be confined to the question before the Committee, and the Chairman may call a speaker to order if his remarks are not relevant to the subject under discussion.

Rule 37

During the discussion of any matter, a member may, at any time, raise a point of order, and such point of order shall immediately be decided upon by the Chairman in accordance with the rules of procedure. Any appeal against the ruling of the Chairman shall immediately be put to the vote, and the ruling of the Chairman shall stand unless overruled by a majority of the members present and voting. A member raising a point of order may not speak on the substance of the matter under discussion.

Rule 38

During the discussion of any matter, a member may move the adjournment of the debate on the item under discussion. In addition to the proposer of the motion, one member may speak in favour of and one against the motion, after which the motion shall immediately be put to the vote.

Rule 39

The Committee may limit the time allowed to each speaker on any question. When debate is limited and a member or representative exceeds his allotted time, the Chairman shall call him to order without delay.

Rule 40

During the course of a debate, the Chairman may announce the list of speakers and, with the consent of the Committee, declare the list closed. The Chairman may, however, accord the right of reply to any member or representative if a speech delivered after he has declared the list closed makes this desirable. When the debate on an item is concluded because there are no other speakers, the Chairman shall declare the debate closed. Such closure shall have the same effect as closure by the consent of the Committee.

Rule 41

A member may, at any time, move the closure of the debate on the item under discussion, whether or not any other member or representative has signified his wish to speak. Permission to speak on the closure of the debate shall be accorded only to two speakers opposing the closure, after which the motion shall immediately be put to the vote.

Rule 42

During the discussion of any matter, a member may move the suspension or the adjournment of the meeting. No discussion on such motions shall be permitted, and they shall immediately be put to the vote.

Rule 43

Subject to rule 37, the following motions shall have precedence in the following order over all other proposals or motions before the meeting:
(a) To suspend the meeting;
(b) To adjourn the meeting;
(c) To adjourn the debate on the item under discussion;
(d) For the closure of the debate on the item under discussion.

Rule 44

Unless otherwise decided by the Committee, proposals and substantive amendments or motions submitted by members shall be introduced in writing and handed to the Secretariat of the Committee, and their consideration shall, if so requested by any member, be deferred until the next meeting on a following day.

Rule 45

Subject to rule 43, any motion by a member calling for a decision on the competence of the Committee to adopt a proposal submitted to it shall be put to the vote immediately before a vote is taken on the proposal in question.

Rule 46

A motion may be withdrawn by the member who proposed it at any time before voting on it has commenced, provided that the motion has not been amended. A motion which has thus been withdrawn may be reintroduced by any member.

Rule 47

When a proposal has been adopted or rejected, it may not be reconsidered at the same session unless the Committee, by a two-thirds majority of its members present and voting, so decides. Permission to speak on a motion to reconsider shall be accorded only to two speakers in favour of the motion and to two speakers opposing the motion, after which it shall be immediately put to the vote.

X. VOTING

Rule 48

Each member of the Committee shall have one vote.

Rule 49

Except as otherwise provided in the Convention and elsewhere in these rules, decisions of the Committee shall be made by a majority of the members present and voting. For the purpose of these rules, "members present and voting" means members casting an affirmative or negative vote. Members who abstain from voting are considered as not voting.

Rule 50

Subject to rule 56, the Committee normally shall vote by show of hands, except that any member may request a roll-call, which shall be taken in the English alphabetical order of the names of the members of the Committee.

Rule 51

The vote of each member participating in any roll-call shall be inserted in the record.

Rule 52

After the voting has commenced, there shall be no interruption of the voting except on a point of order by a member in connexion with the actual conduct of the voting. Brief statements by members consisting solely in explanations of their votes may be permitted by the Chairman before the voting has commenced or after the voting has been completed.

Rule 53

Parts of a proposal shall be voted on separately if a member requests that the proposal be divided. Those parts of the proposal which have been approved shall then be put to the vote as a whole; if all the operative parts of a proposal have been rejected, the proposal shall be considered to have been rejected as a whole.

Rule 54

1.   When an amendment to a proposal is moved, the amendment shall be voted on first. When two or more amendments to a proposal are moved, the Committee shall first vote on the amendment furthest removed in substance from the original proposal and then on the amendment next furthest removed therefrom, and so on, until all amendments have been put to the vote. If one or more amendments are adopted, the amended proposal shall then be voted upon.

2.   A motion is considered an amendment to a proposal if it merely adds to, deletes from or revises part of that proposal.

Rule 55

1.   If two or more proposals relate to the same question, the Committee shall, unless it decides otherwise, vote on the proposals in the order in which they have been submitted.

2.   The Committee may, after each vote on a proposal, decide whether to vote on the next proposal.

3.   Any motions requiring that no decision be taken on the substance of such proposals, however, shall be considered as previous questions and shall be put to the vote before them.

Rule 56

All elections shall be decided by secret ballot.

Rule 57

When only one person or member is to be elected and no candidate obtains in the first ballot the majority required, a second ballot shall be taken, which shall be restricted to the two candidates obtaining the largest number of votes. If in the second ballot the votes are equally divided, and a majority is required, the Chairman shall decide between the candidates by drawing lots. If a two-thirds majority is required, the balloting shall be continued until one candidate secures two-thirds of the votes cast, provided that, after the third inconclusive ballot, votes may be cast for any eligible member. If three such unrestricted ballots are inconclusive, the next three ballots shall be restricted to the two candidates who obtain the greatest number of votes in the third of the unrestricted ballots, and the following three ballots thereafter shall be unrestricted, and so on until a person or member is elected.

Rule 58

When two or more elective places are to be filled at one time under the same conditions, those candidates obtaining in the first ballot the majority required shall be elected. If the number of candidates obtaining such majority is less than the number of persons or members to be elected, there shall be additional ballots to fill the remaining places, the voting being restricted to the candidates obtaining the greatest number of votes in the previous ballot, to a number not more than twice the places remaining to be filled, provided that, after the third inconclusive ballot, votes may be cast for any eligible person or member. If three such unrestricted ballots are inconclusive, the next three ballots shall be restricted to the candidates who obtained the greatest number of votes in the third of the unrestricted ballots, to a number not more than twice the places remaining to be filled, and the following three ballots thereafter shall be unrestricted, and so on until all the places have been filled.

Rule 59

If a vote is equally divided on matters other than elections, the proposal shall be regarded as rejected.

XI. SUBSIDIARY BODIES

Rule 60

1. The Committee may in accordance with the provisions of the Convention and subject to the provisions of rule 25, set up such subcommittees and other *ad hoc* subsidiary bodies as it deems necessary and define their composition and mandates.

2. Each subsidiary body shall elect its own officers and adopt its own rules of procedure.

XII. REPORTS OF THE COMMITTEE

Rule 61

The Committee shall report annually through the Secretary General to the General Assembly, as provided in the Convention.

Rule 62

The texts of reports, formal decisions and other official documents of the Committee and its subsidiary bodies shall be distributed by the Secretariat to all members of the Committee, to all States Parties to the Convention and, as may be determined by the Committee, to others directly concerned.

XIII. AMENDMENTS
Rule 63

These rules of procedure may be amended by a decision of the Committee.

PART II. PROVISIONAL RULES OF PROCEDURE RELATING TO THE FUNCTIONS OF THE COMMITTEE

XIV. REPORTS AND INFORMATION FROM STATES PARTIES UNDER ARTICLE 9 OF THE CONVENTION

Rule 64

The Committee may, through the Secretary-General, inform the States Parties of its wishes regarding the form and contents of the periodic reports required to be submitted under article 9 of the Convention.

Rule 64A

The Committee shall, through the Secretary-General, notify the States Parties (as early as possible) of the opening date, duration and place of the session at which their respective reports will be examined. Representatives of the States Parties may be present at the meetings of the Committee when their reports are examined. The Committee may also inform a State Party from which it decides to seek further information that it may authorize its representative to be present at a specified meeting. Such a representative should be able to answer questions which may be put to him by the Committee and make statements on reports already submitted by his State, and may also submit additional information from his State.

Rule 65

If the Committee decides to request an additional report or further information from a State Party under the provisions of article 9, paragraph 1, of the Convention, it may indicate the manner as well as the time within which such additional report or further information shall be supplied and shall transmit its decision to the Secretary-General for communication, within two weeks, to the State Party concerned.

Rule 66

1. At each session, the Secretary-General shall notify the Committee of all cases of non-receipt of reports or additional information, as the case may be, provided for under article 9 of the Convention. The Committee, in such cases, may transmit to the State Party concerned, through the Secretary-General, a reminder concerning the submission of the report or additional information.

2. If even after the reminder, referred to in paragraph 1 of this Rule, the State Party does not submit the report or additional information required under article 9 of the Convention, the Committee shall include a reference to this effect in its annual report to the General Assembly.

Rule 66A

1. When considering a report submitted by a State Party under article 9, the Committee shall first determine whether the report provides the information referred to in the relevant communications of the Committee.

2. If a report of the State Party to the Convention, in the opinion of the Committee, does not contain sufficient information, the Committee may request that State to furnish additional information.

3. If, on the basis of its examination of the reports and information supplied by the State Party, the Committee determines that some of the obligations of that State under the Convention have not been discharged, it may make suggestions and general recommendations in accordance with article 9, paragraph 2, of the Convention.

Rule 67

1. Suggestions and general recommendations made by the Committee based on the examination of the reports and information received from States Parties under article 9, paragraph 2, of the Convention shall be communicated by the Committee through the Secretary-General to the States Parties for their comments.

2. The Committee may, where necessary, indicate a time-limit within which comments from States Parties are to be received.

3. Suggestions and general recommendations of the Committee referred to in paragraph 1, shall be reported to the General Assembly, together with comments, if any, from States Parties.

XV. Communications from States Parties Under Article 11 of the Convention

Rule 68

1. When a matter is brought to the attention of the Committee by a State Party in accordance with article 11, paragraph 1, of the Convention, the Committee shall examine it at a private meeting and shall then transmit it to the State Party concerned through the Secretary-General. The Committee in examining the communication shall not consider its substance. Any action at this stage by the Committee in respect of the communication shall in no way be construed as an expression of its views on the substance of the communication.

2. If the Committee is not in session, the Chairman shall bring the matter to the attention of its members by transmitting copies of the communication and requesting their consent to transmit such communication, on behalf of the Committee, to the State Party concerned in compliance with article 11, paragraph 1. The Chairman shall also specify a time-limit of three weeks for their replies.

3. Upon receipt of the consent of the majority of the members, or, if within the specified time-limit no replies are received, the Chairman shall transmit the communication to the State Party concerned, through the Secretary-General, without delay.

4. In the event of any replies being received which represent the views of the majority of the Committee, the Chairman, while acting in accordance with such replies, shall bear in mind the requirement of urgency in transmitting on behalf of the Committee the communication to the State Party concerned.

5. The Committee, or the Chairman on behalf of the Committee, shall remind the receiving State that the time-limit for submission of its written explanations or statement under the Convention is three months.

6. When the Committee receives the explanations or statements of the receiving State, the procedure laid down above shall be followed with respect to the transmission of those explanations or statements to the State Party submitting the initial communication.

Rule 69

The Committee may call upon the States Parties concerned to supply information relevant to the application of article 11 of the Convention. The Committee may indicate the manner as well as the time within which such information shall be supplied.

Rule 70

If any matter is submitted for consideration by the Committee under paragraph 2 of article 11 of the Convention, the Chairman, through the Secretary-General, shall inform the States Parties concerned of the forthcoming consideration of this matter not later than thirty days in advance of the first meeting of the Committee, in the case of a regular session, and at least eighteen days in advance of the first meeting of the Committee, in the case of a special session.

XVI. ESTABLISHMENT AND FUNCTIONS OF THE *Ad Hoc* CONCILIATION COMMITTEE UNDER ARTICLES 12 AND 13 OF THE CONVENTION

Rule 71

After the Committee has obtained and collated all the information it thinks necessary as regards a dispute that has arisen under article 11, paragraph 2, of the Convention, the Chairman shall notify the States Parties to the dispute and undertake consultations with them concerning the composition of the *Ad Hoc* Conciliation Commission (hereinafter referred to as "the Commission"), in accordance with article 12 of the Convention.

Rule 72

Upon receiving the unanimous consent of the States Parties to the dispute regarding the composition of the Commission, the Chairman shall proceed to the appointment of the members of the Commission and shall inform the States Parties to the dispute of the composition of the Commission.

Rule 73

1. If within three months of the Chairman's notification as provided in rule 71 above, the States Parties to the dispute fail to reach agreement on all or part of the composition of the Commission, the Chairman shall then bring the situation to the attention of the Committee which shall proceed according to article 12, paragraph 1(b), of the Convention at its next session.

2. Upon the completion of the election, the Chairman shall inform the States Parties to the dispute of the composition of the Commission.

Rule 74

Upon assuming his duties, each member of the Commission shall make the following solemn declaration at the first meeting of the Commission:

"I solemnly declare that I will perform my duties and exercise my powers as a member of the *Ad Hoc* Conciliation Commission honourably, faithfully, impartially and conscientiously."

Rule 75

Whenever a vacancy arises in the Commission, the Chairman of the Committee shall fill the vacancy as soon as possible in accordance with procedures laid down in rules 71 to 73. He shall proceed with filling such vacancy upon receipt of a report from the Commission or upon a notification by the Secretary-General.

Rule 76

The information obtained and collated by the Committee shall be made available by its Chairman, through the Secretary-General, to the members of the Commission at the time of notifying the members of the Commission of the date of the first meeting of the Commission.

Rule 77

1. The Chairman of the Committee shall communicate the report of the Commission referred to in article 13 of the Convention as soon as possible after its receipt to each of the States Parties to the dispute and to the members of the Committee.

2. The States Parties to the dispute, shall, within three months after the receipt of the Commission's report, inform the Chairman of the Committee whether or not they accept the recommendations contained in the report of the Commission. The Chairman shall transmit the information received from the States Parties to the dispute to the members of the Committee.

3. After the expiry of the time-limit provided for in the preceding paragraph, the Chairman of the Committee shall communicate the report of the Commission and any declaration of States Parties concerned to the other States Parties to the Convention.

Rule 78

The Chairman of the Committee shall keep the members of the Committee informed of his actions under rules 72 to 77.

6. COMMUNICATION CONCERNING REPORTS FROM THE STATES PARTIES UNDER ARTICLE 9 OF THE CONVENTION ON THE ELIMINATION OF RACIAL DISCRIMINATION
UN Doc. CERD/C/R.12; 25 GAOR, Suppl. No. 27 (A/8027), at 32-34 (1970).

The Committee on the Elimination of Racial Discrimination, established under the International Convention on the Elimination of All Forms of Racial Discrimination, having regard to the functions entrusted to it under article 9 of the Convention, wishes to draw the attention of the States Parties to the provisions of paragraph 1 of article 9, according to which States Parties "undertake to submit to the Secretary-General of the United Nations, for consideration by the Committee a report on the legislative, judicial, administrative or other measures which they have adopted and which give effect to the provisions of this Convention: (a) within one year after the entry into force of the Convention for the State concerned; and (b) thereafter every two years and whenever the Committee so requests." Paragraph 1 also provides that "the Committee may request further information from the States Parties."

The Committee attaches great importance to these reports. It is unanimously of the view that, being a principal source of information, these reports provide the Committee with an essential element for discharging one of its most important responsibilities, namely, reporting to the General Assembly of the United Nations under article 9, paragraph 2, of the Convention.

In order for these reports to be of assistance to the Committee, and in order for them to reflect the progress towards the achievement of the principles and objectives of the Convention, which include the condemnation of racial discrimination and colonialism, the Committee feels that information contained in them on "the legislative, judicial, administrative or other measures" might be presented on the following lines:

1. Information on the legislative, judicial, administrative or other measures that have been adopted and that give effect to the following provisions of the Convention:

    (a)   Condemnation of racial segregation and *apartheid*, in accordance with article 3;

    (b)   Prohibition and elimination of racial discrimination in all its forms, as enumerated in article 5, especially in the field of political, civil, economic, social and cultural rights and the right of access to any place or service intended for use by the general public;

    (c)   Assuring "everyone within their jurisdiction effective protection and remedies, through the competent national tribunals and other State institutions, against any acts of racial discrimination which violate his human rights and fundamental freedoms contrary to this Convention, as well as the right to seek from such tribunals just and adequate reparation or satisfaction for any damage suffered as a result of such discrimination," in accordance with article 6.

2. Information on the legislative, judicial, administrative or other measures that have been adopted and that give effect to the following provisions of the Convention:

(a) The undertaking "to engage in no act or practice of racial discrimination against persons, groups of persons or institutions and to ensure that all public authorities and public institutions, national and local, shall act in conformity with this obligation," in accordance with article 2, paragraph 1(a);

(b) The undertaking "not to sponsor, defend or support racial discrimination by any persons or organizations," in accordance with article 2, paragraph 1(b);

(c) The undertaking "not [to] permit public authorities or public institutions, national or local, to promote or incite racial discrimination," in accordance with article 4(c).

3. Information on the legislative, judicial, administrative or other measures that have been adopted and that give effect to the following provisions of the Convention:

(a) The undertaking "to review governmental, national and local policies, and to amend, rescind or nullify any laws and regulations which have the effect of creating or perpetuating racial discrimination wherever it exists," in accordance with article 2, paragraph 1(c);

(b) The undertaking to "prohibit and bring to an end, by all appropriate means, including legislation as required by circumstances, racial discrimination by any persons, group or organization," in accordance with article 2, paragraph 1(d);

(c) The undertaking to prevent, prohibit and eradicate, in territories under their jurisdiction, all practices of racial segregation and *apartheid,* in accordance with article 3;

(d) The undertaking to "declare an offence punishable by law all dissemination of ideas based on racial superiority or hatred, incitement to racial discrimination, as well as all acts of violence or incitement to such acts against any race or group of persons of another colour or ethnic origin, and also the provision of any assistance to racist activities, including the financing thereof," in accordance with article 4(a);

(e) The undertaking to "declare illegal and prohibit organizations, and also organized and all other propaganda activities, which promote and incite racial discrimination, and shall recognize participation in such organizations or activities as an offence punishable by law," in accordance with article 4(b).

4. Information on the legislative, judicial, administrative or other measures that have been adopted and that give effect to the following provisions of the Convention:

(a) The undertaking "to encourage, where appropriate, integrationist multi-racial organizations and movements and other means of eliminating barriers between races, and to discourage anything which tends to strengthen racial division," in accordance with article 2, paragraph 1(e);

(b) The undertaking to take, "when the circumstances so warrant" "in the social, economic, cultural and other fields, special and concrete measures to ensure the adequate development and protection of certain racial groups or individuals belonging to them, for the purpose of guaranteeing them the full and equal enjoyment of human rights and fundamental freedoms," in accordance with article 2, paragraph 2;

(c) The undertaking "to adopt immediate and effective measures, particularly in the fields of teaching, education, culture and information, with a view to combating prejudices which lead to racial discrimination and to promoting understanding, tolerance and friendship among nations and racial or ethnic groups, as well as to propagating the purposes and principles of the Charter of the United Nations, the Universal Declaration of Human Rights, the United Nations Declaration on the Elimination of All Forms of Racial Discrimination, and this Convention," in accordance with article 7.

The Committee trusts that, in reporting on the "legislative, judicial, administrative or other measures," the States Parties would provide information regarding national procedures within their countries to implement those measures.

It would also be useful for the Committee if the reports were to contain information on the practice of the Courts relating to cases of racial discrimination.

The Committee is addressing this communication to all States Parties in the hope that all those States Parties which have already submitted their first reports may, nevertheless, wish to supplement them by additional information as outlined in the foregoing paragraphs.

As regards the first reports of the States Parties provided for in article 9, paragraph 1(a), of the Convention, it would be most helpful to the Committee if the reports were to relate to legislative, judicial, administrative or other measures taken to give effect to the provisions of the Convention before and since entry into force of the Convention. The Committee fully understands that the subsequent reports at two-year intervals provided for under article 9, paragraph 1(b), may deal primarily with such measures as will be taken during the two-year interval between reports.

7. PROCEDURES FOR DEALING WITH COMMUNICATIONS REVEALING A CONSISTENT PATTERN OF GROSS VIOLATIONS OF HUMAN RIGHTS

a. Resolution 1503 (XLVIII) of the Economic and Social Council, 27 May 1970.
48 ESCOR, Suppl. No. 1A (E/4832/Add.1), at 8-9.

The Economic and Social Council,

Noting resolutions 7 (XXVI) and 17 (XXV) of the Commission on Human Rights and resolution 2 (XXI) of the Sub-Commission on Prevention of Discrimination and Protection of Minorities,

1. *Authorizes* the Sub-Commission on Prevention of Discrimination and Protection of Minorities to appoint a working group consisting of not more than five of its members, with due regard to geographical distribution, to meet once a year in private meetings for a period not exceeding ten days immediately before the sessions of the Sub-Commission to consider all communications, including replies of Governments thereon, received by the Secretary-General under Council resolution 728 F (XXVIII) of 30 July 1959 with a view to bringing to the attention of the Sub-Commission those communications, together with replies of Governments, if any, which appear to reveal a consistent pattern of gross and reliably attested violations of human rights and fundamental freedoms within the terms of reference of the Sub-Commission;

2. *Decides* that the Sub-Commission on Prevention of Discrimination and Protection of Minorities should, as the first stage in the implementation of the present resolution, devise at its

twenty-third session appropriate procedures for dealing with the question of admissibility of communications received by the Secretary-General under Council resolution 728 F (XXVIII) and in accordance with Council resolution 1235 (XLII) of 6 June 1967;

3. *Requests* the Secretary-General to prepare a document on the question of admissibility of communications for the Sub-Commission's consideration at its twenty-third session;

4. *Further requests* the Secretary-General:

(a) To furnish to the members of the Sub-Commission every month a list of communications prepared by him in accordance with Council resolution 728 F (XXVIII) and a brief description of them, together with the text of any replies received from Governments;

(b) To make available to the members of the working group at their meetings the originals of such communications listed as they may request, having due regard to the provisions of paragraph 2 (b) of Council resolution 728 F (XXVIII) concerning the divulging of the identity of the authors of communications;

(c) To circulate to the members of the Sub-Commission, in the working languages, the originals of such communications as are referred to the Sub-Commission by the working group;

5. *Requests* the Sub-Commission on Prevention of Discrimination and Protection of Minorities to consider in private meetings, in accordance with paragraph 1 above, the communications brought before it in accordance with the decision of a majority of the members of the working group and any replies of Governments relating thereto and other relevant information, with a view to determining whether to refer to the Commission on Human Rights particular situations which appear to reveal a consistent pattern of gross and reliably attested violations of human rights requiring consideration by the Commission;

6. *Requests* the Commission on Human Rights after it has examined any situation referred to it by the Sub-Commission to determine:

(a) Whether it requires a thorough study by the Commission and a report and recommendations thereon to the Council in accordance with paragraph 3 of Council resolution 1235 (XLII);

(b) Whether it may be a subject of an investigation by an *ad hoc* committee to be appointed by the Commission which shall be undertaken only with the express consent of the State concerned and shall be conducted in constant co-operation with that State and under conditions determined by agreement with it. In any event, the investigation may be undertaken only if:

    (i) All available means at the national level have been resorted to and exhausted;

    (ii) The situation does not relate to a matter which is being dealt with under other procedures prescribed in the constituent instruments of, or conventions adopted by, the United Nations and the specialized agencies, or in regional conventions, or which the State concerned wishes to submit to other procedures in accordance with general or special international agreements to which it is a party.

7. *Decides* that if the Commission on Human Rights appoints an *ad hoc* committee to carry on an investigation with the consent of the State concerned:

(*a*) The composition of the committee shall be determined by the Commission. The members of the committee shall be independent persons whose competence and impartiality is beyond question. Their appointment shall be subject to the consent of the Government concerned;

(*b*) The committee shall establish its own rules of procedure. It shall be subject to the quorum rule. It shall have authority to receive communications and hear witnesses, as necessary. The investigation shall be conducted in co-operation with the Government concerned;

(*c*) The committee's procedure shall be confidential, its proceedings shall be conducted in private meetings and its communications shall not be publicized in any way;

(*d*) The committee shall strive for friendly solutions before, during and even after the investigation;

(*e*) The committee shall report to the Commission on Human Rights with such observations and suggestions as it may deem appropriate;

8. *Decides* that all actions envisaged in the implementation of the present resolution by the Sub-Commission on Prevention of Discrimination and Protection of Minorities or the Commission on Human Rights shall remain confidential until such time as the Commission may decide to make recommendations to the Economic and Social Council;

9. *Decides* to authorize the Secretary-General to provide all facilities which may be required to carry out the present resolution, making use of the existing staff of the Division of Human Rights of the United Nations Secretariat;

10. *Decides* that the procedure set out in the present resolution for dealing with communications relating to violations of human rights and fundamental freedoms should be reviewed if any new organ entitled to deal with such communications should be established within the United Nations or by international agreement.

b. Resolution 1(XXIV) of the Sub-Commission on Prevention of Discrimination and Protection of Minorities, 13 August 1971.
Report of the Sub-Commission . . . on its 24th Session, UN Doc. E/CN.4/1070(1971), at 50-52.

The Sub-Commission on Prevention of Discrimination and Protection of Minorities,

Considering that the Economic and Social Council, by its resolution 1503 (XLVIII), decided that the Sub-Commission should devise appropriate procedures for dealing with the question of admissibility of communications received by the Secretary-General under Council resolution 728 F (XXVIII) of 30 July 1959 and in accordance with Council resolution 1235 (XLII) of 6 June 1967,

Adopts the following provisional procedures for dealing with the question of admissibility of communications referred to above:

(1) *Standards and criteria*

(a) The object of the communication must not be inconsistent with the relevant principles of the Charter, of the Universal Declaration of Human Rights and of the other applicable instruments in the field of human rights.

(b) Communications shall be admissible only if, after consideration thereof, together with the replies if any of the Governments concerned, there are reasonable grounds to believe that they may reveal a consistent pattern of gross and reliably attested violations of human rights and fundamental freedoms, including policies of racial discrimination and segregation and of *apartheid,* in any country, including colonial and other dependent countries and peoples.

(2) *Source of communications*

(a) Admissible communications may originate from a person or group of persons who, it can be reasonably presumed, are victims of the violations referred to in subparagraph (1) (b) above, any person or group of persons who have direct and reliable knowledge of those violations, or non-governmental organizations acting in good faith in accordance with recognized principles of human rights, not resorting to politically motivated stands contrary to the provisions of the Charter of the United Nations and having direct and reliable knowledge of such violations.

(b) Anonymous communications shall be inadmissible; subject to the requirements of subparagraph 2(b) of resolution 728 F (XXVIII) of the Economic and Social Council, the author of a communication, whether an individual, a group of individuals or an organization, must be clearly identified.

(c) Communications shall not be inadmissible solely because the knowledge of the individual authors is second-hand, provided that they are accompanied by clear evidence.

(3) *Contents of communications and nature of allegations*

(a) The communication must contain a description of the facts and must indicate the purpose of the petition and the rights that have been violated.

(b) Communications shall be inadmissible if their language is essentially abusive and in particular if they contain insulting references to the State against which the complaint is directed. Such communications may be considered if they meet the other criteria for admissibility after deletion of the abusive language.

(c) A communication shall be inadmissible if it has manifestly political motivations and its subject is contrary to the provisions of the Charter of the United Nations.

(d) A communication shall be inadmissible if it appears that it is based exclusively on reports disseminated by mass media.

(4) *Existence of other remedies*

(a) Communications shall be inadmissible if their admission would prejudice the functions of the specialized agencies of the United Nations system.

(b) Communications shall be inadmissible if domestic remedies have not been exhausted, unless it appears that such remedies would be ineffective or unreasonably prolonged. Any failure to exhaust remedies should be satisfactorily established.

(c) Communications relating to cases which have been settled by the State concerned in accordance with the principles set forth in the Universal Declaration of Human Rights and other applicable documents in the field of human rights will not be considered.

(5) *Timeliness*

A communication shall be inadmissible if it is not submitted to the United Nations within a reasonable time after the exhaustion of the domestic remedies as provided above.

SECTION C. DOCUMENTS RELATING TO NON-SELF-GOVERNING PEOPLES

1. DECLARATION ON THE GRANTING OF INDEPENDENCE TO COLONIAL COUNTRIES AND TERRITORIES

Resolution 1514 (XV) of the General Assembly, 14 December 1960.
15 GAOR, Suppl. No. 16 (A/4684), at 66-67.

The General Assembly,

Mindful of the determination proclaimed by the peoples of the world in the Charter of the United Nations to reaffirm faith in fundamental human rights, in the equal rights of men and women and of nations large and small and to promote social progress and better standards of life in larger freedom,

Conscious of the need for the creation of conditions of stability and well-being and peaceful and friendly relations based on respect for the principles of equal rights and self-determination of all peoples, and of universal respect for, and observance of, human rights and fundamental freedoms for all without distinction as to race, sex, language or religion,

Recognizing the passionate yearning for freedom in all dependent peoples and the decisive role of such peoples in the attainment of their independence,

Aware of the increasing conflicts resulting from the denial of or impediments in the way of the freedom of such peoples, which constitute a serious threat to world peace,

Considering the important role of the United Nations in assisting the movement for independence in Trust and Non-Self-Governing Territories,

Recognizing that the peoples of the world ardently desire the end of colonialism in all its manifestations,

Convinced that the continued existence of colonialism prevents the development of international economic co-operation, impedes the social, cultural and economic development of dependent peoples and militates against the United Nations ideal of universal peace,

Affirming that peoples may, for their own ends, freely dispose of their natural wealth and resources without prejudice to any obligations arising out of international economic co-operation, based upon the principle of mutual benefit, and international law,

Believing that the process of liberation is irresistible and irreversible and that, in order to avoid serious crises, an end must be put to colonialism and all practices of segregation and discrimination associated therewith,

Welcoming the emergence in recent years of a large number of dependent territories into freedom and independence, and recognizing the increasingly powerful trends towards freedom in such territories which have not yet attained independence,

Convinced that all peoples have an inalienable right to complete freedom, the exercise of their sovereignty and the integrity of their national territory,

Solemnly proclaims the necessity of bringing to a speedy and unconditional end colonialism in all its forms and manifestations;

And to this end

Declares that:

1. The subjection of peoples to alien subjugation, domination and exploitation constitutes a denial of fundamental human rights, is contrary to the Charter of the United Nations and is an impediment to the promotion of world peace and co-operation.

2. All peoples have the right to self-determination; by virtue of that right they freely determine their political status and freely pursue their economic, social and cultural development.

3. Inadequacy of political, economic, social or educational preparedness should never serve as a pretext for delaying independence.

4. All armed action or repressive measures of all kinds directed against dependent peoples shall cease in order to enable them to exercise peacefully and freely their right to complete independence, and the integrity of their national territory shall be respected.

5. Immediate steps shall be taken, in Trust and Non-Self-Governing Territories or all other territories which have not yet attained independence, to transfer all powers to the peoples of those territories, without any conditions or reservations, in accordance with their freely expressed will and desire, without any distinction as to race, creed or colour, in order to enable them to enjoy complete independence and freedom.

6. Any attempt aimed at the partial or total disruption of the national unity and the territorial integrity of a country is incompatible with the purposes and principles of the Charter of the United Nations.

7. All States shall observe faithfully and strictly the provisions of the Charter of the United Nations, the Universal Declaration of Human Rights and the present Declaration on the basis of equality, non-interference in the internal affairs of all States, and respect for the sovereign rights of all peoples and their territorial integrity.

2. TRUSTEESHIP AGREEMENT FOR THE TERRITORY
OF NEW GUINEA

Approved by Resolution 63(I) of the General Assembly, 13 December 1946.
1 (pt. 2) GAOR, Resolutions (A/64/Add.1), at 122. Text from 8 UNTS 181
(1947). The texts of all trusteeship agreements approved by the General
Assembly in 1946 may be found in 1 (pt. 2) GAOR, Suppl. No. 5 (1947).

Whereas the Territory of New Guinea has been administered in accordance with Article 22 of the Covenant of the League of Nations and in pursuance of a mandate conferred upon His Britannic Majesty and exercised on his behalf by the Government of the Commonwealth of Australia; and

Whereas, the Charter of the United Nations, signed at San Francisco on 26 June 1945, provides, by Article 75 for the establishment of an International Trusteeship System for the administration and supervision of such territories as may be placed thereunder by subsequent individual agreements; and

Whereas the Government of Australia now undertakes to place the Territory of New Guinea under the Trusteeship System, on the terms set forth in the present Trusteeship Agreement,

Therefore the General Assembly of the United Nations, acting in pursuance of Article 85 of the Charter, approves the following terms of trusteeship for the Territory of New Guinea, in substitution for the terms of the mandate under which the Territory has been administered:

Article 1. The Territory to which this Trusteeship Agreement applies (hereinafter called the Territory) consists of that portion of the island of New Guinea and the groups of islands administered therewith under the mandate dated 17 December 1920, conferred upon His Britannic Majesty and exercised by the Government of Australia.

Article 2. The Government of Australia (hereinafter called the Administering Authority) is hereby designated as the sole authority which shall exercise the administration of the Territory.

Article 3. The Administering Authority undertakes to administer the Territory in accordance with the provisions of the Charter and in such a manner as to achieve, in the Territory, the basic objectives of the International Trusteeship System, which are set forth in Article 76 of the Charter.

Article 4. The Administering Authority shall be responsible for the peace, order, good government and defence of the Territory and for this purpose shall have the same powers of legislation, administration and jurisdiction in and over the Territory as if it were an integral part of Australia, and will be entitled to apply to the Territory, subject to such modifications as it deems desirable, such laws of the Commonwealth of Australia as it deems appropriate to the needs and conditions of the Territory.

Article 5. It is agreed that the Administering Authority, in the exercise of its powers under article 4, shall be at liberty to bring the Territory into a customs, fiscal or administrative union or federation with other dependent territories under its jurisdiction or control, and to establish common services between the Territory and any or all of these territories, if, in its opinion, it would be in the interests of the Territory and not inconsistent with the basic objectives of the Trusteeship System to do so.

Article 6. The Administering Authority further undertakes to apply, in the Territory, the provisions of such international agreements and such recommendations of the specialized agencies referred to in Article 57 of the Charter as are, in the opinion of the Administering Authority, suited to the needs and conditions of the Territory and conducive to the achievement of the basic objectives of the Trusteeship System.

Article 7. The Administering Authority may take all measures in the Territory which it considers desirable to provide for the defence of the Territory and for maintenance of international peace and security.

Article 8. The Administering Authority undertakes the discharge of its obligations under article 3 of this Agreement:

1. To co-operate with the Trusteeship Council in the discharge of all the Council's functions under Articles 87 and 88 of the Charter;

2. In accordance with its established policy:

(a) To take into consideration the customs and usages of the inhabitants of New Guinea and respect the rights and safeguard the interests, both present and future, of the indigenous inhabitants of the Territory; and in particular, to ensure that no rights over native land in favour of any person not an indigenous inhabitant of New Guinea may be created or transferred except with the consent of the competent public authority;

(b) To promote, as may be appropriate to the circumstances of the Territory, the educational and cultural advancement of the inhabitants;

(c) To assure to the inhabitants of the Territory, as may be appropriate to the particular circumstances of the Territory and its peoples, a progressively increasing share in the administrative and other services of the Territory;

(d) To guarantee to the inhabitants of the Territory, subject only to the requirements of public order, freedom of speech, of the press, of assembly and of petition, freedom of conscience and worship and freedom of religious teaching.

3. TRUSTEESHIP AGREEMENT FOR THE FORMER JAPANESE MANDATED ISLANDS

Draft proposed by the United States on 17 February 1947, with changes made by the Security Council, when it approved the agreement on 2 April 1947. Words added by the Council are in italics; omitted words are in brackets. Adapted from 2 SCOR, Suppl. No. 8; 8 UNTS 190 (1947).

Whereas Article 75 of the Charter of the United Nations provides for the establishment of an international trusteeship system for the administration and supervision of such territories as may be placed thereunder by subsequent agreements; and

Whereas under Article 77 of the said Charter the trusteeship system may be applied to territories now held under mandate; and

Whereas on 17 December 1920 the Council of the League of Nations confirmed a mandate for the former German islands north of the equator to Japan, to be administered in accordance with Article 22 of the Covenant of the League of Nations; and

Whereas Japan, as a result of the Second World War, has ceased to exercise any authority in these islands;

Now therefore, the Security Council of the United Nations, having satisfied itself that the relevant Articles of the Charter have been complied with, hereby resolves to approve the following terms of trusteeship for the Pacific islands formerly under mandate to Japan.

Article 1. The territory of the Pacific islands, consisting of the islands formerly held by Japan under mandate in accordance with Article 22 of the Covenant of the League of Nations, is hereby designated as a strategic area and placed under the trusteeship system established in the Charter of the United Nations. The territory of the Pacific islands is hereinafter referred to as the Trust Territory.

Article 2. The United States of America is designated as the Administering Authority of the Trust Territory.

Article 3. The Administering Authority shall have full powers of administration, legislation, and jurisdiction over the territory subject to the provisions of this Agreement [as an integral part of the United States], and may apply to the Trust Territory, subject to any modifications which the Administering Authority may consider desirable, such of the laws of the United States as it may deem appropriate to local conditions and requirements.

Article 4. The Administering Authority, in discharging the obligations of trusteeship in the Trust Territory, shall act in accordance with the Charter of the United Nations and the provisions of this Agreement, and shall, as specified in Article 83, paragraph 2, of the Charter, apply the objectives of the international trusteeship system, as set forth in Article 76 of the Charter, to the people of the Trust Territory.

Article 5. In discharging its obligations under Article 76a and Article 84 of the Charter, the Administering Authority shall ensure that the Trust Territory shall play its part, in accordance with the Charter of the United Nations, in the maintenance of international peace and security. To this end the Administering Authority shall be entitled:

1. To establish naval, military and air bases and to erect fortifications in the Trust Territory;

2. To station and employ armed forces in the Territory; and

3. To make use of volunteer forces, facilities and assistance from the Trust Territory in carrying out the obligations towards the Security Council undertaken in this regard by the Administering Authority, as well as for the local defence and the maintenance of law and order within the Trust Territory.

Article 6. In discharging its obligations under Article 76b of the Charter, the Administering Authority shall:

1. Foster the development of such political institutions as are suited to the Trust Territory, and shall promote the development of the inhabitants of the Trust Territory towards self-government *or independence, as may be appropriate to the particular circumstances of the Trust Territory and its peoples and the freely expressed wishes of the peoples concerned;* and to this end shall give to the inhabitants of the Trust Territory a progressively increasing share in the administrative services in the Territory; shall develop their participation in [local] government; shall give due recognition to the customs of the inhabitants in providing a system of law for the Territory; and shall take other appropriate measures towards these ends;

2. Promote the economic advancement and self-sufficiency of the inhabitants, and to this end shall regulate the use of natural resources; encourage the development of fisheries, agriculture, and industries; protect the inhabitants against the loss of their lands and resources; and improve the means of transportation and communication;

3. Promote the social advancement of the inhabitants, and to this end shall protect the rights and fundamental freedoms of all elements of the population without discrimination; protect the

health of the inhabitants; control the traffic in arms and ammunition, opium and other dangerous drugs, and alcohol and other spirituous beverages; and institute such other regulations as may be necessary to protect the inhabitants against social abuses; and

4. Promote the educational advancement of the inhabitants, and to this end shall take steps toward the establishment of a general system of elementary education; facilitate the vocational and cultural advancement of the population; and shall encourage qualified students to pursue higher education, including training on the professional level.

Article 7. [In discharging its obligations under Article 76c of the Charter, the Administering Authority, subject only to the requirements of public order and security, shall guarantee to the inhabitants of the Trust Territory freedom of speech, of the press, and of assembly; freedom of conscience, of worship, and of religious teaching; and freedom of migration and movement.]

In discharging its obligations under Article 76c of the Charter, the Administering Authority shall guarantee to the inhabitants of the Trust Territory freedom of conscience, and, subject only to the requirements of public order and security, freedom of speech, of the press and of assembly; freedom of worship and of religious teaching; and freedom of migration and movement.

Article 8.—1. In discharging its obligations under Article 76d of the Charter, as defined by Article 83, paragraph 2, of the Charter, the Administering Authority, subject to the requirements of security and the obligation to promote the advancement of the inhabitants, shall accord to nationals of each Member of the United Nations and to companies and associations organized in conformity with the laws of such Members, treatment in the Trust Territory no less favourable than that accorded therein to nationals, companies and associations of any other United Nation except the Administering Authority.

2. The Administering Authority shall ensure equal treatment to the Members of the United Nations and their nationals in the administration of justice.

3. Nothing in this article shall be so construed as to accord traffic rights to aircraft flying into and out of the Trust Territory. Such rights shall be subject to agreement between the Administering Authority and the State whose nationality such aircraft possesses.

4. The Administering Authority may negotiate and conclude commercial and other treaties and agreements with Members of the United Nations and other States, designed to attain for the inhabitants of the Trust Territory treatment by the Members

of the United Nations and other States no less favourable than that granted by them to the nationals of other States. The Security Council may recommend, or invite other organs of the United Nations to consider and recommend, what rights the inhabitants of the Trust Territory should acquire in consideration of the rights obtained by Members of the United Nations in the Trust Territory.

Article 9. The Administering Authority shall be entitled to constitute the Trust Territory into a customs, fiscal, or administrative union or federation with other territories under United States jurisdiction and to establish common services between such territories and the Trust Territory where such measures are not inconsistent with the basic objectives of the international trusteeship system and with the terms of this agreement.

Article 10. The Administering Authority, acting under the provisions of Article 3 of this Agreement, may accept membership in any regional advisory commission, regional authority, or technical organization, or other voluntary association of States, may co-operate with specialized international bodies, public or private, and may engage in other forms of international co-operation.

Article 11.—1. The Administering Authority shall take the necessary steps to provide the status of citizenship of the Trust Territory for the inhabitants of the Trust Territory.

2. The Administering Authority shall afford diplomatic and consular protection to inhabitants of the Trust Territory when outside the territorial limits of the Trust Territory or of the Territory of the Administering Authority.

Article 12. The Administering Authority shall enact such legislation as may be necessary to place the provisions of this Agreement in effect in the Trust Territory.

Article 13. The provisions of Articles 87 and 88 of the Charter shall be applicable to the Trust Territory, provided that the Administering Authority may determine the extent of their applicability to any areas which may from time to time be specified by it as closed for security reasons.

Article 14. The Administering Authority undertakes to apply in the Trust Territory the provisions of any international conventions and recommendations which may be appropriate to the particular circumstances of the Trust Territory and which would be conducive to the achievement of the basic objectives of article 6 of this agreement.

Article 15. The terms of the present Agreement shall not be altered, amended or terminated without the consent of the Administering Authority.

Article 16. The present Agreement shall come into force when approved by the Security Council of the United Nations and by the Government of the United States after due constitutional process.

PART II. EUROPE

1. [EUROPEAN] CONVENTION FOR THE PROTECTION OF HUMAN RIGHTS AND FUNDAMENTAL FREEDOMS

Signed at Rome, 4 November 1950; entered into force on 3 September 1953. Council of Europe, European Convention on Human Rights: Collected Texts, Section 1, Doc. 1 (7th ed., Strasbourg, 1971).

The Governments signatory hereto, being Members of the Council of Europe,

Considering the Universal Declaration of Human Rights proclaimed by the General Assembly of the United Nations on 10th December 1948;

Considering that this Declaration aims at securing the universal and effective recognition and observance of the Rights therein declared;

Considering that the aim of the Council of Europe is the achievement of greater unity between its Members and that one of the methods by which that aim is to be pursued is the maintenance and further realisation of Human Rights and Fundamental Freedoms;

Reaffirming their profound belief in those Fundamental Freedoms which are the foundation of justice and peace in the world and are best maintained on the one hand by an effective political democracy and on the other by a common understanding and observance of the Human Rights upon which they depend;

Being resolved, as the Governments of European countries which are like-minded and have a common heritage of political traditions, ideals, freedom and the rule of law, to take the first steps for the collective enforcement of certain of the Rights stated in the Universal Declaration;

Have agreed as follows:

Article 1

The High Contracting Parties shall secure to everyone within their jurisdiction the rights and freedoms defined in Section I of this Convention.

SECTION I

Article 2

(1) Everyone's right to life shall be protected by law. No one shall be deprived of his life intentionally save in the execution of a sentence of a court following his conviction of a crime for which this penalty is provided by law.

(2) Deprivation of life shall not be regarded as inflicted in contravention of this Article when it results from the use of force which is no more than absolutely necessary:

(a)   in defence of any person from unlawful violence;

(b)   in order to effect a lawful arrest or to prevent the escape of a person lawfully detained;

(c)   in action lawfully taken for the purpose of quelling a riot or insurrection.

Article 3

No one shall be subjected to torture or to inhuman or degrading treatment or punishment.

Article 4

(1)   No one shall be held in slavery or servitude.

(2)   No one shall be required to perform forced or compulsory labour.

(3)   For the purpose of this Article the term "forced or compulsory labour" shall not include:

(a)   any work required to be done in the ordinary course of detention imposed according to the provisions of Article 5 of this Convention or during conditional release from such detention;

(b)   any service of a military character or, in case of conscientious objectors in countries where they are recognised, service exacted instead of compulsory military service;

(c)   any service exacted in case of an emergency or calamity threatening the life or well-being of the community;

(d)   any work or service which forms part of normal civic obligations.

Article 5

(1)   Everyone has the right to liberty and security of person.

No one shall be deprived of his liberty save in the following cases and in accordance with a procedure prescribed by law:

(a)   the lawful detention of a person after conviction by a competent court;

(b)   the lawful arrest or detention of a person for non-compliance with the lawful order of a court or in order to secure the fulfilment of any obligation prescribed by law;

(c)   the lawful arrest or detention of a person effected for the purpose of bringing him before the competent legal authority on reasonable suspicion of having committed an offence or when it is reasonably considered necessary to prevent his committing an offence or fleeing after having done so;

(d)   the detention of a minor by lawful order for the purpose of educational supervision or his lawful detention for the purpose of bringing him before the competent legal authority;

(e)   the lawful detention of persons for the prevention of the spreading of infectious diseases, of persons of unsound mind, alcoholic or drug addicts or vagrants;

(f)   the lawful arrest or detention of a person to prevent his effecting an unauthorised entry into the country or of a person against whom action is being taken with a view to deportation or extradition.

(2)   Everyone who is arrested shall be informed promptly, in a language which he understands, of the reasons for his arrest and of any charge against him.

(3)   Everyone arrested or detained in accordance with the provisions of paragraph 1 (c) of this Article shall be brought promptly before a judge or other officer authorised by law to exercise judicial power and shall be entitled to trial within a reasonable time or to release pending trial. Release may be conditioned by guarantees to appear for trial.

(4)   Everyone who is deprived of his liberty by arrest or detention shall be entitled to take proceedings by which the lawfulness of his detention shall be decided speedily by a court and his release ordered if the detention is not lawful.

(5)   Everyone who has been the victim of arrest or detention in contravention of the provisions of this Article shall have an enforceable right to compensation.

Article 6

(1)   In the determination of his civil rights and obligations or of any criminal charge against him, everyone is entitled to a fair and public hearing within a reasonable time by an independent and impartial tribunal established by law. Judgment shall be pronounced publicly but the press and public may be excluded from all or part of the trial in the interests of morals, public order or national security in a democratic society, where the interests of juveniles or the protection of the private life of the parties so require, or to the extent strictly necessary in the opinion of the court in special circumstances where publicity would prejudice the interests of justice.

(2)   Everyone charged with a criminal offence shall be presumed innocent until proved guilty according to law.

(3)   Everyone charged with a criminal offence has the following minimum rights:

(a)   to be informed promptly, in a language which he understands and in detail, of the nature and cause of the accusation
against him;

(b)   to have adequate time and facilities for the preparation
of his defence;

(c)   to defend himself in person or through legal assistance
of his own choosing or, if he has not sufficient means to pay for
legal assistance, to be given it free when the interests of justice
so require;

(d)   to examine or have examined witnesses against him and
to obtain the attendance and examination of witnesses on his
behalf under the same conditions as witnesses against him;

(e)   to have the free assistance of an interpreter if he cannot
understand or speak the language used in court.

Article 7

(1)   No one shall be held guilty of any criminal offence on
account of any act or omission which did not constitute a criminal
offence under national or international law at the time when it
was committed. Nor shall a heavier penalty be imposed than the
one that was applicable at the time the criminal offence was
committed.

(2)   This Article shall not prejudice the trial and punishment
of any person for any act or omission which, at the time when
it was committed, was criminal according to the general principles
of law recognised by civilised nations.

Article 8

(1)   Everyone has the right to respect for his private and family
life, his home and his correspondence.

(2)   There shall be no interference by a public authority with
the exercise of this right except such as is in accordance with the
law and is necessary in a democratic society in the interests of
national security, public safety or the economic well-being of the
country, for the prevention of disorder or crime, for the protection of health or morals, or for the protection of the rights and
freedoms of others.

Article 9

(1)   Everyone has the right to freedom of thought, conscience
and religion; this right includes freedom to change his religion or
belief and freedom, either alone or in community with others and
in public or private, to manifest his religion or belief, in worship,
teaching, practice and observance.

(2) Freedom to manifest one's religion or beliefs shall be subject only to such limitations as are prescribed by law and are necessary in a democratic society in the interests of public safety, for the protection of public order, health or morals, or for the protection of the rights and freedoms of others.

Article 10

(1) Everyone has the right to freedom of expression. This right shall include freedom to hold opinions and to receive and impart information and ideas without interference by public authority and regardless of frontiers. This Article shall not prevent States from requiring the licensing of broadcasting, television or cinema enterprises.

(2) The exercise of these freedoms, since it carries with it duties and responsibilities, may be subject to such formalities, conditions, restrictions or penalties as are prescribed by law and are necessary in a democratic society, in the interests of national security, territorial integrity or public safety, for the prevention of disorder or crime, for the protection of health or morals, for the protection of the reputation or rights of others, for preventing the disclosure of information received in confidence, or for maintaining the authority and impartiality of the judiciary.

Article 11

(1) Everyone has the right to freedom of peaceful assembly and to freedom of association with others, including the right to form and to join trade unions for the protection of his interests.

(2) No restrictions shall be placed on the exercise of these rights other than such as are prescribed by law and are necessary in a democratic society in the interests of national security or public safety, for the prevention of disorder or crime, for the protection of health or morals or for the protection of the rights and freedoms of others. This Article shall not prevent the imposition of lawful restrictions on the exercise of these rights by members of the armed forces, of the police or of the administration of the State.

Article 12

Men and women of marriageable age have the right to marry and to found a family, according to the national laws governing the exercise of this right.

Article 13

Everyone whose rights and freedoms as set forth in this Convention are violated shall have an effective remedy before a national authority notwithstanding that the violation has been committed by persons acting in an official capacity.

Article 14

The enjoyment of the rights and freedoms set forth in this Convention shall be secured without discrimination on any ground such as sex, race, colour, language, religion, political or other opinion, national or social origin, association with a national minority, property, birth or other status.

Article 15

(1)   In time of war or other public emergency threatening the life of the nation any High Contracting Party may take measures derogating from its obligations under this Convention to the extent strictly required by the exigencies of the situation, provided that such measures are not inconsistent with its other obligations under international law.

(2)   No derogation from Article 2, except in respect of deaths resulting from lawful acts of war, or from Articles 3, 4 (paragraph 1) and 7 shall be made under this provision.

(3)   Any High Contracting Party availing itself of this right of derogation shall keep the Secretary-General of the Council of Europe fully informed of the measures which it has taken and the reasons therefor. It shall also inform the Secretary-General of the Council of Europe when such measures have ceased to operate and the provisions of the Convention are again being fully executed.

Article 16

Nothing in Articles 10, 11 and 14 shall be regarded as preventing the High Contracting Parties from imposing restrictions on the political activity of aliens.

Article 17

Nothing in this Convention may be interpreted as implying for any State, group or person any right to engage in any activity or perform any act aimed at the destruction of any of the rights and freedoms set forth herein or at their limitation to a greater extent than is provided for in the Convention.

Article 18

The restrictions permitted under this Convention to the said rights and freedoms shall not be applied for any purpose other than those for which they have been prescribed.

SECTION II

Article 19

To ensure the observance of the engagements undertaken by the High Contracting Parties in the present Convention, there shall be set up:

(1) A European Commission of Human Rights hereinafter referred to as "the Commission";

(2) A European Court of Human Rights, hereinafter referred to as "the Court."

SECTION III

Article 20

The Commission shall consist of a number of members equal to that of the High Contracting Parties. No two members of the Commission may be nationals of the same State.

Article 21

(1) The members of the Commission shall be elected by the Committee of Ministers by an absolute majority of votes, from a list of names drawn up by the Bureau of the Consultative Assembly; each group of the Representatives of the High Contracting Parties in the Consultative Assembly shall put forward three candidates, of whom two at least shall be its nationals.

(2) As far as applicable, the same procedure shall be followed to complete the Commission in the event of other States subsequently becoming Parties to this Convention, and in filling casual vacancies.

Article 22

(1) The members of the Commission shall be elected for a period of six years. They may be re-elected. However, of the members elected at the first election, the terms of seven members shall expire at the end of three years.

(2) The members whose terms are to expire at the end of the initial period of three years shall be chosen by lot by the Secretary-General of the Council of Europe immediately after the first election has been completed.

(3) A member of the Commission elected to replace a member whose term of office has not expired shall hold office for the remainder of his predecessor's term.

(4) The members of the Commission shall hold office until replaced. After having been replaced, they shall continue to deal with such cases as they already have under consideration.

Article 23

The members of the Commission shall sit on the Commission in their individual capacity.

Article 24

Any High Contracting Party may refer to the Commission, through the Secretary-General of the Council of Europe, any alleged breach of the provisions of the Convention by another High Contracting Party.

Article 25

(1)   The Commission may receive petitions addressed to the Secretary-General of the Council of Europe from any person, non-governmental organisation or group of individuals claiming to be the victim of a violation by one of the High Contracting Parties of the rights set forth in this Convention, provided that the High Contracting Party against which the complaint has been lodged has declared that it recognises the competence of the Commission to receive such petitions. Those of the High Contracting Parties who have made such a declaration undertake not to hinder in any way the effective exercise of this right.

(2)   Such declarations may be made for a specific period.

(3)   The declarations shall be deposited with the Secretary-General of the Council of Europe who shall transmit copies thereof to the High Contracting Parties and publish them.

(4)   The Commission shall only exercise the powers provided for in this Article when at least six High Contracting Parties are bound by declarations made in accordance with the preceding paragraphs.

Article 26

The Commission may only deal with the matter after all domestic remedies have been exhausted, according to the generally recognised rules of international law, and within a period of six months from the date on which the final decision was taken.

Article 27

(1)   The Commission shall not deal with any petition submitted under Article 25 which

(a)   is anonymous, or

(b)   is substantially the same as a matter which has already been examined by the Commission or has already been submitted to another procedure of international investigation or settlement and if it contains no relevant new information.

(2)   The Commission shall consider inadmissible any petition submitted under Article 25 which it considers incompatible with

the provisions of the present Convention, manifestly ill-founded, or an abuse of the right of petition.

(3)   The Commission shall reject any petition referred to it which it considers inadmissible under Article 26.

Article 28

In the event of the Commission accepting a petition referred to it:

(a)   it shall, with a view to ascertaining the facts, undertake together with the representatives of the parties an examination of the petition and, if need be, an investigation, for the effective conduct of which the States concerned shall furnish all necessary facilities, after an exchange of views with the Commission;

(b)   it shall place itself at the disposal of the parties concerned with a view to securing a friendly settlement of the matter on the basis of respect for Human Rights as defined in this Convention.

Article 29

(1)   The Commission shall perform the functions set out in Article 28 by means of a Sub-Commission consisting of seven members of the Commission.

(2)   Each of the parties concerned may appoint as members of this Sub-Commission a person of its choice.

(3)   The remaining members shall be chosen by lot in accordance with arrangements prescribed in the Rules of Procedure of the Commission.

Article 30

If the Sub-Commission succeeds in effecting a friendly settlement in accordance with Article 28, it shall draw up a Report which shall be sent to the States concerned, to the Committee of Ministers and to the Secretary-General of the Council of Europe for publication. This Report shall be confined to a brief statement of the facts and of the solution reached.

Article 31

(1)   If a solution is not reached, the Commission shall draw up a Report on the facts and state its opinion as to whether the facts found disclose a breach by the State concerned of its obligations under the Convention. The opinions of all the members of the Commission on this point may be stated in the Report.

(2)   The Report shall be transmitted to the Committee of Ministers. It shall also be transmitted to the States concerned, who shall not be at liberty to publish it.

(3)   In transmitting the Report to the Committee of Ministers the Commission may make such proposals as it thinks fit.

Article 32

(1)   If the question is not referred to the Court in accordance with Article 48 of this Convention within a period of three months from the date of the transmission of the Report to the Committee of Ministers, the Committee of Ministers shall decide by a majority of two-thirds of the members entitled to sit on the Committee whether there has been a violation of the Convention.

(2)   In the affirmative case the Committee of Ministers shall prescribe a period during which the High Contracting Party concerned must take the measures required by the decision of the Committee of Ministers.

(3)   If the High Contracting Party concerned has not taken satisfactory measures within the prescribed period, the Committee of Ministers shall decide by the majority provided for in paragraph (1) above what effect shall be given to its original decision and shall publish the Report.

(4)   The High Contracting Parties undertake to regard as binding on them any decision which the Committee of Ministers may take in application of the preceding paragraphs.

Article 33

The Commission shall meet in camera.

Article 34

The Commission shall take its decisions by a majority of the Members present and voting; the Sub-Commission shall take its decisions by a majority of its members.

Article 35

The Commission shall meet as the circumstances require. The meetings shall be convened by the Secretary-General of the Council of Europe.

Article 36

The Commission shall draw up its own rules of procedure.

Article 37

The secretariat of the Commission shall be provided by the Secretary-General of the Council of Europe.

SECTION IV

Article 38

The European Court of Human Rights shall consist of a number of judges equal to that of the Members of the Council of Europe. No two judges may be nationals of the same State.

Article 39

(1)   The members of the Court shall be elected by the Consultative Assembly by a majority of the votes cast from a list of persons nominated by the Members of the Council of Europe; each Member shall nominate three candidates, of whom two at least shall be its nationals.

(2)   As far as applicable, the same procedure shall be followed to complete the Court in the event of the admission of new Members of the Council of Europe, and in filling casual vacancies.

(3)   The candidates shall be of high moral character and must either possess the qualifications required for appointment to high judicial office or be jurisconsults of recognised competence.

Article 40

(1)   The members of the Court shall be elected for a period of nine years. They may be re-elected. However, of the members elected at the first election the terms of four members shall expire at the end of three years, and the terms of four more members shall expire at the end of six years.

(2)   The members whose terms are to expire at the end of the initial periods of three and six years shall be chosen by lot by the Secretary-General immediately after the first election has been completed.

(3)   A member of the Court elected to replace a member whose term of office has not expired shall hold office for the remainder of his predecessor's term.

(4)   The members of the Court shall hold office until replaced. After having been replaced, they shall continue to deal with such cases as they already have under consideration.

Article 41

The Court shall elect its President and Vice-President for a period of three years. They may be re-elected.

Article 42

The members of the Court shall receive for each day of duty a compensation to be determined by the Committee of Ministers.

Article 43

For the consideration of each case brought before it the Court shall consist of a Chamber composed of seven judges. There shall sit as an ex officio member of the Chamber the judge who is a national of any State party concerned, or, if there is none, a person of its choice who shall sit in the capacity of judge; the names of the other judges shall be chosen by lot by the President before the opening of the case.

Article 44

Only the High Contracting Parties and the Commission shall have the right to bring a case before the Court.

Article 45

The jurisdiction of the Court shall extend to all cases concerning the interpretation and application of the present Convention which the High Contracting Parties or the Commission shall refer to it in accordance with Article 48.

Article 46

(1) Any of the High Contracting Parties may at any time declare that it recognises as compulsory *ipso facto* and without special agreement the jurisdiction of the Court in all matters concerning the interpretation and application of the present Convention.

(2) The declarations referred to above may be made unconditionally or on condition of reciprocity on the part of several or certain other High Contracting Parties or for a specified period.

(3) These declarations shall be deposited with the Secretary-General of the Council of Europe who shall transmit copies thereof to the High Contracting Parties.

Article 47

The Court may only deal with a case after the Commission has acknowledged the failure of efforts for a friendly settlement and within the period of three months provided for in Article 32.

Article 48

The following may bring a case before the Court, provided that the High Contracting Party concerned, if there is only one, or the High Contracting Parties concerned, if there is more than one, are subject to the compulsory jurisdiction of the Court or, failing that, with the consent of the High Contracting Party concerned, if there is only one, or of the High Contracting Parties concerned if there is more than one:

(a) the Commission;

(b) a High Contracting Party whose national is alleged to be a victim;

(c) a High Contracting Party which referred the case to the Commission;

(d) a High Contracting Party against which the complaint has been lodged.

Article 49

In the event of dispute as to whether the Court has jurisdiction, the matter shall be settled by the decision of the Court.

Article 50

If the Court finds that a decision or a measure taken by a legal authority or any other authority of a High Contracting Party is completely or partially in conflict with the obligations arising from the present Convention, and if the internal law of the said Party allows only partial reparation to be made for the consequences of this decision or measure, the decision of the Court shall, if necessary, afford just satisfaction to the injured party.

Article 51

(1)   Reasons shall be given for the judgment of the Court.

(2)   If the judgment does not represent in whole or in part the unanimous opinion of the judges, any judge shall be entitled to deliver a separate opinion.

Article 52

The judgment of the Court shall be final.

Article 53

The High Contracting Parties undertake to abide by the decision of the Court in any case to which they are parties.

Article 54

The judgment of the Court shall be transmitted to the Committee of Ministers which shall supervise its execution.

Article 55

The Court shall draw up its own rules and shall determine its own procedure.

Article 56

(1)   The first election of the members of the Court shall take place after the declarations by the High Contracting Parties mentioned in Article 46 have reached a total of eight.

(2)   No case can be brought before the Court before this election.

SECTION V

Article 57

On receipt of a request from the Secretary-General of the Council of Europe any High Contracting Party shall furnish an explanation of the manner in which its internal law ensures the effective implementation of any of the provisions of this Convention.

Article 58

The expenses of the Commission and the Court shall be borne by the Council of Europe.

Article 59

The members of the Commission and of the Court shall be entitled, during the discharge of their functions, to the privileges and immunities provided for in Article 40 of the Statute of the Council of Europe and in the agreements made thereunder.

Article 60

Nothing in this Convention shall be construed as limiting or derogating from any of the human rights and fundamental freedoms which may be ensured under the laws of any High Contracting Party or under any other agreement to which it is a Party.

Article 61

Nothing in this Convention shall prejudice the powers conferred on the Committee of Ministers by the Statute of the Council of Europe.

Article 62

The High Contracting Parties agree that, except by special agreement, they will not avail themselves of treaties, conventions or declarations in force between them for the purpose of submitting, by way of petition, a dispute arising out of the interpretation or application of this Convention to a means of settlement other than those provided for in this Convention.

Article 63

(1)   Any State may at the time of its ratification or at any time thereafter declare by notification addressed to the Secretary-General of the Council of Europe that the present Convention shall extend to all or any of the territories for whose international relations it is responsible.

(2)   The Convention shall extend to the territory or territories named in the notification as from the thirtieth day after the receipt of this notification by the Secretary-General of the Council of Europe.

(3)   The provisions of this Convention shall be applied in such territories with due regard, however, to local requirements.

(4)   Any State which has made a declaration in accordance with paragraph 1 of this Article may at any time thereafter declare on behalf of one or more of the territories to which the declaration relates that it accepts the competence of the Commission to receive petitions from individuals, non-governmental organisations or groups of individuals in accordance with Article 25 of the present Convention.

Article 64

(1)   Any State may, when signing this Convention or when depositing its instrument of ratification, make a reservation in respect of any particular provision of the Convention to the extent that any law then in force in its territory is not in conformity with the provision. Reservations of a general character shall not be permitted under this Article.

(2)   Any reservation made under this Article shall contain a brief statement of the law concerned.

Article 65

(1)   A High Contracting Party may denounce the present Convention only after the expiry of five years from the date on which it became a Party to it and after six months' notice contained in a notification addressed to the Secretary-General of the Council of Europe, who shall inform the other High Contracting Parties.

(2)   Such a denunciation shall not have the effect of releasing the High Contracting Party concerned from its obligations under this Convention in respect of any act which, being capable of constituting a violation of such obligations, may have been performed by it before the date at which the denunciation became effective.

(3)   Any High Contracting Party which shall cease to be a Member of the Council of Europe shall cease to be a Party to this Convention under the same conditions.

(4)   The Convention may be denounced in accordance with the provisions of the preceding paragraphs in respect of any territory to which it has been declared to extend under the terms of Article 63.

Article 66

(1)   This Convention shall be open to the signature of the Members of the Council of Europe. It shall be ratified. Ratifications shall be deposited with the Secretary-General of the Council of Europe.

(2)   The present Convention shall come into force after the deposit of ten instruments of ratification.

(3) As regards any signatory ratifying subsequently, the Convention shall come into force at the date of the deposit of its instrument of ratification.

(4) The Secretary-General of the Council of Europe shall notify all the Members of the Council of Europe of the entry into force of the Convention, the names of the High Contracting Parties who have ratified it, and the deposit of all instruments of ratification which may be effected subsequently.

2. PROTOCOL [NO. 1] TO THE [EUROPEAN] CONVENTION FOR THE PROTECTION OF HUMAN RIGHTS AND FUNDAMENTAL FREEDOMS

Signed at Paris, 20 March 1952; entered into force on 18 May 1954. Council of Europe, European Convention on Human Rights: Collected Texts, Section 1, Doc. 2 (7th ed., Strasbourg, 1971). This Protocol added three additional rights to those protected by the Convention.

The Governments signatory hereto, being Members of the Council of Europe,

Being resolved to take steps to ensure the collective enforcement of certain rights and freedoms other than those already included in Section I of the Convention for the Protection of Human Rights and Fundamental Freedoms signed at Rome on 4th November 1950 (hereinafter referred to as "the Convention"),

Have agreed as follows:

Article 1

Every natural or legal person is entitled to the peaceful enjoyment of his possessions. No one shall be deprived of his possessions except in the public interest and subject to the conditions provided for by law and by the general principles of international law.

The preceding provisions shall not, however, in any way impair the right of a State to enforce such laws as it deems necessary to control the use of property in accordance with the general interest or to secure the payment of taxes or other contributions or penalties.

Article 2

No person shall be denied the right to education. In the exercise of any functions which it assumes in relation to education and to teaching, the State shall respect the right of parents to ensure such education and teaching in conformity with their own religious and philosophical convictions.

Article 3

The High Contracting Parties undertake to hold free elections at reasonable intervals by secret ballot, under conditions which will ensure the free expression of the opinion of the people in the choice of the legislature.

Article 4

Any High Contracting Party may at the time of signature or ratification or at any time thereafter communicate to the Secretary-General of the Council of Europe a declaration stating the extent to which it undertakes that the provisions of the present Protocol shall apply to such of the territories for the international relations of which it is responsible as are named therein.

Any High Contracting Party which has communicated a declaration in virtue of the preceding paragraph may from time to time communicate a further declaration modifying the terms of any former declaration or terminating the application of the provisions of this Protocol in respect of any territory.

A declaration made in accordance with this Article shall be deemed to have been made in accordance with Paragraph (1) of Article 63 of the Convention.

Article 5

As between the High Contracting Parties the provisions of Articles 1, 2, 3 and 4 of this Protocol shall be regarded as additional Articles to the Convention and all the provisions of the Convention shall apply accordingly.

Article 6

This Protocol shall be open for signature by the Members of the Council of Europe, who are the signatories of the Convention; it shall be ratified at the same time as or after the ratification of the Convention. It shall enter into force after the deposit of ten instruments of ratification. As regards any signatory ratifying subsequently, the Protocol shall enter into force at the date of the deposit of its instrument of ratification.

The instruments of ratification shall be deposited with the Secretary-General of the Council of Europe, who will notify all Members of the names of those who have ratified.

3. PROTOCOL NO. 2 TO THE [EUROPEAN] CONVENTION FOR THE PROTECTION OF HUMAN RIGHTS AND FUNDAMENTAL FREEDOMS

Signed at Strasbourg, 6 May 1963; entered into force on 21 September 1970. Council of Europe, European Convention on Human Rights: Collected Texts, Section 1, Doc. 3 (7th ed., Strasbourg, 1971). This Protocol conferred upon the European Court of Human Rights competence to give advisory opinions.

The member States of the Council of Europe signatory hereto:

Having regard to the provisions of the Convention for the Protection of Human Rights and Fundamental Freedoms signed at Rome on 4th November 1950 (hereinafter referred to as "the Convention") and, in particular, Article 19 instituting, among other bodies, a European Court of Human Rights (hereinafter referred to as "the Court");

Considering that it is expedient to confer upon the Court competence to give advisory opinions subject to certain conditions;

Have agreed as follows:

Article 1

1. The Court may, at the request of the Committee of Ministers, give advisory opinions on legal questions concerning the interpretation of the Convention and the Protocols thereto.

2. Such opinions shall not deal with any question relating to the content or scope of the rights or freedoms defined in Section 1 of the Convention and in the Protocols thereto, or with any other question which the Commission, the Court or the Committee of Ministers might have to consider in consequence of any such proceedings as could be instituted in accordance with the Convention.

3. Decisions of the Committee of Ministers to request an advisory opinion of the Court shall require a two-thirds majority vote of the representatives entitled to sit on the Committee.

Article 2

The Court shall decide whether a request for an advisory opinion submitted by the Committee of Ministers is within its consultative competence as defined in Article 1 of this Protocol.

Article 3

1. For the consideration of requests for an advisory opinion, the Court shall sit in plenary session.

2. Reasons shall be given for advisory opinions of the Court.

3. If the advisory opinion does not represent in whole or in part the unanimous opinion of the judges, any judge shall be entitled to deliver a separate opinion.

4. Advisory opinions of the Court shall be communicated to the Committee of Ministers.

Article 4

The powers of the Court under Article 55 of the Convention shall extend to the drawing up of such rules and the determination of such procedure as the Court may think necessary for the purposes of this Protocol.

Article 5

1. This Protocol shall be open to signature by member States of the Council of Europe, signatories to the Convention, who may become Parties to it by:

(a) signature without reservation in respect of ratification or acceptance;

(b) signature with reservation in respect of ratification or acceptance, followed by ratification or acceptance.

Instruments of ratification or acceptance shall be deposited with the Secretary-General of the Council of Europe.

2. This Protocol shall enter into force as soon as all States Parties to the Convention shall have become Parties to the Protocol, in accordance with the provisions of paragraph 1 of this Article.

3. From the date of the entry into force of this Protocol, Articles 1 to 4 shall be considered an integral part of the Convention.

4. The Secretary-General of the Council of Europe shall notify the member States of the Council of:

(a) any signature without reservation in respect of ratification or acceptance;

(b) any signature with reservation in respect of ratification or acceptance;

(c) the deposit of any instrument of ratification or acceptance;

(d) the date of entry into force of this Protocol in accordance with paragraph 2 of this Article.

4. PROTOCOL NO. 3 TO THE [EUROPEAN] CONVENTION FOR THE PROTECTION OF HUMAN RIGHTS AND FUNDAMENTAL FREEDOMS

Signed at Strasbourg, 6 May 1963; entered into force on 21 September 1970. Council of Europe, European Convention on Human Rights: Collected Texts, Section 1, Doc. 4 (7th ed., Strasbourg, 1971). This Protocol amended Articles 29, 30 and 34 of the Convention.

The member States of the Council of Europe, signatories to this Protocol,

Considering that it is advisable to amend certain provisions of the Convention for the Protection of Human Rights and Fundamental Freedoms signed at Rome on 4th November 1950 (hereinafter referred to as "the Convention") concerning the procedure of the European Commission of Human Rights,

Have agreed as follows:

Article 1

1. Article 29 of the Convention is deleted.

2. The following provisions shall be inserted in the Convention:

"Article 29

After it has accepted a petition submitted under Article 25, the Commission may nevertheless decide unanimously to reject the petition if, in the course of its examination, it finds that the existence of one of the grounds for non-acceptance provided for in Article 27 has been established.

In such a case, the decision shall be communicated to the parties."

Article 2

In Article 30 of the Convention, the word "Sub-Commission" shall be replaced by the word "Commission."

Article 3

1. At the beginning of Article 34 of the Convention, the following shall be inserted:

"Subject to the provisions of Article 29 . . ."

2. At the end of the same Article, the sentence "the Sub-Commission shall take its decisions by a majority of its members" shall be deleted.

Article 4

1. This Protocol shall be open to signature by the member States of the Council of Europe signatories to the Convention, who may become Parties to it either by:

(a) signature without reservation in respect of ratification or acceptance, or

(b) signature with reservation in respect of ratification or acceptance, followed by ratification or acceptance.

Instruments of ratification or acceptance shall be deposited with the Secretary-General of the Council of Europe.

2. This Protocol shall enter into force as soon as all States Parties to the Convention shall have become Parties to the Protocol, in accordance with the provisions of paragraph 1 of this Article.

3. The Secretary-General of the Council of Europe shall notify the member States of the Council of:

(a)   any signature without reservation in respect of ratification or acceptance;

(b)   any signature with reservation in respect of ratification or acceptance;

(c)   the deposit of any instrument of ratification or acceptance;

(d)   the date of entry into force of this Protocol in accordance with paragraph 2 of this Article.

5.   PROTOCOL NO. 4 TO THE [EUROPEAN] CONVENTION FOR THE PROTECTION OF HUMAN RIGHTS AND FUNDAMENTAL FREEDOMS

Signed at Strasbourg, 16 September 1963; entered into force on 2 May 1968. Council of Europe, European Convention on Human Rights: Collected Texts, Section 1, Doc. 5 (7th ed., Strasbourg, 1971). This Protocol added four additional rights to those protected by the Convention.

The Governments signatory hereto, being Members of the Council of Europe,

Being resolved to take steps to ensure the collective enforcement of certain rights and freedoms other than those already included in Section I of the Convention for the Protection of Human Rights and Fundamental Freedoms signed at Rome on 4th November 1950 (hereinafter referred to as "the Convention") and in Articles 1 to 3 of the First Protocol to the Convention, signed at Paris on 20th March 1952,

Have agreed as follows:

Article 1

No one shall be deprived of his liberty merely on the ground of inability to fulfil a contractual obligation.

Article 2

1.   Everyone lawfully within the territory of a State shall, within that territory, have the right to liberty of movement and freedom to choose his residence.

2.   Everyone shall be free to leave any country, including his own.

3.   No restrictions shall be placed on the exercise of these rights other than such as are in accordance with law and are necessary in a democratic society in the interests of national security or public safety, for the maintenance of *ordre public*, for the prevention of crime, for the protection of health or morals, or for the protection of the rights and freedoms of others.

4.   The rights set forth in paragraph 1 may also be subject, in particular areas, to restrictions imposed in accordance with law and justified by the public interest in a democratic society.

Article 3

1. No one shall be expelled, by means either of an individual or of a collective measure, from the territory of the State of which he is a national.

2. No one shall be deprived of the right to enter the territory of the State of which he is a national.

Article 4

Collective expulsion of aliens is prohibited.

Article 5

1. Any High Contracting Party may, at the time of signature or ratification of this Protocol, or at any time thereafter, communicate to the Secretary-General of the Council of Europe a declaration stating the extent to which it undertakes that the provisions of this Protocol shall apply to such of the territories for the international relations of which it is responsible as are named therein.

2. Any High Contracting Party which has communicated a declaration in virtue of the preceding paragraph may, from time to time, communicate a further declaration modifying the terms of any former declaration or terminating the application of the provisions of this Protocol in respect of any territory.

3. A declaration made in accordance with this Article shall be deemed to have been made in accordance with paragraph 1 of Article 63 of the Convention.

4. The territory of any State to which this Protocol applies by virtue of ratification or acceptance by that State, and each territory to which this Protocol is applied by virtue of a declaration by that State under this Article, shall be treated as separate territories for the purpose of the references in Articles 2 and 3 to the territory of a State.

Article 6

1. As between the High Contracting Parties the provisions of Articles 1 to 5 of this Protocol shall be regarded as additional Articles to the Convention, and all the provisions of the Convention shall apply accordingly.

2. Nevertheless, the right of individual recourse recognised by a declaration made under Article 25 of the Convention, or the acceptance of the compulsory jurisdiction of the Court by a declaration made under Article 46 of the Convention, shall not be effective in relation to this Protocol unless the High Contracting Party concerned has made a statement recognising such right, or

accepting such jurisdiction, in respect of all or any of Articles 1 to 4 of the Protocol.

Article 7

1.   This Protocol shall be open for signature by the Members of the Council of Europe who are the signatories of the Convention; it shall be ratified at the same time as or after the ratification of the Convention. It shall enter into force after the deposit of five instruments of ratification. As regards any signatory ratifying subsequently, the Protocol shall enter into force at the date of the deposit of its instrument of ratification.

2.   The instruments of ratification shall be deposited with the Secretary-General of the Council of Europe, who will notify all Members of the names of those who have ratified.

6. PROTOCOL NO. 5 TO THE [EUROPEAN] CONVENTION FOR THE PROTECTION OF HUMAN RIGHTS AND FUNDAMENTAL FREEDOMS

Signed at Strasbourg, 20 January 1966; not yet in force. Council of Europe, European Convention on Human Rights: Collected Texts, Section 1, Doc. 6 (7th ed., Strasbourg, 1971). The purpose of this Protocol is to amend Articles 22 and 40 of the Convention.

The Governments signatory hereto, being Members of the Council of Europe,

Considering that certain inconveniences have arisen in the application of the provisions of Articles 22 and 40 of the Convention for the Protection of Human Rights and Fundamental Freedoms signed at Rome on 4th November 1950 (hereinafter referred to as "the Convention") relating to the length of the terms of office of the members of the European Commission of Human Rights (hereinafter referred to as "the Commission") and of the European Court of Human Rights (hereinafter referred to as "the Court");

Considering that it is desirable to ensure as far as possible an election every three years of one half of the members of the Commission and of one third of the members of the Court;

Considering therefore that it is desirable to amend certain provisions of the Convention,

Have agreed as follows:

Article 1

In Article 22 of the Convention, the following two paragraphs shall be inserted after paragraph (2):

"(3)   In order to ensure that, as far as possible, one half of the membership of the Commission shall be renewed every three years, the Committee of Ministers may decide, before proceeding to any subsequent election, that the term or terms of office of one or more members to be elected shall be for a period other than six years but not more than nine and not less than three years.

"(4) In cases where more than one term of office is involved and the Committee of Ministers applies the preceding paragraph, the allocation of the terms of office shall be effected by the drawing of lots by the Secretary-General, immediately after the election."

Article 2

In Article 22 of the Convention, the former paragraphs (3) and (4) shall become respectively paragraphs (5) and (6).

Article 3

In Article 40 of the Convention, the following two paragraphs shall be inserted after paragraph (2):

"(3) In order to ensure that, as far as possible, one third of the membership of the Court shall be renewed every three years, the Consultative Assembly may decide, before proceeding to any subsequent election, that the term or terms of office of one or more members to be elected shall be for a period other than nine years but not more than twelve and not less than six years.

"(4) In cases where more than one term of office is involved and the Consultative Assembly applies the preceding paragraph, the allocation of the terms of office shall be effected by the drawing of lots by the Secretary-General immediately after the election."

Article 4

In Article 40 of the Convention, the former paragraphs (3) and (4) shall become respectively paragraphs (5) and (6).

Article 5

1. This Protocol shall be open to signature by Members of the Council of Europe, signatories to the Convention, who may become Parties to it by:

(a) signature without reservation in respect of ratification or acceptance;

(b) signature with reservation in respect of ratification or acceptance, followed by ratification or acceptance.

Instruments of ratification or acceptance shall be deposited with the Secretary-General of the Council of Europe.

2. This Protocol shall enter into force as soon as all Contracting Parties to the Convention shall have become Parties to the Protocol, in accordance with the provisions of paragraph 1 of this Article.

3. The Secretary-General of the Council of Europe shall notify the Members of the Council of:

(a) any signature without reservation in respect of ratification or acceptance;

(b) any signature with reservation in respect of ratification or acceptance;

(c) the deposit of any instrument of ratification or acceptance;

(d) the date of entry into force of this Protocol in accordance with paragraph 2 of this Article.

7. RULES OF PROCEDURE OF THE EUROPEAN COMMISSION OF HUMAN RIGHTS

Adopted by the Commission, 2 April 1955; with amendments to 18 December 1970. Council of Europe, European Convention on Human Rights: Collected Texts, Section 2 (7th ed., Strasbourg, 1971).

The Commission,

Having regard to the Convention for the Protection of Human Rights and Fundamental Freedoms and Protocols, hereinafter called the Convention;

Pursuant to Article 36 of the Convention;

Adopts the present Rules:

TITLE I. ORGANISATION AND WORKING OF THE COMMISSION

CHAPTER I. MEMBERS OF THE COMMISSION

Rule 1

1. The duration of the term of office of members of the Commission elected on 18th May 1954 shall be calculated as from this date. Similarly, the duration of the term of office of any member elected as a consequence of a State becoming a Party to the Convention after 18th May 1954 shall be calculated as from his election.

2. However, when a member is re-elected on the expiry of his term of office or is elected to replace a member whose term of office has expired or is about to expire, the duration of his term of office shall, in either case, be calculated as from the date of such expiry.

3. In accordance with Article 22, paragraph (3), of the Convention, a member elected to replace a member whose term of office has not expired shall hold office for the remainder of his predecessor's term.

4. In accordance with Article 22, paragraph (4), of the Convention, members shall hold office until replaced. After having

been replaced, they shall continue to deal with such cases as they already have under consideration.

Rule 2

Before taking up his duties, each member of the Commission shall, at the first meeting of the Commission at which he is present after his election, make the following oath or solemn declaration:

"I swear," or "I solemnly declare"—"that I will exercise all my powers and duties honourably and faithfully, impartially and conscientiously and that I will keep secret all deliberations."

Rule 3

1. Members of the Commission shall take precedence after the President and Vice-President according to the length of time they have been in office.

2. Members having the same length of time in office shall take precedence according to age.

3. Re-elected members shall take precedence having regard to the duration of their previous terms of office.

Rule 4

Resignation of a member shall be notified to the President who shall transmit it to the Secretary-General of the Council of Europe. Subject to the provisions of Rule 1, paragraph (4), it shall constitute vacation of office.

Chapter II. Presidency of the Commission

Rule 5

1. The Commission shall elect the President and Vice-President during the month following the date of the entry into office of members elected at periodical elections of part of the Commission in accordance with paragraph (1) of Article 22 of the Convention.

2. If the President or Vice-President, before the normal expiry of his term of office as President or Vice-President, ceases to be a member of the Commission or resigns his office, the Commission shall elect a successor to hold office for the remainder of the said term.

3. The elections referred to in this Rule shall be by secret ballot; only the members present shall take part. Election shall be by an absolute majority of votes.

If no member receives an absolute majority, a second ballot shall take place. The member receiving the most votes shall then be elected. In the case of equal voting the member having precedence under Rule 3 shall be elected.

Rule 6

The President shall direct the work and preside at the meetings of the Commission.

Rule 7

The Vice-President shall take the place of the President if the latter is unable to carry out his duties or if the office of President is vacant.

Rule 8

If the President and Vice-President are at the same time unable to carry out their duties or if their offices are at the same time vacant, the duties of President shall be carried out by another member according to the order of precedence laid down in Rule 3.

Rule 9

If the President is a national of a High Contracting Party which is party to a case brought before the Commission, he shall relinquish the office of President in respect of that case.

Rule 10

If the President of the Commission for some special reason considers that he should relinquish the office of President in a particular case, he shall so inform the Vice-President or the member acting in his place.

CHAPTER III. SECRETARIAT OF THE COMMISSION

Rule 11

1. Pursuant to Article 37 of the Convention, the Secretariat of the Commission shall be provided by the Secretary-General of the Council of Europe.

2. The Secretary-General shall appoint the Secretary of the Commission.

Rule 12

The Secretary

(a) shall assist the Commission and its members in the fulfilment of their duties;

(b) shall be the channel for all communications concerning the Commission;

(c) shall have custody of the seals, stamps and archives of the Commission.

Rule 13

1. A special register shall be kept at the Secretariat in which all cases, relevant pleadings and exhibits shall be entered in the order of their submission and without intervening spaces or deletions. Nothing shall be written in the register in abbreviated form.

2. A note of the entry in the register shall be endorsed by the Secretary of the Commission on the original documents and, at the request of the parties, on copies presented by them for that purpose.

3. Entries in the register and the notes of entries provided for in paragraph (2) of this Rule shall have effect as certified matters of record.

4. The manner of keeping the register shall be laid down by the President in agreement with the Secretary.

Rule 14

The duties of the Secretariat shall be laid down by the President in agreement with the Secretary-General of the Council of Europe.

Rules 15 to 21
(deleted)

CHAPTER IV.   THE WORKING OF THE COMMISSION

Rule 22

The seat of the Commission shall be at the seat of the Council of Europe at Strasbourg. The Commission or any of its organs may, however, if they think fit, carry out their duties elsewhere.

Rule 23

1. The Commission shall meet at the decision of the President when the latter considers that circumstances so require. It shall also meet if at least one third of its members so request.

2. Pursuant to Article 35 of the Convention, the Commission shall be convened by the Secretary-General of the Council of Europe.

Rule 24

The date and time of meetings shall be laid down by the President of the Commission.

Rule 25

A quorum of the Commission shall be nine members. However, seven members shall constitute a quorum when the Commission considers the admissibility of an application submitted under

Article 25 of the Convention and provided that the group of three members referred to in Rule 34 has unanimously reported that the application appears to be inadmissible.

Rule 26

Sessions of the Commission shall be held in camera.

Rule 27

1. The Commission shall deliberate in private. Its deliberations shall be and shall remain secret.

2. Only the members of the Commission shall take part in the deliberations of the Commission.

3. The Secretary shall as a rule be present at the deliberations. No other person may be admitted except by decision of the Commission.

Rule 28

Every member present at the deliberations shall state his opinion and the reasons therefor. The junior member according to the order of precedence laid down in Rule 3 shall speak first.

Rule 29

1. Subject to the provisions of Article 29 of the Convention, decisions of the Commission shall be taken by a majority of members present and voting.

2. The votes shall be cast in the inverse order to the order of precedence laid down in Rule 3.

3. If the voting is equal, the President shall have a casting vote.

Rule 30

The minutes of deliberations shall be secret; they shall be limited to a record of the subject of the discussions, the votes taken, the names of those voting for and against a motion and any statements expressly made for insertion in the minutes.

Rule 31

1. Members who are prevented by illness or other serious reason from taking part in the meetings shall, as soon as possible, give notice thereof to the Secretary of the Commission who shall inform the President.

2. If the President and a member who has been prevented from being present at the hearing of oral explanations by the parties, or the hearing of experts or witnesses, cannot reach a conclusion on the question whether or not that member shall take part in the deliberations or decision of the Commission subse-

quent to such hearing, the President shall refer the question for a decision by the Commission.

Rule 32

1.   If a member for some special reason considers that he should not take part in the examination of a particular case, the President and the member concerned shall consult together. In the event of disagreement, the Commission shall decide.

2.   If the President considers that a member should not, for some special reason, take part in the examination of a particular case, he shall so notify the member concerned and refer the question for a decision by the Commission.

Rule 33

Members of the Commission may not take part in the examination of any case in which they have previously acted as the agents, advisers or legal representatives of one of the parties or concerning which they have been required to state an opinion as members of a tribunal, commission of enquiry, or in any other capacity. In the event of doubt or dispute, the Commission shall decide.

Rule 34

1.   The Commission shall, as circumstances require, constitute one or more groups, each consisting of three of its members, to carry out the duties laid down in Rule 45. It shall also appoint two substitute members for each group.

2.   During the interval between sessions of the Commission, the President may, if necessary, either constitute a group or replace any member who is unable to take part in the work of a group already constituted.

3.   The President of each group shall be the member of that group who has precedence under Rule 3.

TITLE II.   PROCEDURE

CHAPTER I.   GENERAL RULES

Rule 35

1.   The official languages of the Commission shall be French and English.

2.   The President may authorise a member to speak in another language.

Rule 36

1.   The High Contracting Parties shall be represented before the Commission by their agents who may have the assistance of counsel or advocates.

2.   The persons, non-governmental organisations and groups of individuals referred to in Article 25 of the Convention may represent their case in person before the Commission. They may be assisted or represented by a member of the Bar, by a solicitor or by a professor of law, or by any other lawyer approved by the Commission.

Rule 37

The Commission may, at the request of a party or of a person representing or assisting that party, permit the use by such party or person of a language other than English or French.

Rule 38

1.   The Commission shall deal with cases in the order in which they become ready for hearing. It may, however, decide to give precedence to a particular case.

2.   The Commission or, if it is not in session, its President may at the request of a party or *ex officio* order a case to be adjourned.

Rule 39

The Commission may, if it considers necessary, order the joinder of two or more cases.

CHAPTER II.   INSTITUTION OF PROCEEDINGS

Rule 40

1.   Any claims submitted under Article 24 or 25 of the Convention shall be submitted in the form of an application in writing and shall be signed by the applicant or his representative.

2.   Where an application is submitted by a non-governmental organisation or by a group of individuals, it shall be signed by those persons competent to represent such organisation or group, if such organisation or group is properly constituted according to the laws of the State to which it is subject. The application shall in all other cases be signed by the persons composing the group submitting the application.

Rule 41

1.   The application shall mention:

(*a*)   the name of the applicant;

(*b*)   the name of the High Contracting Party against which the claim is made;

(*c*)   the object of the claim;

(*d*)   as far as possible the provision of the Convention alleged to have been violated;

(*e*)   a statement of the facts and argument;

(*f*)   any attached documents.

2.   The applicant shall provide information enabling it to be shown that the conditions laid down in Article 26 of the Convention have been satisfied.

Rule 42

Where the applicant intends to claim damages for an alleged injury, the amount of damages claimed may be stated in the application.

Rule 43

The Secretary-General of the Council of Europe shall transmit the application and any relevant documents to the President of the Commission.

Rule 44

Where, pursuant to Article 24 of the Convention, an application is brought before the Commission by a High Contracting Party, the President of the Commission shall through the Secretary-General of the Council of Europe give notice of such application to the High Contracting Party against which the claim is made and shall invite it to submit to the Commission its observations in writing on the admissibility of such application.

Rule 45

1.   Any application submitted pursuant to Article 25 of the Convention shall be referred by the President of the Commission to the group of three members mentioned in Rule 34, which shall make a preliminary examination as to its admissibility. The group of three members shall then submit to the Commission a Report on such preliminary examination.

2.   If the group of three members unanimously reports that the application appears to be admissible, the President of the Commission shall through the Secretary-General of the Council of Europe give notice of such application to the High Contracting Party against which the claim is made and shall invite it to submit to the Commission its observations in writing on the admissibility of such application.

3.   If the group of three members does not unanimously report that the application appears to be admissible, the Commission shall consider the application and may

(*a*)   either, declare at once that the application is inadmissible,

(*b*)   or, through the Secretary-General of the Council of Europe give notice of such application to the High Contracting Party against which the claim is made and invite it to submit to the Commission its observations in writing on the admissibility of such application.

Rule 46

1. Except for the case provided for in Rule 45, paragraph (3) (a), the Commission, before it decides as to the admissibility of an application, may, if it thinks fit, invite the parties to submit to it their further comments in writing. It may also invite the parties to make oral explanations.

2. During the interval between sessions of the Commission, the President may, if he thinks fit, exercise the powers mentioned in paragraph (1) of this Rule.

3. The decision of the Commission in regard to the admissibility of the application shall be accompanied by reasons. The Secretary of the Commission shall communicate such decision to the applicant and, except for the case provided for in Rule 45, paragraph 3 (a), to the respondent party.

CHAPTER III. PROCEDURE AFTER THE ACCEPTANCE OF AN APPLICATION

Rule 47

When the Commission accepts an application, the President shall lay down the time-limits within which the parties shall file their submissions and evidence.

Rule 48

1. Each pleading shall be signed in the original by the party or its representative.

2. Each pleading shall be dated. For the purpose of determining any time-limits, the date of the filing of the pleading with the Secretariat-General of the Council of Europe shall alone be taken into consideration.

3. Any document submitted as an appendix and written in a language other than the official languages shall, unless the President otherwise decides, be accompanied by translation into one of the official languages. Translations of extracts may be submitted, however, in the case of lengthy documents. The Commission may at any time require a more complete translation or a certified translation to be submitted.

Rule 49
(deleted)

Rule 50

1. The Commission may take any measure which it considers expedient in order to carry out the duties laid down in Article 28 of the Convention.

2. The Commission shall take formal note of the refusal of a party to comply with such measures.

Rule 51

1. The Commission may charge one or more of its members to carry out an enquiry or any other form of investigation or to perform any other task necessary for the proper execution of its functions under Article 28 of the Convention. Such member or members shall duly report to the Commission.

2. The Commission may also appoint one of its members as rapporteur.

Rule 52
(deleted)

Rule 53

1. The Commission may put questions to the parties and request them to give explanations.

2. Each member of the Commission shall have the same right and shall give notice to the President if he wishes to exercise it.

Rule 54

1. The Commission may, at the request of a party or *proprio motu,* decide to hear as a witness or expert or in any other capacity any person whose evidence or statements seem likely to assist it in the carrying out of its task.

2. Any witness, expert or other person whom the Commission decides to hear shall be summoned by the Secretary. The summons shall indicate:

—the names, first names, occupation and domicile of the parties in the case;

—the facts or points regarding which the person concerned will be heard;

—the arrangements made, in accordance with paragraph 3, paragraph 4 or paragraph 5 of this Rule, to reimburse the person concerned for any expenses incurred by him.

3. The expenses incurred by any witness, expert or other person whom the Commission decides to hear at the request of a High Contracting Party shall be borne by that Party.

4. The expenses incurred by any witness, expert or other person whom the Commission decides to hear at the request of a

person, non-governmental organisation or group of individuals which has referred a matter to the Commission under Article 25 of the Convention, shall be borne either by the applicant or by the Council of Europe as the Commission may decide. In the latter case they shall be fixed by the President.

5. The expenses incurred by any witness, expert or other person whom the Commission *proprio motu* decides to hear shall be fixed by the President and be borne by the Council of Europe.

6. Any witness, expert or other person whom the Commission decides to hear may, if he has not sufficient knowledge of English or French, be authorised by the President to speak in another language.

Rule 55

1. After establishing the identity of the witnesses or experts, the President or the member or members mentioned in Rule 51, paragraph 1, shall request them to take the following oath:

(*a*)   for witnesses: "I swear that I will speak the truth, the whole truth and nothing but the truth."

(*b*)   for experts: "I swear that my statement will be in accordance with my sincere belief."

2. Instead of taking the oath in the terms set out in paragraph (1) of this Rule, the witnesses or experts may make the following declaration:

(*a*)   for witnesses: "I solemnly declare upon my honour and conscience that I will speak the truth, the whole truth and nothing but the truth."

(*b*)   for experts: "I solemnly declare upon my honour and conscience that my statement will be in accordance with my sincere belief."

Rule 56

Questions may be put to the witnesses, experts or other persons mentioned in Rule 54, paragraph (1):

(*a*)   by the President or any member of the Commission;

(*b*)   by a party, with the permission of the President or of the member or members mentioned in Rule 51, paragraph 1.

Rule 57

Where, without good reason, a witness, expert or other person who has been duly required to appear, fails to appear or refuses to give evidence, the Secretary-General of the Council of Europe shall, at the request of the President, so inform that High Contracting Party to whose jurisdiction the person concerned is subject. The same provisions shall apply where a witness or expert has, in the opinion of the Commission, violated the oath or solemn declaration mentioned in Rule 55.

Rule 58

If the Commission considers that it is expedient to examine a case in a place other than the seat of the Council of Europe, it shall, through the Secretary-General of the Council of Europe, request any High Contracting Party concerned to grant it all necessary facilities, as mentioned in paragraph (*a*) of Article 28 of the Convention, in order that it may carry out its task.

Rule 59

The Secretariat shall draw up the minutes of the hearings. The minutes shall be signed by the President and by the Secretary. They shall constitute certified matters of record.

Rule 59a

Where the Commission decides to reject an application under Article 29 of the Convention, its decision shall be accompanied by reasons. The Secretary shall communicate the Commission's decision to the parties.

CHAPTER IV.   THE REPORT OF THE COMMISSION

Rule 60

The Report provided for in Article 30 of the Convention shall contain:
—the date on which it was drawn up;
—the names of the President and members of the Commission;
—a description of the parties;
—the names of the representatives and counsel of the parties;
—a statement of the facts;
—the terms of the solution reached.

Rule 61

The Report referred to in Rule 60 shall be signed by the President and by the Secretary. It shall be sent to the High Contracting Parties concerned, to the Committee of Ministers and to the Secretary-General of the Council of Europe for publication.

Rules 62 to 64
(deleted)

Rule 65

The Report provided for in Article 31 of the Convention shall be drawn up after deliberation by the Commission in plenary session.

Rule 66

The Report shall contain:

—the date on which it was drawn up;

—the names of the President and members who took part in the deliberation mentioned in Rule 65;

—a description of the parties;

—the names of the representatives and counsel of the parties;

—a statement of the proceedings;

—a statement of the facts;

—the opinion of the Commission as to whether the facts found disclose a breach by the High Contracting Party concerned of its obligations under the Convention;

—the reasons on which that opinion is based;

—a statement of the number of members forming the majority;

—any proposal which the Commission may consider appropriate.

Rule 67

Each member may, in accordance with paragraph (1) of Article 31 of the Convention, include in the Report a statement of his opinion.

Rule 68

Where the Commission decides to make proposals concerning damages as envisaged in Rule 42, it shall make them in pursuance of paragraph (3) of Article 31 of the Convention.

Rule 69

The Report and any proposals shall be signed by the President and by the Secretary. They shall be sent through the Secretary-General of the Council of Europe to the Committee of Ministers and only to those High Contracting Parties which are concerned.

Rule 70

During the period of three months following the transmission of the Report of the Committee of Ministers, the Commission shall consider at a plenary session whether or not to bring the case before the European Court of Human Rights in pursuance of Article 48, paragraph (a), of the Convention.

TITLE III. RELATIONS OF THE COMMISSION
WITH THE COURT

Rule 71

The Commission shall assist the European Court of Human Rights in any case brought before the Court. For this purpose and in accordance with Rule 29, paragraph (1) of the Rules of Court, the Commission shall as soon as possible appoint, at a plenary session, one or more of its members to take part, as a delegate, in the consideration of the case before the Court. These delegates may be assisted by any person appointed by the Commission. In discharging their functions they shall act in accordance with such directives as they may receive from the Commission.

Rule 72

1. When, in pursuance of Article 48, paragraph (a) of the Convention, the Commission decides to bring a case before the Court, it shall, in accordance with Rule 31, paragraph (2) of the Rules of Court, draw up a request indicating in particular:

   (*a*) the parties to the proceedings before the Commission;

   (*b*) the date on which the Commission adopted its Report;

   (*c*) the date on which, as certified by the Secretary of the Commission in a document attached to the request, the Report was transmitted to the Committee of Ministers;

   (*d*) the names and addresses of its delegates.

2. The Secretary of the Commission shall transmit to the Registry of the Court thirty copies of the request referred to in paragraph (1) of this Rule.

Rule 73

When, in pursuance of Article 48, paragraph (b), (c) or (d) of the Convention, a High Contracting Party brings a case before the Court, the Secretary of the Commission shall communicate to the Registry of the Court as soon as possible:

   (*a*) the names and addresses of the Commission's delegates;

   (*b*) any other information which the Commission may consider appropriate.

Rule 74

The Secretary of the Commission shall, as soon as he has transmitted the request referred to in Rule 72, paragraph (2) above, or has received the communication mentioned in Rule 32, paragraph (1) (c) of the Rules of Court, file with the Registry of the Court an adequate number of copies of the Commission's Report.

Rule 75

The Commission shall communicate to the Court, at its request, any memorial, evidence, document or information concerning the case, with the exception of documents relating to the attempt to secure a friendly settlement in accordance with Article 28, paragraph (b) of the Convention. The communication of those documents shall be subject in each case to a decision of the Commission.

Rule 76

When a case brought before the Commission in pursuance of Article 25 of the Convention is subsequently referred to the Court, the Secretary of the Commission shall immediately notify the applicant. Unless the Commission shall otherwise decide, the Secretary shall also in due course communicate to him the Commission's Report, informing him that he may, within a time-limit fixed by the President, submit to the Commission his written observations on the said Report. The Commission shall decide what action, if any, shall be taken in respect of those observations.

ADDENDUM TO RULES OF PROCEDURE

LEGAL AID

Rule 1

The Commission may, either at the request of an applicant lodging an application under Article 25 of the Convention or *proprio motu*, grant free legal aid to that applicant for the representation of his case before the Commission:

(a)   where observations in writing on the admissibility of that application have been received from the respondent Government in pursuance of Rule 45, paragraphs 2 or 3 (b), or where the time-limit for their submission has expired, or

(b)   where the application has been declared admissible.

Rule 2

Free legal aid shall only be granted where the Commission is satisfied:

(a)   that it is essential for the proper discharge of the Commission's duties;

(b)   that the applicant has not sufficient means to meet all or part of the costs involved.

Rule 3

(a)   In order to determine whether or not the applicant has sufficient means to meet all or part of the costs involved, the Commission shall require him to complete a form of declaration stating his income, capital assets and any financial commitments in respect of dependents, or any other financial obligations. Such declaration shall be certified by the appropriate domestic authority or authorities.

(*b*) Before making a grant of free legal aid, the Commission shall request the respondent Government to submit its comments in writing.

(*c*) The Commission shall, after receiving the information mentioned in paragraphs (*a*) and (*b*), decide whether or not to grant free legal aid and shall inform the parties accordingly.

(*d*) The President shall fix the time-limits within which the parties shall be requested to supply the information referred to in this Rule.

Rule 4

(*a*) Fees shall be payable only to a barrister-at-law, solicitor or professionally qualified person of similar status. Fees may, where appropriate, be paid to more than one such lawyer as defined above.

(*b*) Legal aid may be granted to cover not only lawyers' fees but also travelling and subsistence expenses and other necessary out-of-pocket expenses incurred by the applicant or appointed lawyer.

Rule 5

(*a*) On the Commission deciding to grant legal aid, the Secretary shall, by agreement with the appointed lawyer, fix the rate of fees to be paid to him.

(*b*) The Secretary shall as soon as possible notify the Secretary-General of the Council of Europe of the rate of fees so agreed.

Rule 6

The Commission may, at any time, if it finds that the conditions set out in Rule 2 are no longer satisfied, revoke its grant of free legal aid to an applicant, in whole or in part, and shall at once notify the parties thereof.

8. RULES OF COURT OF THE EUROPEAN COURT OF HUMAN RIGHTS

Adopted by the Court, 18 September 1959; with amendments to 29 May 1970. Council of Europe, European Convention on Human Rights: Collected Texts, Section 3 (7th ed., Strasbourg, 1971).

The European Court of Human Rights,

Having regard to the Convention for the Protection of Human Rights and Fundamental Freedoms and the Protocols thereto

Makes the present Rules:

Rule 1
(Definitions)

For the purposes of these Rules:

(a)   the term "Convention" means the Convention for the Protection of Human Rights and Fundamental Freedoms and the Protocols thereto;

(b)   the expression "Protocol No. 2" means Protocol No. 2 to the Convention conferring upon the European Court of Human Rights competence to give advisory opinions;

(c)   the expression "plenary Court" means the European Court of Human Rights sitting in plenary session;

(d)   the term "Chamber" means any Chamber constituted in pursuance of Article 43 of the Convention;

(e)   the term "Court" means either the plenary Court or the Chambers;

(f)   the expression *"ad hoc* judge" means any person, other than an elected judge, chosen by a Contracting Party in pursuance of Article 43 of the Convention to sit as a member of a Chamber;

(g)   the term "judge" or "judges" means the judges elected by the Consultative Assembly of the Council of Europe or *ad hoc* judges;

(h)   the term "Parties" means those Contracting Parties which are the Applicant and Respondent Parties;

(i)   the term "Commission" means the European Commission of Human Rights;

(j)   the expression "delegates of the Commission" means the member or members of the Commission delegated by it to take part in the consideration of a case before the Court;

(k)   the expression "report of the Commission" means the report provided for in Article 31 of the Convention;

(l)   the expression "Committee of Ministers" means the Committee of Ministers of the Council of Europe.

TITLE I.   ORGANISATION AND WORKING OF THE COURT

CHAPTER I.   JUDGES

Rule 2
(Calculation of term of office)

1.   The duration of the term of office of an elected judge shall be calculated as from his election. However, when a judge is re-elected on the expiry of his term of office or is elected to replace a judge whose term of office has expired or is about to expire, the

duration of his term of office shall, in either case, be calculated as from the date of such expiry.

2. In accordance with Article 40, § 3, of the Convention, a judge elected to replace a judge whose term of office has not expired shall hold office for the remainder of his predecessor's term.

3. In accordance with Article 40, § 4, of the Convention, elected judges shall hold office until replaced. After having been replaced, they shall continue to deal with any case, or any part of a case, or any particular point, in connection with which hearings have begun before them.

Rule 3
(Oath or solemn declaration)

1. Before taking up his duties, each elected judge shall, at the first sitting of the Court at which he is present after his election, take the following oath or make the following solemn declaration:

"I swear," or "I solemnly declare"—"that I will exercise my functions as a judge honourably, independently and impartially and that I will keep secret all deliberations."

2. This act shall be recorded in minutes.

Rule 4
(Obstacle to the exercise of the functions of judge)

A judge may not exercise his functions while he is a member of a Government or while he holds a post or exercises a profession which is likely to affect confidence in his independence. In case of need the Court shall decide.

Rule 5
(Precedence)

1. Elected judges shall take precedence after the President and the Vice-President according to their seniority in office; in the event of re-election, even if it is not an immediate re-election, the length of time during which they previously exercised their functions shall be taken into account.

2. Elected judges having the same seniority in office shall take precedence according to age.

3. *Ad hoc* judges shall take precedence after the elected judges according to age.

Rule 6
(Resignation)

Resignation of a judge shall be notified to the President who shall transmit it to the Secretary-General of the Council of Europe.

Subject to the provisions of Rule 2, § 3, resignation shall constitute vacation of office.

CHAPTER II. PRESIDENCY OF THE PLENARY COURT

Rule 7
(Election of the President and Vice-President)

1. The President and Vice-President of the Court shall, in accordance with Article 41 of the Convention, be elected for a period of three years, provided that such period shall not exceed the duration of their term of office as judges. They may be re-elected.

2. The plenary Court shall elect the President and Vice-President following the entry into office of the judges elected at periodical elections of part of the Court in accordance with Article 40, § 1, of the Convention. The President and Vice-President shall continue to exercise their functions until the election of their respective successors.

3. If the President or Vice-President ceases to be a member of the Court or resigns his office before its normal expiry, the plenary Court shall elect a successor for the remainder of the term of that office.

4. The elections referred to in this Rule shall be by secret ballot; only the elected judges who are present shall take part. If no judge receives an absolute majority, a ballot shall take place between the two judges who have received most votes. In the case of equal voting, preference shall be given to the judge having precedence in accordance with Rule 5.

Rule 8
(Functions of the President)

The President shall direct the work and administration of the Court; he shall preside at plenary sessions.

Rule 9
(Functions of the Vice-President)

The Vice-President shall take the place of the President if the latter is unable to carry out his functions or if the office of President is vacant.

Rule 10
(Replacement of the President and Vice-President)

If the President and Vice-President are at the same time unable to carry out their functions or if their offices are at the same time vacant, the office of President shall be assumed by another elected judge in accordance with the order of precedence provided for in Rule 5.

Chapter III.   The Registry

Rule 11
(Election of the Registrar)

1.   The Court shall elect its Registrar after the President has in this respect obtained the opinion of the Secretary-General of the Council of Europe. The candidates must possess the legal knowledge and the experience necessary to carry out the duties of the post and must have an adequate working knowledge of the two official languages of the Court.

2.   The Registrar shall be elected for a term of seven years. He may be re-elected.

3.   The elections referred to in this Rule shall be by secret ballot; only the elected judges who are present shall take part. If no candidate receives an absolute majority, a ballot shall take place between the two candidates who have received most votes. In the case of equal voting, preference shall be given to the oldest candidate.

4.   Before taking up his duties, the Registrar shall take the following oath or make the following solemn declaration before the Court or, if the Court is not in session, before the President:

"I swear," or "I solemnly declare"—"that I will exercise loyally, discreetly and conscientiously the functions conferred upon me as Registrar of the European Court of Human Rights."

Rule 12
(Election of the Deputy Registrar)

1.   The Court shall also elect a Deputy Registrar according to the conditions and in the manner and for the term prescribed in Rule 11.

2.   Before taking up his duties, the Deputy Registrar shall take an oath or make a solemn declaration before the Court, or, if the Court is not in session, before the President, in similar terms to that prescribed in respect of the Registrar.

Rule 13
(Other officials of the Registrar)

The President, or the Registrar on his behalf, shall request the Secretary-General of the Council of Europe to provide the Registrar with the staff, permanent or temporary, equipment and facilities necessary for the Court.

The officials of the Registry, other than the Registrar and the Deputy Registrar, shall be appointed by the Secretary-General, with the agreement of the President or the Registrar.

Rule 14
(Duties of the Registrar)

1. The Registrar shall be the channel for all communications and notifications made by, or addressed to, the Court.

2. The Registrar shall ensure that the dates of despatch and receipt of any communication or notification may be easily verified. Communications or notifications addressed to the agents for the Parties or to the delegates of the Commission shall be considered as having been addressed to the Parties themselves or the Commission itself. The date of receipt shall be noted on each document received by the Registrar who shall transmit to the sender a receipt bearing this date and the number under which the document has been registered.

3. The Registrar shall, subject to the discretion attaching to his duties, reply to all requests for information concerning the work of the Court, in particular, from the Press. He shall announce the date and time fixed for the hearings in open Court.

4. General instructions drawn up by the Registrar and sanctioned by the President shall provide for the working of the Registry.

CHAPTER IV. THE WORKING OF THE COURT

Rule 15
(Seat of the Court)

The seat of the European Court of Human Rights shall be at the seat of the Council of Europe at Strasbourg. The Court may, however, if it considers it expedient, exercise its functions in any territories to which the Convention applies.

Rule 16
(Sessions of the plenary Court)

The plenary sessions of the Court shall be convened by the President and the Court shall be so convened at least once annually.

Rule 17
(Quorum)

1. The quorum of the plenary Court shall be eleven judges.

2. If there is no quorum, the President shall adjourn the sitting.

Rule 18
(Public character of the hearings)

The hearings shall be public, unless the Court shall in exceptional circumstances decide otherwise.

Rule 19
(Deliberations)

1. The Court shall deliberate in private. Its deliberations shall be and shall remain secret.

2. Only the judges shall take part in the deliberations. The Registrar or his substitute shall be present. No other person may be admitted except by special decision of the Court.

3. Each judge present at such deliberations shall state his opinion and the reasons therefor.

4. Any question which is to be voted upon shall be formulated in precise terms in the two official languages and the text shall, if a judge so requests, be distributed before the vote is taken.

5. The minutes of the private sittings of the Court for deliberations shall be secret; they shall be limited to a record of the subject of the discussions, the votes taken, the names of those voting for and against a motion and any statements expressly made for insertion in the minutes.

Rule 20
(Majority required)

1. The decisions of the Court shall be taken by the majority of judges present.

2. The votes shall be cast in the inverse order to the order of precedence provided for in Rule 5.

3. If the voting is equal, the President shall have a second and casting vote.

CHAPTER V.   THE CHAMBERS

Rule 21
(Composition of the Court when constituted in a Chamber)

1. When a case is brought before the Court either by the Commission or by a Contracting Party having the right to do so under Article 48 of the Convention, the Court shall be constituted in a Chamber of seven judges. The judge or judges who have the nationality of the State or States which are Parties to the case shall, in accordance with Article 43 of the Convention, sit as *ex officio* members of this Chamber. The names of the other judges shall be chosen by lot.

2. In making the communications provided for in Rule 32, the Registrar shall invite:

(*a*) the Contracting Party against which the complaint has been lodged before the Commission to supply him within thirty days with the name and address of its agent;

(b) any other Contracting Party which appears to have the right, under Article 48 of the Convention, to bring a case before the Court and which has not availed itself of that right to inform him within thirty days whether it wishes to appear as a Party to the case of which the Court has been seized and, if so, to supply him with the name and address of its agent;

(c) the Commission, if the Commission has not brought the case before the Court, to supply him as soon as possible with the names and addresses of its delegates.

3. In the case of doubt or dispute as to whether a Contracting Party has the right under Article 48 of the Convention to bring a case before the Court, the President shall submit that question to the plenary Court for decision.

4. At the same time as the communication made by the Registrar in accordance with paragraph 2 of this Rule, the President shall notify all the judges that he will proceed to constitute a Chamber by means of drawing lots. If a judge, upon receiving such notification, believes that he will be unable to sit for one of the reasons given in Rule 24 of the Rules of Court he shall inform the President who may exclude the name of such judge from the ballot.

5. The President of the Court shall, in the presence of the Registrar, choose by lot from among those judges who are not unable to sit, have not required to withdraw or are not dispensed from sitting under Rule 24 of the Rules of Court, the names of those called upon to compose or complete the Chamber and of three substitutes. The substitutes shall be those judges whose names are drawn last, other than the President or Vice-President who shall in all cases be considered to be appointed titular judges.

6. If the President of the Court finds that two cases concern the same Party or Parties and relate wholly or in part to the same Article or Articles of the Convention, he may refer the second case to the Chamber already constituted, or in the course of constitution, for the consideration of the first case, or, if there is none, proceed to the constitution of one Chamber to consider both cases.

7. The office of President of the Chamber shall be held *ex officio* by the President of the Court if he has been chosen by lot as member of the Chamber; if he has not been so chosen, the Vice-President, if chosen by lot, shall preside. In the absence of both the President and Vice-President, the office of President

shall be held by the senior judge of the judges chosen by lot according to the order of precedence provided for in Rule 5. The same rule shall apply where the person called upon to act as President is unable to attend or withdraws.

Rule 22
(Substitute judges)

1.   The substitute judges shall be called upon to sit according to the order determined by the drawing of lots, in place of any judges chosen by lot who are unable to sit or have withdrawn. After being replaced, a judge chosen by lot shall cease to be a member of the Chamber.

2.   The substitute judges shall be supplied with the documents relating to the proceedings. The President may convoke one or more of them, according to the above order of precedence, to attend the hearings and deliberations without taking part therein.

Rule 23
(*Ad hoc* judges)

1.   If the Court does not include an elected judge having the nationality of a Party or if the judge called upon to sit in that capacity is unable to sit or withdraws, the President of the Court shall invite the agent of the Party concerned to inform him within thirty days whether his Government wishes to appoint to sit as judge either another elected judge or, as an *ad hoc* judge, any other person possessing the qualifications required under Article 39, § 3, of the Convention and, if so, to state the name of the person so appointed. The same rule shall apply if an *ad hoc* judge is unable to sit or withdraws.

2.   If a reply has not been received within thirty days, the Government concerned shall be presumed to have waived such right of appointment and, if the seat falls vacant during the proceedings, a substitute judge shall be called upon to fill that vacancy, according to the order in which such judges have been chosen by lot.

3.   An *ad hoc* judge shall, at the opening of the first sitting fixed for the consideration of the case for which he has been appointed, take the oath or make the solemn declaration provided for in Rule 3.

Rule 24
(Inability to attend, withdrawal or exemption)

1.   Any judge who is prevented by illness or other serious reasons from taking part in sittings for which he has been convoked shall, as soon as possible, give notice thereof to the President of the Chamber.

2. A judge may not take part in the consideration of any case in which he has a personal interest or in which he has previously acted either as the agent, advocate or adviser of a Party or of a person having an interest in the case, or as member of a tribunal or commission of enquiry, or in any other capacity.

3. If a judge considers that he should withdraw from consideration of a particular case or if the President considers such withdrawal to be desirable, the President and the judge shall consult together. In case of disagreement, the President shall decide.

4. Similarly, any judge who has been called upon to sit on one or more previous cases may, at his request, be exempted from sitting on a new case provided his services can be dispensed with.

Rule 25
(Common interest)

1. If several Parties have a common interest, they shall for the purposes of the provisions of this Chapter, be deemed to be one Party. The President of the Court shall invite them to agree to appoint a single elected judge or *ad hoc* judge in accordance with Article 43 of the Convention. If the Parties are unable to agree, the President shall choose by lot, from among the persons proposed as judges by these Parties, the judge called upon to sit *ex officio*. The names of the other judges and substitute judges shall then be chosen by lot by the President of the Court from among the elected judges who are not nationals of any of these Parties.

2. In the case of dispute as to the existence of a common interest, the plenary Court shall decide.

TITLE II. PROCEDURE

CHAPTER I. GENERAL RULES

Rule 26
(Possibility of particular derogations)

The provisions of this Title shall not prevent the Court from derogating from them for the consideration of a particular case with the agreement of the Party or Parties and after having obtained the opinion of the delegates of the Commission.

Rule 27
(Official languages)

1. The official languages of the Court shall be French and English.

2.   The Court may authorise any Party to use a language other than French or English. In that event, the Party concerned shall attach to the original of each document submitted by it a translation into French or English; it shall be responsible for the interpretation into French or English of the oral arguments or statements made by its agents, advocates or advisers and shall, to the extent which the Court may determine in each case, bear the other extra expenses involved in the use of a non-official language.

3.   Any witness, expert or other person appearing before the Court may use his own language if he does not have sufficient knowledge of either of the two official languages. The Court shall, in that event, make the necessary arrangements for the interpretation into French or English of the statements of the witness, expert or other person concerned.

4.   All decisions of the Court shall be given in French and English and the Court shall state which of the two texts shall be authentic.

Rule 28
(Representation of the Parties)

The Parties shall be represented by agents who may have the assistance of advocates or advisers.

Rule 29
(Relations between the Court and the Commission)

1.   The Commission shall delegate one or more of its members to take part in the consideration of a case before the Court. The delegates may, if they so desire, have the assistance of any person of their choice.

2.   The Court shall, whether a case is referred to it by a Contracting Party or by the Commission, take into consideration the report of the latter.

Rule 30
(Communications, notifications and summonses addressed to persons other than the agents of the Parties or the delegates of the Commission)

1.   If, for any communication, notification or summons addressed to persons other than the agents of the Parties or the delegates of the Commission, the Court considers it necessary to have the assistance of the Government of the State on whose territory such communication, notification or summons is to have effect, the President shall apply directly to that Government in order to obtain the necessary facilities.

2.   The same rule shall apply when the Court desires to make or arrange for the making of an investigation on the spot in order

to establish the facts or to procure evidence or when it orders the appearance of a person resident in, or having to cross, that territory.

CHAPTER II. INSTITUTION OF PROCEEDINGS

Rule 31
(Filing of the application or request)

1.   Any Contracting Party which intends to bring a case before the Court in accordance with the provisions of Article 48 of the Convention shall file with the Registry an application, in forty copies, indicating:

(a)   the parties to the proceedings before the Commission;

(b)   the date on which the Commission adopted its report;

(c)   the date on which the report was transmitted to the Committee of Ministers;

(d)   the object of the application, including any objections made to the opinion of the Commission;

(e)   the name and address of the person appointed as agent.

2.   If the Commission intends to bring a case before the Court in accordance with the provisions of Article 48 of the Convention, it shall file with the Registry a request, in forty copies, signed by its President and containing the particulars set out in sub-paragraphs (a), (b) and (c) of paragraph 1 of this Rule together with the names and addresses of the delegates of the Commission.

Rule 32
(Communication of the application or request)

1.   On receipt of an application or request, the Registrar shall immediately transmit a copy thereof:

(a)   to the President, Vice-President and judges;

(b)   to any Contracting Party mentioned in Article 48 of the Convention which has not brought the application before the Court;

(c)   to the President and members of the Commission if the Commission has not brought the case before the Court.

He shall also inform the Committee of Ministers, through the Secretary-General of the Council of Europe, of the filing of the application or request.

2.   The communications mentioned in sub-paragraphs (a) and (b) of paragraph 1 of this Rule shall include a copy of the report of the Commission.

Rule 33
(Notice of composition of the Chamber)

As soon as a Chamber has been constituted for the consideration of a case, the Registrar shall communicate its composition to the judges, to the agents of the Parties and to the President of the Commission.

Rule 34
(Interim measures)

1. Before the constitution of a Chamber, the President of the plenary Court may, at the request of a Party, of the Commission, of any person concerned or *proprio motu,* bring to the attention of the Parties any interim measure the adoption of which seems desirable. The Chamber, when constituted, or, if the Chamber is not in session, its President, shall have the same right.

2. Notice of these measures shall be immediately given to the Committee of Ministers.

CHAPTER III. EXAMINATION OF CASES

Rule 35
(Written Procedure)

1. After the Chamber has been constituted, the President of the Chamber shall, after ascertaining the views of the agents of the Parties and the delegates of the Commission or, if they have not yet been appointed, the President of the Commission, upon the procedure to be followed, direct whether, and if so in what order and within what time-limits, memorials, counter-memorials and other documents are to be filed.

2. If in pursuance of Rule 21, § 6, a Chamber is seized of two cases, its President may, in the interest of the proper administration of justice and after having obtained the opinion of the agents of the Parties and the delegates of the Commission, order that the proceedings in both cases be conducted simultaneously, without prejudice to the decision of the Chamber on the joinder of the cases.

3. The memorials, counter-memorials and documents annexed thereto shall be filed with the Registry in forty copies. The Registrar shall transmit copies of all these documents to the judges, to the agents of the Parties and to the delegates of the Commission.

Rule 36
(Fixing of the date of the opening of the oral proceedings and release of the report of the Commission)

When the case is ready for hearing, the President of the Chamber shall, after consulting the agents of the Parties and the delegates of the Commission, fix the date of the opening of the oral proceedings. From that moment, the report of the Commission, excluding any particulars relating to the attempt to reach a friendly settlement, may be made public through the Registrar.

Rule 37
(Conduct of the hearings)

The President of the Chamber shall direct the hearings. He shall prescribe the order in which the agents, the advocates or advisers of the Parties and the delegates of the Commission, as well as any other person appointed by them in accordance with Rule 29, § 1, shall be called upon to speak.

Rule 38
(Enquiry, expert opinion and other measures for obtaining information)

1. The Chamber may, at the request of a Party or of delegates of the Commission or *proprio motu,* decide to hear as a witness or expert or in any other capacity any person whose evidence or statements seem likely to assist it in the carrying out of its task.

2. The Chamber may, at any time during the proceedings, depute one or more of its members to conduct an enquiry, to carry out an investigation on the spot or to obtain information in any other manner.

3. The Chamber may entrust any body, office, commission or authority of its choice with the task of obtaining information, expressing an opinion, or making a report, upon any specific point.

4. Any report prepared in accordance with the preceding paragraphs shall be addressed to the Registrar.

Rule 39
(Convocation of witnesses, experts and other persons; expenses of their appearance)

1. Witnesses, experts or other persons whom the Chamber decides to hear shall be summoned by the Registrar. If they are called by a Party, the expenses of their appearance shall be taxed by the President and, unless the Chamber shall otherwise decide in pursuance of Rule 50, § 1 (k), shall be borne by that Party. In other cases, such expenses shall be fixed by the President and borne by the Council of Europe.

2. The summons shall indicate:

—the names of the Party or Parties;

—the object of the enquiry, expert opinion or any other measure for obtaining information as ordered by the Chamber;

—any provisions for the payment of the sum due to the person summoned.

Rule 40
(Oath or solemn declaration by witnesses and experts)

1. After the establishment of his identity and before giving evidence, every witness shall take the following oath or make the following solemn declaration:

"I swear"—or "I solemnly declare upon my honour and conscience"—"that I will speak the truth, the whole truth and nothing but the truth."

2. After the establishment of his identity and before carrying out his task, every expert shall take the following oath or make the following solemn declaration:

"I swear"—or "I solemnly declare"—"that I will discharge my duty as expert honourably and conscientiously."

This oath may be taken or this declaration made before the President of the Chamber or before a judge or local authority nominated by the President.

Rule 41
(Objection to a witness or expert; hearing of a person
for purpose of information)

The Chamber shall decide in the case of any dispute arising from an objection to a witness or expert. Nevertheless, it may, if it considers it necessary, hear for the purpose of information a person who cannot be heard as a witness.

Rule 42
(Questions put during the hearings)

1. The President of the Chamber or any judge may put questions to the agents, advocates or advisers of the Parties, to the witnesses and experts, to the delegates of the Commission, and to any other persons appearing before the Chamber.

2. The witnesses, experts and other persons referred to in Rule 38, § 1, may, subject to the control of the President who has power to decide as to the relevance of the questions put, be examined by the agents, advocates or advisers of the Parties, by the delegates of the Commission, and by any person appointed by them in accordance with Rule 29, § 1.

Rule 43
(Failure to appear or false evidence)

When, without good reason, a witness or any other person who has been duly summoned fails to appear or refuses to give evidence, the Registrar shall, on being so required by the President, inform that Contracting Party to whose jurisdiction such witness or other person is subject. The same provisions shall apply when a witness or expert has, in the opinion of the Chamber, violated the oath or solemn declaration mentioned in Rule 40.

Rule 44
(Minutes of hearings)

1. Minutes shall be made of each hearing and shall be signed by the President and the Registrar.

2. These minutes shall include:

—the names of the judges present;

—the names of the agents, advocates and advisers and of the delegates of the Commission present;

—the surname, first names, description and residence of the witnesses, experts or other persons heard;

—the declarations expressly made for insertion in the minutes on behalf of the Parties or of the Commission;

—a summary record of the questions put by the President or other judges and of the replies made thereto;

—any decision by the Chamber delivered during the hearing.

3. Copies of the minutes shall be given to the agents of the Parties and to the delegates of the Commission.

4. The minutes shall constitute certified matters of record.

Rule 45
(Shorthand note of hearings)

1. The Registrar shall be responsible for the making of a shorthand note of each hearing.

2. The agents, advocates and advisers of the Parties, the delegates of the Commission and the witnesses, experts and other persons mentioned in Rules 29, § 1, and 38, § 1, shall receive the shorthand note of their arguments, statements or evidence, in order that they may, subject to the control of the Registrar or of the Chamber, make corrections within the time-limits laid down by the President.

Rule 46
(Preliminary objections)

1. A preliminary objection must be filed by a Party at the latest before the expiry of the time-limit fixed for the delivery of its first pleading.

2.   If a Party raises a preliminary objection, the Chamber shall, after having received the replies or comments of every other Party and of the delegates of the Commission, give its decision on the objection or join the objection to the merits.

Rule 47
(Discontinuance)

1.   When the Party which has brought the case before the Court notifies the Registrar of its intention not to proceed with the case and when the other Parties agree to such discontinuance, the Chamber shall, after having obtained the opinion of the Commission, decide whether or not it is appropriate to approve the discontinuance and accordingly to strike the case out of its list. In the affirmative, the Chamber shall give a reasoned decision which shall be communicated to the Committee of Ministers in order to allow them to supervise, in accordance with Article 54 of the Convention, the execution of any undertakings which may have been attached to the discontinuance by the order or with the approval of the Chamber.

2.   The Chamber may, having regard to the responsibilities of the Court in pursuance of Article 19 of the Convention, decide that, notwithstanding the notice of discontinuance, it should proceed with the consideration of the case.

3.   When the Commission, after having brought a case before the Court, informs the Court that a friendly settlement which satisfies the conditions of Article 28 of the Convention has subsequently been reached, the Chamber may, after having obtained the opinion, if necessary, of the delegates of the Commission, strike the case out of its list.

Rule 48
(Relinquishment of jurisdiction by the Chamber in favour of the plenary Court)

1.   Where a case pending before a Chamber raises a serious question affecting the interpretation of the Convention, the Chamber may, at any time, relinquish jurisdiction in favour of the plenary Court. The relinquishment of jurisdiction shall be obligatory where the resolution of such question might have a result inconsistent with a judgment previously delivered by a Chamber or by the plenary Court. Reasons need not be given for the decision to relinquish jurisdiction.

2.   The plenary Court, having been seized of the case, may either retain jurisdiction over the whole case or may, after deciding on the question of interpretation, order that the case be referred

back to the Chamber which shall, in regard to the remaining part of the case, recover its original jurisdiction.

3.   Any provisions governing the Chambers shall apply, *mutatis mutandis*, to the proceedings before the plenary Court.

4.   When the Court has been seized, in accordance with paragraph 1 above, of a case pending before a Chamber, any *ad hoc* judge who is a member of that Chamber shall sit as a judge of the plenary Court.

CHAPTER IV.   JUDGMENTS

Rule 49
(Procedure by default)

Where a Party fails to appear or to present its case, the Chamber shall, subject to the provisions of Rule 47, give a decision in the case.

Rule 50
(Contents of the judgment)

1.   The judgment shall contain:

(a)   the names of the President and the judges constituting the Chamber and the name of the Registrar;

(b)   the date on which it was delivered at a hearing in public;

(c)   a description of the Party or Parties;

(d)   the names of the agents, advocates or advisers of the Party or Parties;

(e)   the names of the delegates of the Commission;

(f)   a statement of the proceedings;

(g)   the submissions of the Party or Parties, and, if any, of the delegates of the Commission;

(h)   the facts of the case;

(i)   the reasons in point of law;

(j)   the operative provisions of the judgment;

(k)   the decision, if any, in regard to costs;

(l)   the number of judges constituting the majority;

(m)   a statement as to which of the two texts, French or English, is authentic.

2.   Any judge who has taken part in the consideration of the case shall be entitled to annex to the judgment either a separate opinion, concurring or dissenting with that judgment, or a bare statement of dissent.

Rule 51
(Signature, delivery and communication of the judgment)

1.   The judgment shall be signed by the President and by the Registrar.

2. The judgment shall be read by the President at a public hearing in one of the two official languages. It shall not be necessary for all the other judges to be present. The agents of the Parties and the delegates of the Commission shall be informed in due time of the date of delivery of judgment.

3. The judgment shall be sent by the President to the Committee of Ministers for the purposes of the application of Article 54 of the Convention.

4. The original copy, duly signed and sealed, shall be placed in the archives of the Court. The Registrar shall send certified copies to the Party or Parties, to the Commission, to the Secretary-General of the Council of Europe and to any other person directly concerned.

Rule 52
(Publication of judgments, decisions and other documents)

1. The Registrar shall be responsible for the publication of:

—judgments and other decisions of the Court;

—documents relating to the proceedings including the report of the Commission but excluding any particulars relating to the attempt to reach a friendly settlement;

—reports of public hearings;

—any document the publication of which is considered as useful by the President of the Court.

Publication shall take place in the two official languages in the case of judgments and other decisions, applications or introductory requests for proceedings and the Commission's reports; the other documents shall be published in the official language in which they occur in the proceedings.

2. Documents deposited with the Registrar and not published shall be accessible to the public unless otherwise decided by the President of the Court either on his own initiative, or at the request of a Party, of the Commission or of any other person concerned.

Rule 53
(Request for interpretation of a judgment)

1. A Party or the Commission may request the interpretation of a judgment within a period of three years following the delivery of that judgment.

2. The request shall state precisely the point or points in the operative provisions of the judgment on which interpretation is required.

3. The Registrar shall communicate the request to any other Party and, where appropriate, to the Commission, and shall in-

vite them to submit any written comments within a period fixed by the President of the Chamber.

4. The request for interpretation shall be considered by the Chamber which gave the judgment and which shall, as far as possible, be composed of the same judges. Those judges who have ceased to be members of the Court shall be recalled in order to deal with the case in accordance with Article 40, § 4, of the Convention. In case of death or inability to attend, they shall be replaced in the same manner as was applied for their appointment to the Chamber.

5. The Chamber shall decide by means of a judgment.

Rule 54
(Request for revision of a judgment)

1. A Party or the Commission may, in the event of the discovery of a fact which might by its nature have a decisive influence and which, when a judgment was delivered, was unknown both to the Court and to that Party or the Commission, request the Court, within a period of six months after that Party or the Commission, as the case may be, acquired knowledge of such fact, to revise that judgment.

2. The request shall mention the judgment of which the revision is requested and shall contain the information necessary to show that the conditions laid down in paragraph 1 of this Rule have been complied with. It shall be accompanied by the original or a copy of all supporting documents.

3. The Registrar shall communicate the request to any other Party and, where appropriate, to the Commission, and shall invite them to submit any written comments within a period fixed by the President.

4. The request for revision shall be considered by a Chamber constituted in accordance with Article 43 of the Convention, which shall decide in a first judgment whether the request is admissible or not under paragraph 1 of this Rule. In the affirmative, the Chamber shall refer the request to the Chamber which gave the original judgment or, if in the circumstances that is not reasonably possible, it shall retain the request and give a judgment upon the merits of the case.

5. The Chamber shall decide by means of a judgment.

CHAPTER V. ADVISORY OPINIONS

Rule 55

In proceedings in regard to advisory opinions the Court shall, in addition to the provisions of Protocol No. 2, apply the provisions which follow. It shall also apply the other provisions of these Rules to the extent to which it considers this to be appropriate.

Rule 56

The request for an advisory opinion shall indicate in precise terms the question on which the opinion of the Court is sought. It shall be filed with the Registry in forty copies.

The request shall also indicate:

(a)   the date on which the Committee of Ministers adopted the decision referred to in Article 1, § 3, of Protocol No. 2;

(b)   the names and addresses of the person or persons appointed by the Committee of Ministers to give the Court any explanations which it may require.

The request shall be accompanied by all documents likely to elucidate the question.

Rule 57

1.   On receipt of a request, the Registrar shall immediately transmit a copy thereof to the President, Vice-President and judges, as well as to the Commission.

2.   He shall inform the Contracting Parties that the Court is prepared to receive their written observations. The President may decide that, by reason of the nature of the question, a similar invitation is to be sent to the Commission.

Rule 58

1.   The President shall lay down the time-limits for the filing of written observations or other documents.

2.   Written observations or other documents shall be filed with the Registry in forty copies. The Registrar shall transmit copies thereof to the judges, to the Committee of Ministers, to each of the Contracting Parties and to the Commission.

Rule 59

After the closure of the written procedure, the President shall decide whether the Contracting Parties or the Commission which have submitted written observations are to be given an opportunity to develop them at an oral hearing held for the purpose.

Rule 60

If the Court considers that the request for an advisory opinion is not within its consultative competence as defined in Article 1 of Protocol No. 2, it shall so declare in a reasoned decision.

Rule 61

1. Advisory opinions shall be given by majority vote of the plenary Court. They shall mention the number of judges constituting the majority.

2. Any judge may, if he so desires, attach to the opinion of the Court either a separate opinion, concurring or dissenting from the advisory opinion, or a bare statement of dissent.

Rule 62

The advisory opinion shall be read by the President at a public hearing in one of the two official languages, prior notice having been given to the Committee of Ministers, to each of the Contracting Parties and to the Commission.

Rule 63

The original of the opinion, duly signed and sealed, shall be placed in the archives of the Court. The Registrar shall send certified copies to the Committee of Ministers, to the Contracting Parties, to the Commission and to the Secretary General of the Council of Europe.

PART III. THE AMERICAS

1. AMERICAN DECLARATION OF THE RIGHTS AND DUTIES OF MAN

Resolution XXX, adopted by the Ninth International Conference of American States, held at Bogotá, Colombia, 30 March–2 May 1948. Pan American Union, Final Act of the Ninth Conference of American States 38-45 (Washington, D.C., 1948).

WHEREAS:

The American peoples have acknowledged the dignity of the individual, and their national constitutions recognize that juridical and political institutions, which regulate life in human society, have as their principal aim the protection of the essential rights of man and the creation of circumstances that will permit him to achieve spiritual and material progress and attain happiness;

The American States have on repeated occasions recognized that the essential rights of man are not derived from the fact that he is a national of a certain state, but are based upon attributes of his human personality;

The international protection of the rights of man should be the principal guide of an evolving American law;

The affirmation of essential human rights by the American States together with the guarantees given by the internal regimes of the states establish the initial system of protection considered by the American States as being suited to the present social and juridical conditions, not without a recognition on their part that they should increasingly strengthen that system in the international field as conditions become more favorable,

The Ninth International Conference of American States

AGREES

To adopt the following

AMERICAN DECLARATION OF THE RIGHTS AND DUTIES OF MAN

PREAMBLE

All men are born free and equal, in dignity and in rights, and, being endowed by nature with reason and conscience, they should conduct themselves as brothers one to another.

The fulfillment of duty by each individual is a prerequisite to the rights of all. Rights and duties are interrelated in every social and political activity of man. While rights exalt individual liberty, duties express the dignity of that liberty.

Duties of a juridical nature presuppose others of a moral nature which support them in principle and constitute their basis.

Inasmuch as spiritual development is the supreme end of human existence and the highest expression thereof, it is the duty of man to serve that end with all his strength and resources.

Since culture is the highest social and historical expression of that spiritual development, it is the duty of man to preserve, practice and foster culture by every means within his power.

And, since moral conduct constitutes the noblest flowering of culture, it is the duty of every man always to hold it in high respect.

CHAPTER ONE. RIGHTS

Article I. Every human being has the right to life, liberty and the security of his person.

Right to life, liberty and personal security.

Article II. All persons are equal before the law and have the rights and duties established in this Declaration, without distinction as to race, sex, language, creed or any other factor.

Right to equality before the law.

Article III. Every person has the right freely to profess a religious faith, and to manifest and practice it both in public and in private.

Right to religious freedom and worship.

Article IV. Every person has the right to freedom of investigation, of opinion, and of the expression and dissemination of ideas, by any medium whatsoever.

Right to freedom of investigation, opinion, expression and dissemination.

Article V. Every person has the right to the protection of the law against abusive attacks upon his honor, his reputation, and his private and family life.

Right to protection of honor, personal reputation, and private and family life.

Article VI. Every person has the right to establish a family, the basic element of society, and to receive protection therefor.

Right to a family and to the protection thereof.

Article VII. All women, during pregnancy and the nursing period, and all children have the right to special protection, care and aid.

Right to protection for mothers and children.

Article VIII. Every person has the right to fix his residence within the territory of the state of which he is a

Right to residence and movement.

national, to move about freely within such territory, and not to leave it except by his own will.

Article IX. Every person has the right to the inviolability of his home.

Right to inviolability of the home.

Article X. Every person has the right to the inviolability and transmission of his correspondence.

Right to the inviolability and transmission of correspondence.

Article XI. Every person has the right to the preservation of his health through sanitary and social measures relating to food, clothing, housing and medical care, to the extent permitted by public and community resources.

Right to the preservation of health and to wellbeing.

Article XII. Every person has the right to an education, which should be based on the principles of liberty, morality and human solidarity.

Right to education.

Likewise every person has the right to an education that will prepare him to attain a decent life, to raise his standard of living, and to be a useful member of society.

The right to an education includes the right to equality of opportunity in every case, in accordance with natural talents, merit and the desire to utilize the resources that the state or the community is in a position to provide.

Every person has the right to receive, free, at least a primary education.

Article XIII. Every person has the right to take part in the cultural life of the community, to enjoy the arts, and to participate in the benefits that result from intellectual progress, especially scientific discoveries.

Right to the benefits of culture.

He likewise has the right to the protection of his moral and material interests as regards his inventions or any literary, scientific or artistic works of which he is the author.

Article XIV. Every person has the right to work, under proper conditions, and to follow his vocation freely, in so far as existing conditions of employment permit.

Every person who works has the right to receive such remuneration as will, in proportion to his capacity and skill, assure him a standard of living suitable for himself and for his family.

Right to work and to fair remuneration.

Article XV. Every person has the right to leisure time, to wholesome recreation, and to the opportunity for advantageous use of his free time to his spiritual, cultural and physical benefit.

Right to leisure time and to the use thereof.

Article XVI. Every person has the right to social security which will protect him from the consequences of unemployment, old age, and any disabilities arising from causes beyond his control that make it physically or mentally impossible for him to earn a living.

Right to social security.

Article XVII. Every person has the right to be recognized everywhere as a person having rights and obligations, and to enjoy the basic civil rights.

Right to recognition of juridical personality and of civil rights.

Article XVIII. Every person may resort to the courts to ensure respect for his legal rights. There should likewise be available to him a simple, brief procedure whereby the courts will protect him from acts of authority that, to his prejudice, violate any fundamental constitutional rights.

Right to a fair trial.

Article XIX. Every person has the right to the nationality to which he is entitled by law and to change it, if

Right to nationality.

he so wishes, for the nationality of any other country that is willing to grant it to him.

Article XX. Every person having legal capacity is entitled to participate in the government of his country, directly or through his representatives, and to take part in popular elections, which shall be by secret ballot, and shall be honest, periodic and free.

Right to vote and to participate in government.

Article XXI. Every person has the right to assemble peaceably with others in a formal public meeting or an informal gathering, in connection with matters of common interest of any nature.

Right of assembly.

Article XXII. Every person has the right to associate with others to promote, exercise and protect his legitimate interests of a political, economic, religious, social, cultural, professional, labor union or other nature.

Right of association.

Article XXIII. Every person has a right to own such private property as meets the essential needs of decent living and helps to maintain the dignity of the individual and of the home.

Right to property.

Article XXIV. Every person has the right to submit respectful petitions to any competent authority, for reasons of either general or private interest, and the right to obtain a prompt decision thereon.

Right of petition.

Article XXV. No person may be deprived of his liberty except in the cases and according to the procedures established by pre-existing law.

No person may be deprived of liberty for nonfulfillment of obligations of a purely civil character.

Every individual who has been deprived of his liberty has the right to have the legality of his detention as-

Right to protection from arbitrary arrest.

certained without delay by a court, and the right to be tried without undue delay, or, otherwise, to be released. He also has the right to humane treatment during the time he is in custody.

Article XXVI. Every accused person is presumed to be innocent until proved guilty.

Right to due process of law.

Every person accused of an offense has the right to be given an impartial and public hearing, and to be tried by courts previously established in accordance with pre-existing laws, and not to receive cruel, infamous or unusual punishment.

Article XXVII. Every person has the right, in case of pursuit not resulting from ordinary crimes, to seek and receive asylum in foreign territory, in accordance with the laws of each country and with international agreements.

Right of asylum.

Article XXVIII. The rights of man are limited by the rights of others, by the security of all, and by the just demands of the general welfare and the advancement of democracy.

Scope of the rights of man.

CHAPTER TWO. DUTIES

Article XXIX. It is the duty of the individual so to conduct himself in relation to others that each and every one may fully form and develop his personality.

Duties to society.

Article XXX. It is the duty of every person to aid, support, educate and protect his minor children, and it is the duty of children to honor their parents always and to aid, support and protect them when they need it.

Duties toward children and parents.

Article XXXI. It is the duty of every person to acquire at least an elementary education.

Duty to receive instruction.

Article XXXII. It is the duty of every person to vote in the popular elections of the country of which he is a national, when he is legally capable of doing so.

Duty to vote.

Article XXXIII. It is the duty of every person to obey the law and other legitimate commands of the authorities of his country and those of the country in which he may be.

Duty to obey the law.

Article XXXIV. It is the duty of every able-bodied person to render whatever civil and military service his country may require for its defense and preservation, and, in case of public disaster, to render such services as may be in his power.

It is likewise his duty to hold any public office to which he may be elected by popular vote in the state of which he is a national.

Duty to serve the community and the nation.

Article XXXV. It is the duty of every person to cooperate with the state and the community with respect to social security and welfare, in accordance with his ability and with existing circumstances.

Duties with respect to social security and welfare.

Article XXXVI. It is the duty of every person to pay the taxes established by law for the support of public services.

Duty to pay taxes.

Article XXXVII. It is the duty of every person to work, as far as his capacity and possibilities permit, in order to obtain the means of livelihood or to benefit his community.

Duty to work.

Article XXXVIII. It is the duty of every person to refrain from taking part in political activities that, according to law, are reserved exclusively to the citizens of the state in which he is an alien.

Duty to refrain from political activities in a foreign country.

2.   STATUTE OF THE INTER-AMERICAN COMMISSION ON HUMAN RIGHTS

Approved by the Council of the Organization of American States, 25 May and 8 June 1960; with the changes and amendments made by Resolution XXII of the Second Special Inter-American Conference and by the Council of the Organization of American States, 24 April 1968. Organization of American States Doc. OEA/Ser. L/V/II.26, Doc. 10, at 1-6 (1971).

I.   NATURE AND PURPOSES

Article 1

The Inter-American Commission on Human Rights, created by the Fifth Meeting of Consultation of Ministers of Foreign Affairs, is an autonomous entity[1] of the Organization of American States, the function of which is to promote respect for human rights.

Article 2

For the purpose of this Statute, human rights are understood to be those set forth in the American Declaration of the Rights and Duties of Man.

II.   MEMBERSHIP

Article 3

(a)   The Inter-American Commission on Human Rights shall be composed of seven members, nationals of the member states of the Organization, who shall be persons of high moral character and recognized competence in the field of human rights.

(b)   The members of the Commission shall represent all the member countries of the Organization of American States and act in its name.

Article 4

(a)   The members of the Commission shall be elected in their personal capacity by the Council of the Organization of American States[2] from a list made up of panels of three persons proposed for the purpose by the governments of the member states of the Organization.

(b)   Each of the said governments shall propose a panel of three persons, on which it may include not only its own nationals but also those of the other member states of the Organization. The proponent governments shall submit with their panels biographical data for each candidate.

---

[1] Now one of the organs of the Organization (Article 51 e of the Charter of the OAS).

[2] Now known as the Permanent Council of the Organization (Articles 51 c, 68 and 78 of the Charter of the OAS).

(c) The vote of the Council of the Organization[3] for election of the members of the Commission shall be taken by secret ballot, and the candidates who obtain the greatest number of votes and an absolute majority of the votes of the representatives of the member states shall be declared elected. If, in order to elect all the members of the Commission, it should become necessary to take several votes, the candidates receiving the smaller number of votes shall be eliminated successively in such manner as the Council determines.

(d) Only one national of any one state may be elected a member of the Commission.

(e) Members of the Commission may be re-elected in the same manner as that prescribed for their election.

Article 5

(a) Except in the case of the first election of members of the Commission and elections that must be held to fill vacancies announced pursuant to Article 7, the Secretary General of the Organization of American States shall address the member states of the Organization in writing, through their representatives on the Council, at least six months prior to the date of the election, inviting them to submit their panels of three candidates within a period of three months.

(b) The Secretary General shall prepare an alphabetical list of the candidates thus nominated and transmit it to the Council of the Organization.[4]

(c) The Council of the Organization[5] shall set the date for the election of the members of the Commission and it shall elect them, in the manner prescribed by this Statute, from among the candidates whose names appear on the list referred to in the preceding paragraph.

Article 6

(a) The members of the Commission shall be elected for four years.

(b) Elections of members of the Commission that are held at the expiration of terms of office shall be conducted pursuant to the provisions of the preceding articles.

(c) The Chairman of the Commission shall be elected by an absolute majority of the votes of its members; he shall hold office for two years and he may be re-elected only once.

---

[3] [See footnote 2.]
[4] [See footnote 2.]
[5] [See footnote 2.]

(d)   The Vice-Chairman of the Commission shall be elected in the same manner and for the same term as the Chairman. The Vice-Chairman shall replace the Chairman when the latter is temporarily prevented from performing his duties. In case of the death or the resignation of the Chairman, the Vice-Chairman shall become Chairman, and at its next meeting the Commission shall elect a new Vice-Chairman.

Article 7

(a)   In case of death or resignation of a member of the Commission, the Chairman shall immediately notify the Secretary General of the Organization of American States, who in turn shall inform the member states of the Organization.

(b)   In order to fill vacancies on the Commission when they occur, each government may propose a candidate within a period of one month, the nomination to be accompanied by the pertinent biographical data.

(c)   The Secretary General shall prepare an alphabetical list of the candidates thus nominated and transmit it to the Council of the Organization.[6]

(d)   When the term of office is due to expire within six months following a vacancy, the vacancy shall not be filled.

Article 7 (bis)

The Chairman of the Commission may go to the Commission's headquarters and remain there for such time as may be necessary for the performance of his duties.

Article 8

During their terms of office, the Chairman and the members of the Commission shall receive the emoluments and travel expenses provided for in the budget of the Pan American Union,[7] under such terms and conditions as the Council of the Organization[8] determines, with due regard to the importance of the Commission's tasks.

III. COMPETENCE AND PROCEDURE

Article 9

In carrying out its assignment of promoting respect for human rights, the Commission shall have the following functions and powers:

---

[6] [See footnote 2.]

[7] Now known as the program-budget of the Organization (Article 118 c of the Charter of the OAS).

[8] The program-budget of the Organization is now approved by the General Assembly (Article 52 e of the Charter of the OAS).

(a)   To develop an awareness of human rights among the peoples of America;

(b)   To make recommendations to the governments of the member states in general, if it considers such action advisable, for the adoption of progressive measures in favor of human rights within the framework of their domestic legislation and, in accordance with their constitutional precepts, appropriate measures to further the faithful observance of those rights;

(c)   To prepare such studies or reports as it considers advisable in the performance of its duties;

(d)   To urge the governments of the member states to supply it with information on the measures adopted by them in matters of human rights;

(e)   To serve the Organization of American States as an advisory body in respect of human rights.

Article 9 (bis)

The Commission shall have the following additional functions and powers:

(a)   To give particular attention to observance of the human rights referred to in Articles I, II, III, IV, XVIII, XXV, and XXVI of the American Declaration of the Rights and Duties of Man;

(b)   To examine communications submitted to it and any other available information; to address the government of any American state for information deemed pertinent by the Commission; and to make recommendations, when it deems this appropriate, with the objective of bringing about more effective observance of fundamental human rights;

(c)   To submit a report annually to the Inter-American Conference[9] or to the Meeting of Consultation of Ministers of Foreign Affairs, which should include: (i) a statement of progress achieved in realization of the goals set forth in the American Declaration; (ii) a statement of areas in which further steps are needed to give effect to the human rights set forth in the American Declaration; and (iii) such observations as the Commission may deem appropriate on matters covered in the communications submitted to it and in other information available to the Commission;

(d)   To verify, as a condition precedent to the exercise of the powers set forth in paragraphs (b) and (c) of the present article,

---

[9] This report is now submitted to the General Assembly (Articles 51 *a* and 52 *f* of the Charter of the OAS).

whether the internal legal procedures and remedies of each member state have been duly applied and exhausted.

Article 10

In performing its assignment, the Commission shall act in accordance with the pertinent provisions of the Charter of the Organization and bear in mind particularly that, in conformity with the American Declaration of the Rights and Duties of Man, the rights of each man are limited by the rights of others, by the security of all, and by the just demands of the general welfare and the advancement of democracy.

IV. SEAT AND MEETINGS

Article 11

(a)   The Secretary General of the Organization shall convoke the first meeting of the Commission.

(b)   After its first meeting, the Commission shall meet:

   (i)   For a maximum of eight weeks a year, in one or two regular meetings, as decided by the Commission itself;

   (ii)   In special meetings when so convoked by the Chairman or at the request of a majority of its members.

(c)   The permanent seat of the Commission shall be the Pan American Union.[10]

The Commission may move to the territory of any American state when it so decides by an absolute majority of votes and with the consent of the government concerned.

V. QUORUM AND VOTING

Article 12

An absolute majority of the members of the Commission shall constitute a quorum.

Article 13

Decisions shall be taken by an absolute majority vote of the members of the Commission, except in the case of procedural matters, when decisions shall be taken by a simple majority.

VI. SECRETARIAT

Article 14

The Secretary General of the Organization of American States shall appoint the necessary technical and administrative personnel

---

[10] Now known as the General Secretariat (Articles 51 *f* and 127 of the Charter of the OAS).

to serve as the Secretariat of the Commission. The Secretariat shall form part of the personnel of the Pan American Union and its expenses shall be included in the budget of the Pan American Union.[11]

Article 14 (bis)

The Secretariat services of the Commission shall be provided by a specialized functional unit, which shall be part of the General Secretariat of the Organization and shall be organized so as to have the resources required for performing the tasks entrusted to it by the Commission.

VIII. REGULATIONS AND AMENDMENTS TO THE STATUTE
Article 15

The Commission shall prepare and adopt its own Rules and Regulations, in accordance with the provisions of this Statute.

Article 16

This Statute may be amended by the Council of the Organization.[12]

3. REGULATIONS OF THE INTER-AMERICAN COMMISSION ON HUMAN RIGHTS

Approved by the Commission on 24 October 1960; with amendments to May 1967. OAS Official Records, OEA/Ser.L/V/II.17, Doc. 26 (1967).

Nature and Functioning

Article 1. The Inter-American Commission on Human Rights, an autonomous entity of the Organization of American States, is governed by the provisions of the Charter of the Organization and the American Declaration of the Rights and Duties of Man, and functions in accordance with the provisions of the Statute of the Commission and these Regulations.

The Members of the Commission shall represent all of the countries members of the Organization of American States and act, in a personal capacity in their name.

Membership

Article 2. The membership of the Commission shall be governed in accordance with the provisions of its Statute, and its organs shall be as follows: Chairman, Vice-Chairman, and Secretariat.

---

[11] The Secretariat now forms part of the personnel of the General Secretariat and its expenses are included in the program-budget of the Organization (Articles 51 *f* and 118 *c* and *d* of the Charter of the OAS).

[12] See Articles 112 and 150 of the Charter of the OAS.

Chairman and Vice Chairman

Article 3. The duties of the Chairman shall be:

a. To represent the Commission.

b. To convoke regular and special meetings of the Commission in accordance with the Statute and Regulations.

c. To preside over the meetings of the Commission and to submit for its considerations the topics on the agenda.

d. To grant the floor to the members in the order in which they have requested it.

e. To rule on points of order that may arise during the discussions of the Commission. If any member so requests, prior to the ruling of the Chairman, the point of order shall be submitted to a majority vote.

f. To submit matters to a vote in accordance with the pertinent provisions of these Regulations.

g. To promote the work of the Commission.

Article 4. At the beginning of each regular or special meeting, the Chairman shall present to the Commission a report on the manner in which, during the recess between meetings, he has discharged the duties conferred upon him by these Regulations.

Article 5. In the event of temporary disability of the Chairman, he shall be replaced by the Vice-Chairman, having the same authority, powers, and obligations. In the event of death or resignation of the Chairman, the Vice-Chairman shall assume the post of Chairman and the Commission shall elect a new Vice-Chairman at the following meeting.

Secretariat

Article 6. The Executive Secretary of the Commission, and the technical and administrative personnel required to collaborate with the same, shall be appointed by the Secretary General of the Organization. The Secretariat of the Commission shall be a part of the Pan American Union and its expenses shall be included in the budget thereof.

Article 7. The Executive Secretary may submit to the Commission, orally or in writing, reports on any topic related to his work.

Article 8. The Secretariat shall prepare documents or studies on any question entrusted to it by the Commission; it shall receive, translate, and distribute the summary minutes of the meetings, the recommendations of the Commission, and any other pertinent documents that may be required. The Secretariat shall also keep its files and, in general, perform all the duties that are entrusted to it.

Members of the Commission

Article 9. The members of the Commission shall perform their functions during the course of the meetings, and during the time of recess shall carry out the tasks or preparatory work entrusted to them by the Commission.

Article 10. The other members of the Commission, in accordance with their seniority thereon, shall follow the Chairman and Vice-Chairman in order of precedence. When there are two or more members with the same length of service, precedence shall be determined by age.

Meetings

Article 11. The Commission shall meet for a maximum of eight weeks a year at one or two regular meetings, as decided by the Commission, notwithstanding that special meetings may be convoked by the Chairman, or at the request of a majority of its members.

Article 12. The Commission may establish subcommittees from its membership, in order to fulfill mandates related to human rights, either at headquarters or in the territory of any American State. Each such subcommittee shall submit a report to the Commission so that it may make a decision thereon.

Article 13. There shall be a standing subcommittee, composed of the Chairman, the Vice-Chairman, a third member, and an alternate. The latter two shall serve on the subcommittee for a term of two years.

Article 14. The duties of the standing subcommittee shall be:

a. To study the communications received and make the recommendations to the Commission it deems appropriate as to the way in which such communications should be dealt with;

b. To prepare in consultation with the Secretariat the working agenda for each meeting; and

c. To advise the Chairman of the Commission when he deems it advisable.

Article 15. The meetings of the Commission shall be held as frequently as may be necessary for the satisfactory progress of its activities.

Article 16. The date and time of the meetings, and the respective agendas, will be specified in the notice of convocation.

Article 17. Each meeting shall be held on the date and at the hour specified, subject to change for any justified reason, at the discretion of the Chairman whenever he so decides, or at the previous request of one or more of the members.

Article 18. During the course of any meeting the date and hour of the next one may be set, in which case only the absent members will be notified.

Article 19. The Secretary General and the Assistant Secretary General of the Organization of American States may participate with voice but without vote in the meetings of the Commission, when they deem it necessary or advisable.

Quorum

Article 20. An absolute majority of the members of the Commission shall constitute a quorum.

Discussions

Article 21. The discussions shall be directed by the Chairman of the Commission and, if any member so requests, they may be adjusted to conform with the pertinent provisions of the Regulations of the Council of the Organization of American States. In cases for which no provision has been made, the Commission shall determine the procedure to be adopted.

Article 22. During the discussion of a given subject, any member may raise a point of order, which shall be decided immediately by the Chairman or, as the case may be, by a majority vote, in accordance with Article 3.

Voting

Article 23. Decisions shall be taken by an absolute majority vote of the members of the Commission, except in matters of procedure, in which case the decisions shall be taken by a simple majority of the members present at the respective meeting. Members who are or are not in agreement are entitled to have an explanation of their vote included immediately after such decision.

Minutes

Article 24. Summary minutes of each meeting shall be prepared, giving the date and time of the meeting, the names of members present, the topic or topics discussed, and the decisions taken.

Article 25. Copies of the minutes of each meeting shall be distributed among the members of the Commission as soon as possible after the meeting, and members may submit their observations to the Secretariat at the meeting in which the respective minutes are considered. Corrections in form shall be decided upon by the Chairman.

Studies and Drafts

Article 26. The Commission shall select, at its own initiative, those topics which it proposes to study for the purpose of promoting respect for human rights in the American hemisphere, and may assign the study of those topics and the preparation of a draft report to a member of the Commission who shall act as rapporteur, to a subcommittee, or to the Secretariat of the Commission.

Article 27. In selecting topics for study the Commission shall take into account the requests and recommendations of the governments, of the Inter-American Conferences, of the Meetings of Consultation of Ministers of Foreign Affairs, and of the Council of the Organization of American States.

Article 28. With respect to the topics that have been assigned to them the rapporteurs shall prepare preliminary reports containing the results of their studies and findings, together with their observations and recommendations.

Article 29. Once a preliminary report by a rapporteur is presented to the Commission for consideration, the members shall present their comments and observations as soon as possible to the rapporteur, who shall, if he deems it necessary, prepare a new report taking those comments and observations into account.

Article 30. After consideration of the preliminary report prepared by the rapporteur, the Commission may approve it entirely or in part, amend it, postpone action, return it to the rapporteur for further study, or prepare its own report or draft.

Article 31. When any given project is submitted for discussion, the Commission shall establish the order of discussion and decide whether the question shall be voted as a whole or by parts. If several amendments are submitted they shall be discussed and voted upon in order, priority being given to those which, in the opinion of the Chairman, most alter the substance of the original draft. Any questions that may arise in this respect shall be decided in accordance with the provisions of Article 23.

Article 32. A report or draft of the Commission shall be signed by the members concurring. Members who are or are not in agreement with the decision of the majority are entitled, pursuant to Article 23 of these Regulations, to have an explanation of their vote included immediately after such report or draft.

Article 33. When the Commission approves a report or draft, the Secretariat of the Commission shall publish the report as an official document of the Inter-American Commission on Human Rights, for internal or general circulation as the Commission so decides.

Article 34. In the case of draft inter-American conventions, the Commission upon approving the draft or drafts prepared by the rapporteur according to the procedure set forth in Articles 28, 29, 30, and 31 of these Regulations, shall transmit the draft document through the General Secretariat of the Organization to the governments of the member states of the Organization so that they may formulate any observations deemed appropriate within the period indicated by the Commisson.

Article 35. The observations made by the governments shall be taken into consideration by the Commission when it prepares the definitive drafts, once the period referred to in Article 34 has expired.

Article 36. The studies, reports, or drafts prepared by the Commission shall be transmitted as soon as possible, through the General Secretariat of the Organization, to the appropriate governments or organs of the Organization.

Communications or Claims Addressed to the Commission

Article 37. The Commission shall take cognizance, for the most effective fulfillment of its functions, of signed communications that contain denunciations or complaints of violations of human rights within the American states.

Article 38.—1. Communications addressed to the Commission shall contain:

    a. The name, address and signature of those making the denunciation or claim.

    b. An account of the act or acts denounced and the name or names of the victims of the supposed violation or violations of human rights.

    2. In the event a communication is addressed to the Commission by an association it shall be signed by those who represent it.

    3. If a communication does not fulfill the above requirements, the Secretariat may request the person making the denunciation or claim to complete it.

Article 39. The Commission shall not deal with any communication that is inadmissible because of one or more of the following reasons:

    a. It is anonymous or written in disrespectful or offensive language;

    b. It is substantially the same as a communication that has been studied previously by the Commission;

    c. It is incompatible with the provisions of the Statute, of the Regulations, or obviously unfounded; or

d. It refers to events or situations that bear no relation to a disregard of human rights by the government against which it is directed.

Article 40. Communications denouncing the violation of human rights shall be addressed to the Commission within a reasonable period of time, in the judgment of the Commission, from the date of occurrence of the opposed violation of those rights.

Article 41.—1. The Secretariat shall acknowledge receipt of communications addressed to the Commission, indicating that they will be considered in accordance with these Regulations.

2. If the Secretariat has any question about the admissibility of a particular communication it shall be resolved by the Commission or the Subcommittee if either of them is in session, or by the Chairman if they are in recess between meetings.

3. If a communication is presented omitting the requirements contemplated in Articles 53 or 54 of these Regulations, as the case may be, the person making the denunciation or claim shall be immediately requested to submit to the Commission the information relevant to said Articles; and in making such request the Secretariat shall include a copy of the text of the pertinent provision.

Article 42.—1. The Secretariat shall transmit the pertinent parts of the communications admitted, in accordance with these Regulations, to the governments of the states referred to, when it has been so decided by the Commission during a session of meetings, or by the Chairman during a recess, and shall at the same time request from them the pertinent information and the cooperation necessary in order to obtain such information directly.

2. The mere fact of a request for information from the Government concerned does not constitute in and of itself a judgment in advance, of the admissibility of the denunciation.

Article 43. Whenever the communications refer to several countries, the pertinent parts of the complaints or denunciations contained in the said communications shall be transmitted to the government of the country referred to, in accordance with the provisions of these Regulations.

Article 44. In transmitting the communications to the governments of states referred to, the identity of the writers thereof shall be withheld, along with any other information that might serve to identify them except when they expressly consent to the inclusion of such information.

Article 45. The Secretariat shall distribute to the members of the Commission, prior to each meeting, a list of communications received, with a brief indication of their contents and of the initial action taken. The Chairman shall add to this list his opinion of each case presented.

Article 46. All communications that fall within the category described in Article 39.a shall be placed in the confidential files of the Commission. The Secretariat shall advise the signers of communications of the categories described in Article 39.b, c, or d that the communications are inadmissible.

Article 47. Once a communication has been declared admissible it shall be classified as to the human rights that it is therein alleged have been violated.

Article 48.—1. The Secretariat shall maintain a special register of communications presented in accordance with these Regulations. The register shall contain the pertinent general information on each case and all the actions taken on the claim, in the order in which they are presented, without blank spaces, erasures, or abbreviations.

2. The Secretariat of the Commission shall note on the original documents their entry in the special register and, at the request of the denouncer or claimant, shall also so note on copies presented.

3. The entry in the special register shall be valid for all the purposes of the procedures established by these Regulations.

Article 49. At the conclusion of the findings of fact, the case will be submitted to the consideration of the full Commission for its decision. The Commission may designate from among its members a *rapporteur* to prepare the appropriate draft report respecting whichever of the cases are submitted to it.

Article 50. The Commission shall examine the evidence adduced by the Government concerned or by the person making the denunciation, or the evidence taken from witnesses to the facts, or that obtained from documents, records or official publications, or through observation *in loco*.

Article 51.—1. The occurrence of the events on which information has been requested will be presumed to be confirmed if the Government referred to has not supplied such information within 180 days of the request, provided always, that the invalidity of the events denounced is not shown by other elements of proof.

2. The Commission may make an extension to the term of 180 days in cases in which it finds it justified.

Article 52. If the violation of human rights is proven, on application of the provisions of Articles 37 through 51 of these

Regulations, the Commission may make recommendations when it deems it proper, as provided for in Article 9.b of the Statute of the Commission, to the member States in general, *i.e.*, to all or to any one of them, to the end that they adopt, in accordance with their constitutional provisions, appropriate means to promote the faithful observance of those rights; without prejudice to the preparation and publication of the reports that the Commission may consider proper, in accordance with Article 9.c of its Statute.

Article 53.—a.   The Commission shall examine, by the special procedure set forth in the following articles, communications addressed to it by any person or group of persons or by associations that are legally established, in which there is a denunciation of the violation of any of the following human rights:

i.   Every human being has the right to life, liberty, and the security of his person (Article I of the American Declaration of the Rights and Duties of Man).

ii.   All persons are equal before the law and have the rights and duties established in this Declaration, without distinction as to race, sex, language, creed or any other factor (Article II of the American Declaration of the Rights and Duties of Man).

iii.   Every person has the right freely to profess a religious faith, and to manifest and practice it both in public and in private (Article III of the American Declaration of the Rights and Duties of Man).

iv.   Every person has the right to freedom of investigation, of opinion, and of the expression and dissemination of ideas, by any medium whatsoever (Article IV of the American Declaration of the Rights and Duties of Man).

v.   Every person may resort to the courts to ensure respect for his legal rights. There should likewise be available to him a simple, brief procedure whereby the courts will protect him from acts of authority that, to his prejudice, violate any fundamental constitutional rights (Article XVIII of the American Declaration of the Rights and Duties of Man).

vi.   No person may be deprived of his liberty except in the cases and according to the procedures established by pre-existing law.

No person may be deprived of liberty for nonfulfillment of obligations of a purely civil character.

Every individual who has been deprived of his liberty has the right to have the legality of his detention ascertained without delay by a court, and the right to be tried without undue delay or otherwise, to be released. He also has the right to humane treatment during the time he is in custody (Article XXV of the American Declaration of the Rights and Duties of Man).

vii.   Every accused persons is presumed to be innocent until proved guilty.

Every person accused of an offense has the right to be given an impartial and public hearing, and to be tried by courts previously established in accordance with pre-existing laws, and not to receive cruel, infamous, or unusual punishment (Article XXVI of the American Declaration of the Rights and Duties of Man).

b.   The Commission shall also examine, in accordance with the aforementioned special procedure, communications in which reprisals against signers of communications addressed to the Commission or against any persons mentioned as injured parties in such communications are denounced.

Article 54.   In exercising the powers set forth in Article 53 of these Regulations, the Commission shall verify, as a condition precedent, whether the internal legal procedures and remedies of each member state have been duly applied and exhausted.

Article 55.   Communications that denounce the violation of the human rights set forth in Article 53 must be addressed to the Commission within six months following the date on which, as the case may be, the final domestic decision has been handed down or the signer of the communication has become aware that his recourse to domestic remedy has arbitrarily been hindered or the final domestic decision has been unjustly delayed.

Article 56.   If the occurrence of the violation is confirmed, the Commission shall prepare a report on the case and make appropriate recommendations to the government concerned.

Article 57.—1.   If the government does not, within a reasonable time, adopt the measures recommended by the Commission, the latter may make the observations it considers appropriate in the annual report it is to present to the Inter-American Conference or to the Meeting of Consultation of Ministers of Foreign Affairs, provided for in paragraph c of Article 9 (bis) of its Statute.

2.   If the Inter-American Conference or the Meeting of Consultation does not make any observations on the Commission's recommendations and if the government referred to has not yet adopted the measures recommended, the Commission may publish its report.

Article 58.   In cases before the Commission in which the procedures established in Articles 53 through 57, inclusive, of these Regulations is to be applied, where for any reason there exists some defect or impossibility of proof, then the procedure established in Articles 37 through 51, inclusive, of these Regulations shall be applied instead.

Interpretation of the Regulations

Article 59. If any questions arise with respect to the interpretation or application of the present Regulations, they shall be resolved by an absolute majority of the members of the Commission.

Amendments to the Regulations

Article 60. The present Regulations may be amended by an absolute majority vote of the members of the Commission.

4. AMERICAN CONVENTION ON HUMAN RIGHTS

Signed at the Inter-American Specialized Conference on Human Rights, San José, Costa Rica, 22 November 1969; not yet in force. OAS Treaty Series, No. 36, at 1-21 (OAS Official Records, OEA/SER.A/16, English).

PREAMBLE

The American states signatory to the present Convention,

Reaffirming their intention to consolidate in this hemisphere, within the framework of democratic institutions, a system of personal liberty and social justice based on respect for the essential rights of man;

Recognizing that the essential rights of man are not derived from one's being a national of a certain state, but are based upon attributes of the human personality, and that they therefore justify international protection in the form of a convention reinforcing or complementing the protection provided by the domestic law of the American states;

Considering that these principles have been set forth in the Charter of the Organization of American States, in the American Declaration of the Rights and Duties of Man, and in the Universal Declaration of Human Rights, and that they have been reaffirmed and refined in other international instruments, worldwide as well as regional in scope;

Reiterating that, in accordance with the Universal Declaration of Human Rights, the ideal of free men enjoying freedom from fear and want can be achieved only if conditions are created whereby everyone may enjoy his economic, social, and cultural rights, as well as his civil and political rights; and

Considering that the Third Special Inter-American Conference (Buenos Aires, 1967) approved the incorporation into the Charter of the Organization itself of broader standards with respect to economic, social, and educational rights and resolved that an

inter-American convention on human rights should determine
the structure, competence, and procedure of the organs responsible for these matters,

Have agreed upon the following:

PART I. STATE OBLIGATIONS AND RIGHTS PROTECTED

CHAPTER I. GENERAL OBLIGATIONS

Article 1. *Obligation to Respect Rights*

1. The States Parties to this Convention undertake to respect
the rights and freedoms recognized herein and to ensure to all
persons subject to their jurisdiction the free and full exercise of
those rights and freedoms, without any discrimination for reasons
of race, color, sex, language, religion, political or other opinion,
national or social origin, economic status, birth, or any other
social condition.

2. For the purposes of this Convention, "person" means every
human being.

Article 2. *Domestic Legal Effects*

Where the exercise of any of the rights or freedoms referred
to in Article 1 is not already ensured by legislative or other provisions, the States Parties undertake to adopt, in accordance with
their constitutional processes and the provisions of this Convention, such legislative or other measures as may be necessary to
give effect to those rights or freedoms.

CHAPTER II. CIVIL AND POLITICAL RIGHTS

Article 3. *Right to Juridical Personality*

Every person has the right to recognition as a person before
the law.

Article 4. *Right to Life*

1. Every person has the right to have his life respected. This
right shall be protected by law and, in general, from the moment
of conception. No one shall be arbitrarily deprived of his life.

2. In countries that have not abolished the death penalty, it
may be imposed only for the most serious crimes and pursuant to
a final judgment rendered by a competent court and in accordance with a law establishing such punishment, enacted prior to
the commission of the crime. The application of such punishment shall not be extended to crimes to which it does not pres-
ently apply.

3. The death penalty shall not be reestablished in states that have abolished it.

4. In no case shall capital punishment be inflicted for political offenses or related common crimes.

5. Capital punishment shall not be imposed upon persons who, at the time the crime was committed, were under 18 years of age or over 70 years of age; nor shall it be applied to pregnant women.

6. Every person condemned to death shall have the right to apply for amnesty, pardon, or commutation of sentence, which may be granted in all cases. Capital punishment shall not be imposed while such a petition is pending decision by the competent authority.

Article 5. Right to Humane Treatment

1. Every person has the right to have his physical, mental, and moral integrity respected.

2. No one shall be subjected to torture or to cruel, inhuman, or degrading punishment or treatment. All persons deprived of their liberty shall be treated with respect for the inherent dignity of the human person.

3. Punishment shall not be extended to any person other than the criminal.

4. Accused persons shall, save in exceptional circumstances, be segregated from convicted persons, and shall be subject to separate treatment appropriate to their status as unconvicted persons.

5. Minors while subject to criminal proceedings shall be separated from adults and brought before specialized tribunals, as speedily as possible, so that they may be treated in accordance with their status as minors.

6. Punishments consisting of deprivation of liberty shall have as an essential aim the reform and social readaptation of the prisoners.

Article 6. Freedom from Slavery

1. No one shall be subject to slavery or to involuntary servitude, which are prohibited in all their forms, as are the slave trade and traffic in women.

2. No one shall be required to perform forced or compulsory labor. This provision shall not be interpreted to mean that, in those countries in which the penalty established for certain crimes is deprivation of liberty at forced labor, the carrying out of such a sentence imposed by a competent court is prohibited. Forced labor shall not adversely affect the dignity or the physical or intellectual capacity of the prisoner.

3. For the purposes of this article, the following do not constitute forced or compulsory labor:

  a. work or service normally required of a person imprisoned in execution of a sentence or formal decision passed by the competent judicial authority. Such work or service shall be carried out under the supervision and control of public authorities, and any persons performing such work or service shall not be placed at the disposal of any private party, company, or juridical person;

  b. military service and, in countries in which conscientious objectors are recognized, national service that the law may provide for in lieu of military service;

  c. service exacted in time of danger or calamity that threatens the existence or the well-being of the community; or

  d. work or service that forms part of normal civic obligations.

Article 7. Right to Personal Liberty

1. Every person has the right to personal liberty and security.

2. No one shall be deprived of his physical liberty except for the reasons and under the conditions established beforehand by the constitution of the State Party concerned or by a law established pursuant thereto.

3. No one shall be subject to arbitrary arrest or imprisonment.

4. Anyone who is detained shall be informed of the reasons for his detention and shall be promptly notified of the charge or charges against him.

5. Any person detained shall be brought promptly before a judge or other officer authorized by law to exercise judicial power and shall be entitled to trial within a reasonable time or to be released without prejudice to the continuation of the proceedings. His release may be subject to guarantees to assure his appearance for trial.

6. Anyone who is deprived of his liberty shall be entitled to recourse to a competent court, in order that the court may decide without delay on the lawfulness of his arrest or detention and order his release if the arrest or detention is unlawful. In States Parties whose laws provide that anyone who believes himself to be threatened with deprivation of his liberty is entitled to recourse to a competent court in order that it may decide on the lawfulness of such threat, this remedy may not be restricted or abolished. The interested party or another person in his behalf is entitled to seek these remedies.

7. No one shall be detained for debt. This principle shall not limit the orders of a competent judicial authority issued for non-fulfillment of duties of support.

Article 8.   Right to a Fair Trial

1. Every person has the right to a hearing, with due guarantees and within a reasonable time, by a competent, independent, and impartial tribunal, previously established by law, in the substantiation of any accusation of a criminal nature made against him or for the determination of his rights and obligations of a civil, labor, fiscal, or any other nature.

2. Every person accused of a criminal offense has the right to be presumed innocent so long as his guilt has not been proven according to law. During the proceedings, every person is entitled, with full equality, to the following minimum guarantees:

    a. the right of the accused to be assisted without charge by a translator or interpreter, if he does not understand or does not speak the language of the tribunal or court;

    b. prior notification in detail to the accused of the charges against him;

    c. adequate time and means for the preparation of his defense;

    d. the right of the accused to defend himself personally or to be assisted by legal counsel of his own choosing, and to communicate freely and privately with his counsel;

    e. the inalienable right to be assisted by counsel provided by the state, paid or not as the domestic law provides, if the accused does not defend himself personally or engage his own counsel within the time period established by law;

    f. the right of the defense to examine witnesses present in the court and to obtain the appearance, as witnesses, of experts or other persons who may throw light on the facts;

    g. the right not to be compelled to be a witness against himself or to plead guilty; and

    h. the right to appeal the judgment to a higher court.

3. A confession of guilt by the accused shall be valid only if it is made without coercion of any kind.

4. An accused person acquitted by a nonappealable judgment shall not be subjected to a new trial for the same cause.

5. Criminal proceedings shall be public, except insofar as may be necessary to protect the interests of justice.

Article 9.   Freedom from Ex Post Facto Laws

No one shall be convicted of any act or omission that did not constitute a criminal offense, under the applicable law, at the time it was committed. A heavier penalty shall not be imposed than the one that was applicable at the time the criminal offense was committed. If subsequent to the commission of the offense the law provides for the imposition of a lighter punishment, the guilty person shall benefit therefrom.

Article 10.   Right to Compensation

Every person has the right to be compensated in accordance with the law in the event he has been sentenced by a final judgment through a miscarriage of justice.

Article 11.   Right to Privacy

1.   Everyone has the right to have his honor respected and his dignity recognized.

2.   No one may be the object of arbitrary or abusive interference with his private life, his family, his home, or his correspondence, or of unlawful attacks on his honor or reputation.

3.   Everyone has the right to the protection of the law against such interference or attacks.

Article 12.   Freedom of Conscience and Religion

1.   Everyone has the right to freedom of conscience and of religion. This right includes freedom to maintain or to change one's religion or beliefs and freedom to profess or disseminate one's religion or beliefs, either individually or together with others, in public or in private.

2.   No one shall be subject to restrictions that might impair his freedom to maintain or to change his religion or beliefs.

3.   Freedom to manifest one's religion and beliefs may be subject only to the limitations prescribed by law that are necessary to protect public safety, order, health, or morals, or the rights or freedoms of others.

4.   Parents or guardians, as the case may be, have the right to provide for the religious and moral education of their children or wards that is in accord with their own convictions.

Article 13.   Freedom of Thought and Expression

1.   Everyone has the right to freedom of thought and expression. This right includes freedom to seek, receive, and impart information and ideas of all kinds, regardless of frontiers, either orally, in writing, in print, in the form of art, or through any other medium of one's choice.

2.   The exercise of the right provided for in the foregoing paragraph shall not be subject to prior censorship but shall be

subject to subsequent imposition of liability, which shall be expressly established by law to the extent necessary to ensure:

    a.   respect for the rights or reputations of others; or

    b.   the protection of national security, public order, or public health or morals.

3.   The right of expression may not be restricted by indirect methods or means, such as the abuse of government or private controls over newsprint, radio broadcasting frequencies, or equipment used in the dissemination of information, or by any other means tending to impede the communication and circulation of ideas and opinions.

4.   Notwithstanding the provisions of paragraph 2 above, public entertainments may be subject by law to prior censorship for the sole purpose of regulating access to them for the moral protection of childhood and adolescence.

5.   Any propaganda for war and any advocacy of national, racial, or religious hatred that constitute incitements to lawless violence or to any other similar illegal action against any person or group of persons on any grounds including those of race, color, religion, language, or national origin shall be considered as offenses punishable by law.

Article 14.　Right of Reply

1.   Anyone injured by inaccurate or offensive statements or ideas disseminated to the public in general by a legally regulated medium of communication has the right to reply or to make a correction using the same communications outlet, under such conditions as the law may establish.

2.   The correction or reply shall not in any case remit other legal liabilities that may have been incurred.

3.   For the effective protection of honor and reputation, every publisher, and every newspaper, motion picture, radio, and television company, shall have a person responsible who is not protected by immunities or special privileges.

Article 15.　Right of Assembly

The right of peaceful assembly, without arms, is recognized. No restrictions may be placed on the exercise of this right other than those imposed in conformity with the law and necessary in a democratic society in the interest of national security, public safety or public order, or to protect public health or morals or the rights or freedoms of others.

Article 16.   Freedom of Association

1.   Everyone has the right to associate freely for ideological, religious, political, economic, labor, social, cultural, sports, or other purposes.

2.   The exercise of this right shall be subject only to such restrictions established by law as may be necessary in a democratic society, in the interest of national security, public safety or public order, or to protect public health or morals or the rights and freedoms of others.

3.   The provisions of this article do not bar the imposition of legal restrictions, including even deprivation of the exercise of the right of association, on members of the armed forces and the police.

Article 17.   Rights of the Family

1.   The family is the natural and fundamental group unit of society and is entitled to protection by society and the state.

2.   The right of men and women of marriageable age to marry and to raise a family shall be recognized, if they meet the conditions required by domestic laws, insofar as such conditions do not affect tthe principle of nondiscrimination established in this Convention.

3.   No marriage shall be entered into without the free and full consent of the intending spouses.

4.   The States Parties shall take appropriate steps to ensure the equality of rights and the adequate balancing of responsibilities of the spouses as to marriage, during marriage, and in the event of its dissolution. In case of dissolution, provision shall be made for the necessary protection of any children solely on the basis of their own best interests.

5.   The law shall recognize equal rights for children born out of wedlock and those born in wedlock.

Article 18.   Right to a Name

Every person has the right to a given name and to the surnames of his parents or that of one of them. The law shall regulate the manner in which this right shall be ensured for all, by the use of assumed names if necessary.

Article 19.   Rights of the Child

Every minor child has the right to the measures of protection required by his condition as a minor on the part of his family, society, and the state.

Article 20. Right to Nationality

1. Every person has the right to a nationality.

2. Every person has the right to the nationality of the state in whose territory he was born if he does not have the right to any other nationality.

3. No one shall be arbitrarily deprived of his nationality or of the right to change it.

Article 21. Right to Property

1. Everyone has the right to the use and enjoyment of his property. The law may subordinate such use and enjoyment to the interest of society.

2. No one shall be deprived of his property except upon payment of just compensation, for reasons of public utility or social interest, and in the cases and according to the forms established by law.

3. Usury and any other form of exploitation of man by man shall be prohibited by law.

Article 22. Freedom of Movement and Residence

1. Every person lawfully in the territory of a State Party has the right to move about in it, and to reside in it subject to the provisions of the law.

2. Every person has the right to leave any country freely, including his own.

3. The exercise of the foregoing rights may be restricted only pursuant to a law to the extent necessary in a democratic society to prevent crime or to protect national security, public safety, public order, public morals, public health, or the rights or freedoms of others.

4. The exercise of the rights recognized in paragraph 1 may also be restricted by law in designated zones for reasons of public interest.

5. No one can be expelled from the territory of the state of which he is a national or be deprived of the right to enter it.

6. An alien lawfully in the territory of a State Party to this Convention may be expelled from it only pursuant to a decision reached in accordance with law.

7. Every person has the right to seek and be granted asylum in a foreign territory, in accordance with the legislation of the state and international conventions, in the event he is being pursued for political offenses or related common crimes.

8. In no case may an alien be deported or returned to a country, regardless of whether or not it is his country of origin,

if in that country his right to life or personal freedom is in danger of being violated because of his race, nationality, religion, social status, or political opinions.

9.   The collective expulsion of aliens is prohibited.

Article 23.   Right to Participate in Government

1.   Every citizen shall enjoy the following rights and opportunities:

   a.   to take part in the conduct of public affairs, directly or through freely chosen representatives;

   b.   to vote and to be elected in genuine periodic elections, which shall be by universal and equal suffrage and by secret ballot that guarantees the free expression of the will of the voters; and

   c.   to have access, under general conditions of equality, to the public service of his country.

2.   The law may regulate the exercise of the rights and opportunities referred to in the preceding paragraph only on the basis of age, nationality, residence, language, education, civil and mental capacity, or sentencing by a competent court in criminal proceedings.

Article 24.   Right to Equal Protection

All persons are equal before the law. Consequently, they are entitled, without discrimination, to equal protection of the law.

Article 25.   Right to Judicial Protection

1.   Everyone has the right to simple and prompt recourse, or any other effective recourse, to a competent court or tribunal for protection against acts that violate his fundamental rights recognized by the constitution or laws of the state concerned or by this Convention, even though such violation may have been committed by persons acting in the course of their official duties.

2.   The States Parties undertake:

   a.   to ensure that any person claiming such remedy shall have his rights determined by the competent authority provided for by the legal system of the state;

   b.   to develop the possibilities of judicial remedy; and

   c.   to ensure that the competent authorities shall enforce such remedies when granted.

CHAPTER III. ECONOMIC, SOCIAL, AND CULTURAL RIGHTS

Article 26. Progressive Development

The States Parties undertake to adopt measures, both internally and through international cooperation, especially those of an economic and technical nature, with a view to achieving progressively, by legislation or other appropriate means, the full realization of the rights implicit in the economic, social, educational, scientific, and cultural standards set forth in the Charter of the Organization of American States as amended by the Protocol of Buenos Aires.

CHAPTER IV. SUSPENSION OF GUARANTEES, INTERPRETATION, AND APPLICATION

Article 27. Suspension of Guarantees

1. In time of war, public danger, or other emergency that threatens the independence or security of a State Party, it may take measures derogating from its obligations under the present Convention to the extent and for the period of time strictly required by the exigencies of the situation, provided that such measures are not inconsistent with its other obligations under international law and do not involve discrimination on the ground of race, color, sex, language, religion, or social origin.

2. The foregoing provision does not authorize any suspension of the following articles: Article 3 (Right to Juridical Personality), Article 4 (Right to Life), Article 5 (Right to Humane Treatment), Article 6 (Freedom from Slavery), Article 9 (Freedom from Ex Post Facto Laws), Article 12 (Freedom of Conscience and Religion), Article 17 (Rights of the Family), Article 18 (Right to a Name), Article 19 (Rights of the Child), Article 20 (Right to Nationality), and Article 23 (Right to Participate in Government), or of the judicial guarantees essential for the protection of such rights.

3. Any State Party availing itself of the right of suspension shall immediately inform the other States Parties, through the Secretary General of the Organization of American States, of the provisions the application of which it has suspended, the reasons that gave rise to the suspension, and the date set for the termination of such suspension.

Article 28. Federal Clause

1. Where a State Party is constituted as a federal state, the national government of such State Party shall implement all the

provisions of the Convention over whose subject matter it exercises legislative and judicial jurisdiction.

2. With respect to the provisions over whose subject matter the constituent units of the federal state have jurisdiction, the national government shall immediately take suitable measures, in accordance with its constitution and its laws, to the end that the competent authorities of the constituent units may adopt appropriate provisions for the fulfillment of this Convention.

3. Whenever two or more States Parties agree to form a federation or other type of association, they shall take care that the resulting federal or other compact contains the provisions necessary for continuing and rendering effective the standards of this Convention in the new state that is organized.

Article 29.   Restrictions Regarding Interpretation

No provision of this Convention shall be interpreted as:

a.   permitting any State Party, group, or person to suppress the enjoyment or exercise of the rights and freedoms recognized in this Convention or to restrict them to a greater extent than is provided for herein;

b.   restricting the enjoyment or exercise of any right or freedom recognized by virtue of the laws of any State Party or by virtue of another convention to which one of the said states is a party;

c.   precluding other rights or guarantees that are inherent in the human personality or derived from representative democracy as a form of government; or

d.   excluding or limiting the effect that the American Declaration of the Rights and Duties of Man and other international acts of the same nature may have.

Article 30.   Scope of Restrictions

The restrictions that, pursuant to this Convention, may be placed on the enjoyment or exercise of the rights or freedoms recognized herein may not be applied except in accordance with laws enacted for reasons of general interest and in accordance with the purpose for which such restrictions have been established.

Article 31.   Recognition of Other Rights

Other rights and freedoms recognized in accordance with the procedures established in Articles 76 and 77 may be included in the system of protection of this Convention.

CHAPTER V. PERSONAL RESPONSIBILITIES

Article 32. Relationship Between Duties and Rights

1. Every person has responsibilities to his family, his community, and mankind.

2. The rights of each person are limited by the rights of others, by the security of all, and by the just demands of the general welfare, in a democratic society.

PART II. MEANS OF PROTECTION

CHAPTER VI. COMPETENT ORGANS

Article 33

The following organs shall have competence with respect to matters relating to the fulfillment of the commitments made by the States Parties to this Convention:

a. the Inter-American Commission on Human Rights, referred to as "The Commission"; and

b. the Inter-American Court of Human Rights, referred to as "The Court."

CHAPTER VII. INTER-AMERICAN COMMISSION ON HUMAN RIGHTS

Section 1. Organization

Article 34

The Inter-American Commission on Human Rights shall be composed of seven members, who shall be persons of high moral character and recognized competence in the field of human rights.

Article 35

The Commission shall represent all the member countries of the Organization of American States.

Article 36

1. The members of the Commission shall be elected in a personal capacity by the General Assembly of the Organization from a list of candidates proposed by the governments of the member states.

2. Each of those governments may propose up to three candidates, who may be nationals of the states proposing them or of any other member state of the Organization of American States. When a slate of three is proposed, at least one of the candidates shall be a national of a state other than the one proposing the slate.

Article 37

1. The members of the Commission shall be elected for a term of four years and may be reelected only once, but the terms of three of the members chosen in the first election shall expire at the end of two years. Immediately following that election the General Assembly shall determine the names of those three members by lot.

2. No two nationals of the same state may be members of the Commission.

Article 38

Vacancies that may occur on the Commission for reasons other than the normal expiration of a term shall be filled by the Permanent Council of the Organization in accordance with the provisions of the Statute of the Commission.

Article 39

The Commission shall prepare its Statute, which it shall submit to the General Assembly for approval. It shall establish its own Regulations.

Article 40

Secretariat services for the Commission shall be furnished by the appropriate specialized unit of the General Secretariat of the Organization. This unit shall be provided with the resources required to accomplish the tasks assigned to it by the Commission.

Section 2. Functions

Article 41

The main function of the Commission shall be to promote respect for and defense of human rights. In the exercise of its mandate, it shall have the following functions and powers:

a. to develop an awareness of human rights among the peoples of America;

b. to make recommendations to the governments of the member states, when it considers such action advisable, for the adoption of progressive measures in favor of human rights within the framework of their domestic law and constitutional provisions as well as appropriate measures to further the observance of those rights;

c. to prepare such studies or reports as it considers advisable in the performance of its duties;

d. to request the governments of the member states to supply it with information on the measures adopted by them in matters of human rights;

e. to respond, through the General Secretariat of the Organization of American States, to inquiries made by the member states on matters related to human rights and, within the limits of its possibilities, to provide those states with the advisory services they request;

f. to take action on petitions and other communications pursuant to its authority under the provisions of Articles 44 through 51 of this Convention; and

g. to submit an annual report to the General Assembly of the Organization of American States.

Article 42

The States Parties shall transmit to the Commission a copy of each of the reports and studies that they submit annually to the Executive Committees of the Inter-American Economic and Social Council and the Inter-American Council for Education, Science, and Culture, in their respective fields, so that the Commission may watch over the promotion of the rights implicit in the economic, social, educational, scientific, and cultural standards set forth in the Charter of the Organization of American States as amended by the Protocol of Buenos Aires.

Article 43

The States Parties undertake to provide the Commission with such information as it may request of them as to the manner in which their domestic law ensures the effective application of any provisions of this Convention.

Section 3. Competence
Article 44

Any person or group of persons, or any nongovernmental entity legally recognized in one or more member states of the Organization, may lodge petitions with the Commission containing denunciations or complaints of violation of this Convention by a State Party.

Article 45

1. Any State Party may, when it deposits its instrument of ratification of or adherence to this Convention, or at any later time, declare that it recognizes the competence of the Commission to receive and examine communications in which a State Party alleges that another State Party has committed a violation of a human right set forth in this Convention.

2. Communications presented by virtue of this article may be admitted and examined only if they are presented by a State Party

that has made a declaration recognizing the aforementioned competence of the Commission. The Commission shall not admit any communication against a State Party that has not made such a declaration.

3. A declaration concerning recognition of competence may be made to be valid for an indefinite time, for a specified period, or for a specific case.

4. Declarations shall be deposited with the General Secretariat of the Organization of American States, which shall transmit copies thereof to the member states of that Organization.

Article 46

1. Admission by the Commission of a petition or communication lodged in accordance with Articles 44 or 45 shall be subject to the following requirements:

a. that the remedies under domestic law have been pursued and exhausted in accordance with generally recognized principles of international law;

b. that the petition or communication is lodged within a period of six months from the date on which the party alleging violation of his rights was notified of the final judgment;

c. that the subject of the petition or communication is not pending in another international proceeding for settlement; and

d. that, in the case of Article 44, the petition contains the name, nationality, profession, domicile, and signature of the person or persons or of the legal representative of the entity lodging the petition.

2. The provisions of paragraphs 1.a and 1.b of this article shall not be applicable when:

a. the domestic legislation of the state concerned does not afford due process of law for the protection of the right or rights that have allegedly been violated;

b. the party alleging violation of his rights has been denied access to the remedies under domestic law or has been prevented from exhausting them; or

c. there has been unwarranted delay in rendering a final judgment under the aforementioned remedies.

Article 47

The Commission shall consider inadmissible any petition or communication submitted under Articles 44 or 45 if:

a. any of the requirements indicated in Article 46 has not been met;

b. the petition or communication does not state facts that tend to establish a violation of the rights guaranteed by this Convention;

c. the statements of the petitioner or of the state indicate that the petition or communication is manifestly groundless or obviously out of order; or

d. the petition or communication is substantially the same as one previously studied by the Commission or by another international organization.

Section 4. Procedure
Article 48

1. When the Commission receives a petition or communication alleging violation of any of the rights protected by this Convention, it shall proceed as follows:

a. If it considers the petition or communication admissible, it shall request information from the government of the state indicated as being responsible for the alleged violations and shall furnish that government a transcript of the pertinent portions of the petition or communication. This information shall be submitted within a reasonable period to be determined by the Commission in accordance with the circumstances of each case.

b. After the information has been received, or after the period established has elapsed and the information has not been received, the Commission shall ascertain whether the grounds for the petition or communication still exist. If they do not, the Commission shall order the record to be closed.

c. The Commission may also declare the petition or communication inadmissible or out of order on the basis of information or evidence subsequently received.

d. If the record has not been closed, the Commission shall, with the knowledge of the parties, examine the matter set forth in the petition or communication in order to verify the facts. If necessary and advisable, the Commission shall carry out an investigation, for the effective conduct of which it shall request, and the states concerned shall furnish to it, all necessary facilities.

e. The Commission may request the states concerned to furnish any pertinent information and, if so requested, shall hear oral statements or receive written statements from the parties concerned.

f. The Commission shall place itself at the disposal of the parties concerned with a view to reaching a friendly settlement of the matter on the basis of respect for the human rights recognized in this Convention.

2.   However, in serious and urgent cases, only the presentation of a petition or communication that fulfills all the formal requirements of admissibility shall be necessary in order for the Commission to conduct an investigation with the prior consent of the state in whose territory a violation has allegedly been committed.

Article 49

If a friendly settlement has been reached in accordance with paragraph 1.f of Article 48, the Commission shall draw up a report, which shall be transmitted to the petitioner and to the States Parties to this Convention, and shall then be communicated to the Secretary General of the Organization of American States for publication. This report shall contain a brief statement of the facts and of the solution reached. If any party in the case so requests, the fullest possible information shall be provided to it.

Article 50

1.   If a settlement is not reached, the Commission shall, within the time limit established by its Statute, draw up a report setting forth the facts and stating its conclusions. If the report, in whole or in part, does not represent the unanimous agreement of the members of the Commission, any member may attach to it a separate opinion. The written and oral statements made by the parties in accordance with paragraph 1.e of Article 48 shall also be attached to the report.

2.   The report shall be transmitted to the states concerned, which shall not be at liberty to publish it.

3.   In transmitting the report, the Committee may make such proposals and recommendations as it sees fit.

Article 51

1.   If, within a period of three months from the date of the transmittal of the report of the Commission to the states concerned, the matter has not either been settled or submitted by the Commission or by the state concerned to the Court and its jurisdiction accepted, the Commission may, by the vote of an absolute majority of its members, set forth its opinion and conclusions concerning the question submitted for its consideration.

2.   Where appropriate, the Commission shall make pertinent recommendation and shall prescribe a period within which the state is to take the measures that are incumbent upon it to remedy the situation examined.

3.   When the prescribed period has expired, the Commission shall decide by the vote of an absolute majority of its members

whether the state has taken adequate measures and whether to publish its report.

CHAPTER VIII.   INTER-AMERICAN COURT OF HUMAN RIGHTS

Section 1.   Organization

Article 52

1.   The Court shall consist of seven judges, nationals of the member states of the Organization, elected in an individual capacity from among jurists of the highest moral authority and of recognized competence in the field of human rights, who possess the qualifications required for the exercise of the highest judicial functions in conformity with the law of the state of which they are nationals or of the state that proposes them as candidates.

2.   No two judges may be nationals of the same state.

Article 53

1.   The judges of the Court shall be elected by secret ballot by an absolute majority vote of the States Parties to the Convention, in the General Assembly of the Organization, from a panel of candidates proposed by those states.

2.   Each of the States Parties may propose up to three candidates, nationals of the state that proposes them or of any other member state of the Organization of American States. When a slate of three is proposed, at least one of the candidates shall be a national of a state other than the one proposing the slate.

Article 54

1.   The judges of the Court shall be elected for a term of six years and may be reelected only once. The term of three of the judges chosen in the first election shall expire at the end of three years. Immediately after the election, the names of the three judges shall be determined by lot in the General Assembly.

2.   A judge elected to replace a judge whose term has not expired shall complete the term of the latter.

3.   The judges shall continue in office until the expiration of their term. However, they shall continue to serve with regard to cases that they have begun to hear and that are still pending, for which purposes they shall not be replaced by the newly elected judges.

Article 55

1.   If a judge is a national of any of the States Parties to a case submitted to the Court, he shall retain his right to hear that case.

2. If one of the judges called upon to hear a case should be a national of one the States Parties to the case, any other State Party in the case may appoint a person of its choice to serve on the Court as an *ad hoc* judge.

3. If among the judges called upon to hear a case none is a national of any of the States Parties to the case, each of the latter may appoint an *ad hoc* judge.

4. An *ad hoc* judge shall possess the qualifications indicated in Article 52.

5. If several States Parties to the Convention should have the same interest in a case, they shall be considered as a single party for purposes of the above provisions. In case of doubt, the Court shall decide.

Article 56

Five judges shall constitute a quorum for the transaction of business by the Court.

Article 57

The Commission shall appear in all cases before the Court.

Article 58

1. The Court shall have its seat at the place determined by the States Parties to the Convention in the General Assembly of the Organization; however, it may convene in the territory of any member state of the Organization of American States when a majority of the Court consider it desirable, and with the prior consent of the state concerned. The seat of the Court may be changed by the States Parties to the Convention in the General Assembly by a two-thirds vote.

2. The Court shall appoint its own Secretary.

3. The Secretary shall have his office at the place where the Court has its seat and shall attend the meetings that the Court may hold away from its seat.

Article 59

The Court shall establish its Secretariat, which shall function under the direction of the Secretary of the Court, in accordance with the administrative standards of the General Secretariat of the Organization in all respect not incompatible with the independence of the Court. The staff of the Court's Secretariat shall be appointed by the Secretary General of the Organization, in consultation with the Secretary of the Court.

Article 60

The Court shall draw up its Statute which it shall submit to the General Assembly for approval. It shall adopt its own Rules of Procedure.

Section 2. *Jurisdiction and Functions*

Article 61

1.   Only the States Parties and the Commission shall have the right to submit a case to the Court.

2.   In order for the Court to hear a case, it is necessary that the procedures set forth in Articles 48 to 50 shall have been completed.

Article 62

1.   A State Party may, upon depositing its instrument of ratification or adherence to this Convention, or at any subsequent time, declare that it recognizes as binding, *ipso facto,* and not requiring special agreement, the jurisdiction of the Court on all matters relating to the interpretation or application of this Convention.

2.   Such declaration may be made unconditionally, on the condition of reciprocity, for a specified period, or for specific cases. It shall be presented to the Secretary General of the Organization, who shall transmit copies thereof to the other member states of the Organization and to the Secretary of the Court.

3.   The jurisdiction of the Court shall comprise all cases concerning the interpretation and application of the provisions of this Convention that are submitted to it, provided that the States Parties to the case recognize or have recognized such jurisdiction, whether by special declaration pursuant to the preceding paragraphs, or by a special agreement.

Article 63

1.   If the Court finds that there has been a violation of a right or freedom protected by this Convention, the Court shall rule that the injured party be ensured the enjoyment of his right or freedom that was violated. It shall also rule, if appropriate, that the consequences of the measure or situation that constituted the breach of such right or freedom be remedied and that fair compensation be paid to the injured party.

2.   In cases of extreme gravity and urgency, and when necessary to avoid irreparable damage to persons, the Court shall adopt such provisional measures as it deems pertinent in matters it has under consideration. With respect to a case not yet submitted to the Court, it may act at the request of the Commission.

Article 64

1. The member states of the Organization may consult the Court regarding the interpretation of this Convention or of other treaties concerning the protection of human rights in the American states. Within their spheres of competence, the organs listed in Chapter X of the Charter of the Organization of American States, as amended by the Protocol of Buenos Aires, may in like manner consult the Court.

2. The Court, at the request of a member state of the Organization, may provide that state with opinions regarding the compatibility of any of its domestic laws with the aforesaid international instruments.

Article 65

To each regular session of the General Assembly of the Organization of American States the Court shall submit, for the Assembly's consideration, a report on its work during the previous year. It shall specify, in particular, the cases in which a state has not complied with its judgments, making any pertinent recommendations.

Section 3. Procedure

Article 66

1. Reasons shall be given for the judgment of the Court.

2. If the judgment does not represent in whole or in part the unanimous opinion of the judges, any judge shall be entitled to have his dissenting or separate opinion attached to the judgment.

Article 67

The judgment of the Court shall be final and not subject to appeal. In case of disagreement as to the meaning or scope of the judgment, the Court shall interpret it at the request of any of the parties, provided the request is made within ninety days from the date of notification of the judgment.

Article 68

1. The States Parties to the Convention undertake to comply with the judgment of the Court in any case to which they are parties.

2. That part of a judgment that stipulates compensatory damages may be executed in the country concerned in accordance with domestic procedure governing the execution of judgments against the state.

Article 69

The parties to the case shall be notified of the judgment of the Court and it shall be transmitted to the States Parties to the Convention.

CHAPTER IX.   COMMON PROVISIONS

Article 70

1.   The judges of the Court and the members of the Commission shall enjoy, from the moment of their election and throughout their term of office, the immunities extended to diplomatic agents in accordance with international law. During the exercise of their official function they shall, in addition, enjoy the diplomatic privileges necessary for the performance of their duties.

2.   At no time shall the judges of the Court or the members of the Commission be held liable for any decisions or opinions issued in the exercise of their functions.

Article 71

The position of judge of the Court or member of the Commission is incompatible with any other activity that might affect the independence or impartiality of such judge or member, as determined in the respective statutes.

Article 72

The judges of the Court and the members of the Commission shall receive emoluments and travel allowances in the form and under the conditions set forth in their statutes, with due regard for the importance and independence of their office. Such emoluments and travel allowances shall be determined in the budget of the Organization of American States, which shall also include the expenses of the Court and its Secretariat. To this end, the Court shall draw up its own budget and submit it for approval to the General Assembly through the General Secretariat. The latter may not introduce any changes in it.

Article 73

The General Assembly may, only at the request of the Commission or the Court, as the case may be, determine sanctions to be applied against members of the Commission or judges of the Court when there are justifiable grounds for such action as set forth in the respective statutes. A vote of a two-thirds majority of the member states of the Organization shall be required for a decision in the case of members of the Commission and, in the case of judges of the Court, a two-thirds majority vote of the States Parties to the Convention shall also be required.

PART III.   GENERAL AND TRANSITORY PROVISIONS

CHAPTER X.   SIGNATURE, RATIFICATION, RESERVATIONS, AMENDMENTS, PROTOCOLS, AND DENUNCIATION

Article 74

1.   This Convention shall be open for signature and ratification by or adherence of any member state of the Organization of American States.

2.   Ratification of or adherence to this Convention shall be made by the deposit of an instrument of ratification or adherence with the General Secretariat of the Organization of American States. As soon as eleven states have deposited their instruments of ratification or adherence, the Convention shall enter into force. With respect to any state that ratifies or adheres thereafter, the Convention shall enter into force on the date of the deposit of its instrument of ratification or adherence.

3.   The Secretary General shall inform all member states of the Organization of the entry into force of the Convention.

Article 75

This Convention shall be subject to reservations only in conformity with the provisions of the Vienna Convention on the Law of Treaties signed on May 23, 1969.

Article 76

1.   Proposals to amend this Convention may be submitted to the General Assembly for the action it deems appropriate by any State Party directly, and by the Commission or the Court through the Secretary General.

2.   Amendments shall enter into force for the states ratifying them on the date when two-thirds of the States Parties to this Convention have deposited their respective instruments of ratification. With respect to the other States Parties, the amendments shall enter into force on the dates on which they deposit their respective instruments of ratification.

Article 77

1.   In accordance with Article 31, any State Party and the Commission may submit proposed protocols to this Convention for consideration by the States Parties at the General Assembly

with a view to gradually including other rights and freedoms within its system of protection.

2. Each protocol shall determine the manner of its entry into force and shall be applied only among the States Parties to it.

Article 78

1. The States Parties may denounce this Convention at the expiration of a five-year period starting from the date of its entry into force and by means of notice given one year in advance. Notice of the denunciation shall be addressed to the Secretary General of the Organization, who shall inform the other States Parties.

2. Such a denunciation shall not have the effect of releasing the State Party concerned from the obligations contained in this Convention with respect to any act that may constitute a violation of those obligations and that has been taken by that state prior to the effective date of denunciation.

CHAPTER XI. TRANSITORY PROVISIONS

Section 1. Inter-American Commission on Human Rights

Article 79

Upon the entry into force of this Convention, the Secretary General shall, in writing, request each member state of the Organization to present, within ninety days, its candidates for membership on the Inter-American Commission on Human Rights. The Secretary General shall prepare a list in alphabetical order of the candidates presented, and transmit it to the member states of the Organization at least thirty days prior to the next session of the General Assembly.

Article 80

The members of the Commission shall be elected by secret ballot of the General Assembly from the list of candidates referred to in Article 79. The candidates who obtain the largest number of votes and an absolute majority of the votes of the representatives of the member states shall be declared elected. Should it become necessary to have several ballots in order to elect all the members of the Commission, the candidates who receive the smallest number of votes shall be eliminated successively, in the manner determined by the General Assembly.

Section 2.   Inter-American Court
of Human Rights
Article 81

Upon the entry into force of this Convention, the Secretary General shall, in writing, request each State Party to present, within ninety days, its candidates for membership on the Inter-American Court of Human Rights. The Secretary General shall prepare a list in alphabetical order of the candidates presented and transmit it to the States Parties at least thirty days prior to the next session of the General Assembly.

Article 82

The judges of the Court shall be elected from the list of candidates referred to in Article 81, by secret ballot of the States Parties to the Convention in the General Assembly. The candidates who obtain the largest number of votes and an absolute majority of the votes of the representatives of the States Parties shall be declared elected. Should it become necessary to have several ballots in order to elect all the judges of the Court, the candidates who receive the smallest number of votes shall be eliminated successively, in the manner determined by the States Parties.

PART IV.   DOCUMENTS OF HISTORICAL IMPORTANCE

1.   TREATY OF PARIS, 30 MARCH 1856

Translation from 2 E. Hertslet, The Map of Europe by Treaty 1250, at 1254-55 (London, 1875).

Article VII.   Her Majesty the Queen of the United Kingdom of Great Britain and Ireland, His Majesty the Emperor of Austria, His Majesty the Emperor of the French, His Majesty the King of Prussia, His Majesty the Emperor of All the Russias, and His Majesty the King of Sardinia, declare the Sublime Porte admitted to participate in the advantages of the Public Law and System (*Concert*) of Europe. Their Majesties engage, each on his part, to respect the Independence and the Territorial Integrity of the Ottoman Empire; Guarantee in common the strict observance of that engagement; and will, in consequence, consider any act tending to its violation as a question of general interest.

Article VIII.   If there should arise between the Sublime Porte and one or more of the other Signing Powers, any misunderstanding which might endanger the maintenance of their relations, the Sublime Porte, and each of such Powers, before having recourse to the use of force, shall afford the other Contracting Parties the opportunity of preventing such an extremity by means of their Mediation.

Article IX.   His Imperial Majesty the Sultan having, in his constant solicitude for the welfare of his subjects, issued a Firman which, while ameliorating their condition without distinction of Religion or of Race, records his generous intentions towards the Christian population of his Empire, and wishing to give a further proof of his sentiments in that respect, has resolved to communicate to the Contracting Parties the said Firman, emanating spontaneously from his Sovereign will.

The Contracting Powers recognise the high value of this communication. It is clearly understood that it cannot, in any case, give to the said Powers the right to interfere, either collectively or separately, in the relations of His Majesty the Sultan with his subjects, nor in the Internal Administration of his Empire.

2.   TREATY OF BERLIN, 13 JULY 1878

Translation from 4 E. Hertslet, The Map of Europe by Treaty 2759, at 2790-91 (London, 1891).

Article XLIV.   In Roumania the difference of religious creeds and confessions shall not be alleged against any person as a

235

ground for exclusion or incapacity in matters relating to the enjoyment of civil and political rights, admission to public employments, functions, and honours, or the exercise of the various professions and industries in any locality whatsoever.

The freedom and outward exercise of all forms of worship shall be assured to all persons belonging to the Roumanian State, as well as to foreigners, and no hindrance shall be offered either to the hierarchical organization of the different communions, or to their relations with their spiritual chiefs.

The subjects and citizens of all the Powers, traders or others, shall be treated in Roumania, without distinction of creed, on a footing of perfect equality.

[Similar provisions, with the exception of the last paragraph, were included in this Treaty with respect to Bulgaria (Art. V), Montenegro (Art. XXVII) and Serbia (Art. XXXV).]

3. COVENANT OF THE LEAGUE OF NATIONS

Part I of the Treaty of Peace, signed at Versailles, 28 June 1919. Text from 3 Malloy-Redmond, Treaties . . . between the United States and Other Powers, 1910-1923, p. 3329, at 3342-44 (Washington, D.C., 1923).

Article 22

To those colonies and territories which as a consequence of the late war have ceased to be under the sovereignty of the States which formerly governed them and which are inhabited by peoples not yet able to stand by themselves under the strenuous conditions of the modern world, there should be applied the principle that the well-being and development of such peoples form a sacred trust of civilisation and that securities for the performance of this trust should be embodied in this Covenant.

The best method of giving practical effect to this principle is that the tutelage of such peoples should be entrusted to advanced nations who by reason of their resources, their experience or their geographical position can best undertake this responsibility, and who are willing to accept it, and that this tutelage should be exercised by them as Mandatories on behalf of the League.

The character of the mandate must differ according to the stage of the development of the people, the geographical situation of the territory, its economic conditions, and other similar circumstances.

Certain communities formerly belonging to the Turkish Empire have reached a stage of development where their existence as independent nations can be provisionally recognised subject to the rendering of administrative advice and assistance by a Mandatory until such time as they are able to stand alone. The wishes of these communities must be a principal consideration in the selection of the Mandatory.

Other peoples, especially those of Central Africa, are at such a stage that the Mandatory must be responsible for the administration of the territory under conditions which will guarantee freedom of conscience and religion, subject only to the maintenance of public order and morals, the prohibition of abuses such as the slave trade, the arms traffic, and the liquor traffic, and the prevention of the establishment of fortifications or military and naval bases and of military training of the natives for other than police purposes and the defence of territory, and will also secure equal opportunities for the trade and commerce of other Members of the League.

There are territories, such as South-West Africa and certain of the South Pacific Islands, which, owing to the sparseness of their population, or their small size, or their remoteness from the centres of civilisation, or their geographical contiguity to the territory of the Mandatory, and other circumstances, can be best administered under the laws of the Mandatory as integral portions of its territory, subject to the safeguards above mentioned in the interests of the indigenous population.

In every case of mandate, the Mandatory shall render to the Council an annual report in reference to the territory committed to its charge.

The degree of authority, control, or administration to be exercised by the Mandatory shall, if not previously agreed upon by the Members of the League, be explicitly defined in each case by the Council.

A permanent Commission shall be constituted to receive and examine the annual reports of the Mandatories and to advise the Council on all matters relating to the observance of the mandates.

Article 23

Subject to and in accordance with the provisions of international conventions existing or hereafter to be agreed upon, the Members of the League:

(a) will endeavour to secure and maintain fair and humane conditions of labour for men, women, and children, both in their own countries and in all countries to which their commercial and industrial relations extend, and for that purpose will establish and maintain the necessary international organisations;

(b) undertake to secure just treatment of the native inhabitants of territories under their control;

(c) will entrust the League with the general supervision over the execution of agreements with regard to the traffic in women and children, and the traffic in opium and other dangerous drugs;

(d)   will entrust the League with the general supervision of the trade in arms and ammunition with the countries in which the control of this traffic is necessary in the common interest;

(e)   will make provision to secure and maintain freedom of communications and of transit and equitable treatment for the commerce of all Members of the League. In this connection, the special necessities of the regions devastated during the war of 1914-1918 shall be borne in mind;

(f)   will endeavour to take steps in matters of international concern for the prevention and control of disease.

4.   TREATY BETWEEN THE ALLIED AND ASSOCIATED POWERS AND POLAND CONCERNING PROTECTION OF MINORITIES

Signed at Versailles, 28 June 1919. LN, Protection of Linguistic, Racial and Religious Minorities by the League of Nations 41-45 (LN Publs. 1927.I.B.2).

Whereas, The Allied and Associated Powers have by the success of their arms restored to the Polish nation the independence of which it had been unjustly deprived; and

Whereas, By the proclamation of March 30, 1917, the Government of Russia assented to the re-establishment of an independent Polish State; and

Whereas, The Polish State, which now, in fact, exercises sovereignty over those portions of the former Russian Empire which are inhabited by a majority of Poles, has already been recognized as a sovereign and independent State by the Principal Allied and Associated Powers; and

Whereas, Under the Treaty of Peace concluded with Germany by the Allied and Associated Powers, a Treaty of which Poland is a signatory, certain portions of the former German Empire will be incorporated in the territory of Poland; and

Whereas, Under the terms of the said Treaty of Peace, the boundaries of Poland not already laid down are to be subsequently determined by the Principal Allied and Associated Powers;

The United States of America, the British Empire, France, Italy and Japan, on the one hand, confirming their recognition of the Polish State, constituted within the said limits as a sovereign and independent member of the Family of Nations, and being anxious to ensure the execution of the provisions of Article 93 of the said Treaty of Peace with Germany;

Poland, on the other hand, desiring to conform her institutions to the principles of liberty and justice, and to give a sure guarantee to the inhabitants of the territory over which she has assumed sovereignty;

For this purpose the High Contracting Parties . . . have agreed as follows:

CHAPTER I

Article 1

Poland undertakes that the stipulations contained in Articles 2 to 8 of this Chapter shall be recognized as fundamental laws, and that no law, regulation or official action shall conflict or interfere with these stipulations, nor shall any law, regulation or official action prevail over them.

Article 2

Poland undertakes to assure full and complete protection of life and liberty to all inhabitants of Poland without distinction of birth, nationality, language, race or religion.

All inhabitants of Poland shall be entitled to the free exercise, whether public or private, of any creed, religion or belief, whose practices are not inconsistent with public order or public morals.

Article 3

Poland admits and declares to be Polish nationals *ipso facto* and without the requirement of any formality, German, Austrian, Hungarian or Russian nationals habitually resident at the date of the coming into force of the present Treaty in territory which is or may be recognized as forming part of Poland, but subject to any provisions in the Treaties of Peace with Germany or Austria respectively relating to persons who became resident in such territory after a specified date.

Nevertheless, the persons referred to above who are over eighteen years of age will be entitled under the conditions contained in the said Treaties to opt for any other nationality which may be open to them. Option by a husband will cover his wife and option by parents will cover their children under eighteen years of age.

Persons who have exercised the above right to opt must, except where it is otherwise provided in the Treaty of Peace with Germany, transfer within the succeeding twelve months their place of residence to the State for which they have opted. They will be entitled to retain their immovable property in Polish territory. They may carry with them their movable property of every description. No export duties may be imposed upon them in connexion with the removal of such property.

Article 4

Poland admits and declares to be Polish nationals *ipso facto* and without the requirement of any formality, persons of German, Austrian, Hungarian or Russian nationality who were born in the said territory of parents habitually resident there, even if at the date of the coming into force of the present Treaty they are not themselves habitually resident there.

Nevertheless, within two years after the coming into force of the present Treaty, these persons may make a declaration before the competent Polish authorities in the country in which they are resident, stating that they abandon Polish nationality, and they will then cease to be considered as Polish nationals. In this connexion a declaration by a husband will cover his wife, and a declaration by parents will cover their children under eighteen years of age.

Article 5

Poland undertakes to put no hindrance in the way of the exercise of the right which the persons concerned have, under the Treaties concluded or to be concluded by the Allied and Associated Powers with Germany, Austria, Hungary or Russia, to choose whether or not they will acquire Polish nationality.

Article 6

All persons born in Polish territory who are not born nationals of another State shall *ipso facto* become Polish nationals.

Article 7

All Polish nationals shall be equal before the law and shall enjoy the same civil and political rights without distinction as to race, language or religion.

Differences of religion, creed or confession shall not prejudice any Polish national in matters relating to the enjoyment of civil or political rights, as for instance admission to public employments, functions and honours, or the exercise of professions and industries.

No restriction shall be imposed on the free use by any Polish national of any language in private intercourse, in commerce, in religion, in the press or in publications of any kind, or at public meetings.

Notwithstanding any establishment by the Polish Government of an official language, adequate facilities shall be given to Polish nationals of non-Polish speech for the use of their language, either orally or in writing, before the courts.

Article 8

Polish nationals who belong to racial, religious or linguistic minorities shall enjoy the same treatment and security in law and in fact as the other Polish nationals. In particular they shall have an equal right to establish, manage and control at their own expense charitable, religious and social institutions, schools and other educational establishments, with the right to use their own language and to exercise their religion freely therein.

Article 9

Poland will provide in the public educational system in towns and districts in which a considerable proportion of Polish nationals of other than Polish speech are resident adequate facilities for ensuring that in the primary schools the instruction shall be given to the children of such Polish nationals through the medium of their own language. This provision shall not prevent the Polish Government from making the teaching of the Polish language obligatory in the said schools.

In towns and districts where there is a considerable proportion of Polish nationals belonging to racial, religious or linguistic minorities, these minorities shall be assured an equitable share in the enjoyment and application of the sums which may be provided out of public funds under the State, municipal or other budget, for educational, religious or charitable purposes.

The provisions of this Article shall apply to Polish citizens of German speech only in that part of Poland which was German territory on August 1st, 1914.

Article 10

Educational Committees appointed locally by the Jewish communities of Poland will, subject to the general control of the State, provide for the distribution of the proportional share of public funds allocated to Jewish schools in accordance with Article 9, and for the organization and management of these schools.

The provisions of Article 9 concerning the use of languages in schools shall apply to these schools.

Article 11

Jews shall not be compelled to perform any act which constitutes a violation of their Sabbath, nor shall they be placed under any disability by reason of their refusal to attend courts of law or to perform any legal business on their Sabbath. This provision however shall not exempt Jews from such obligations as shall be imposed upon all other Polish citizens for the necessary purposes of military service, national defence, or the preservation of public order.

Poland declares her intention to refrain from ordering or permitting elections, whether general or local, to be held on a Saturday, nor will registration for electoral or other purposes be compelled to be performed on a Saturday.

Article 12

Poland agrees that the stipulations in the foregoing Articles, so far as they affect persons belonging to racial, religious or linguistic minorities, constitute obligations of international concern and shall be placed under the guarantee of the League of Nations. They shall not be modified without the assent of a majority of the Council of the League of Nations. The United States, the British Empire, France, Italy and Japan hereby agree not to withhold their assent from any modification in these Articles which is in due form assented to by a majority of the Council of the League of Nations.

Poland agrees that any Member of the Council of the League of Nations shall have the right to bring to the attention of the Council any infraction, or any danger of infraction, or any of these obligations, and that the Council may thereupon take such action and give such direction as it may deem proper and effective in the circumstances.

Poland further agrees that any difference of opinion as to questions of law or fact arising out of these Articles between the Polish Government and any one of the Principal Allied and Associated Powers or any other Power, a Member of the Council of the League of Nations, shall be held to be a dispute of an international character under Article 14 of the Covenant of the League of Nations. The Polish Government hereby consents that any such dispute shall, if the other party thereto demands, be referred to the Permanent Court of International Justice. The decision of the Permanent Court shall be final and shall have the same force and effect as an award under Article 13 of the Covenant.

5. MANDATE FOR SOUTH-WEST AFRICA

Approved by the Council of the League of Nations, 17 December 1920. Text from UN, Terms of League of Nations Mandates, UN Doc. A/70, No. 10 (1946). (This volume contains also the texts of the other Mandates.)

THE COUNCIL OF THE LEAGUE OF NATIONS:

Whereas by Article 119 of the Treaty of Peace with Germany signed at Versailles on June 28th, 1919, Germany renounced in favour of the Principal Allied and Associated Powers all her rights over her oversea possessions, including therein German South-West Africa; and

Whereas the Principal Allied and Associated Powers agreed that, in accordance with Article 22, Part I (Covenant of the League of Nations) of the said Treaty, a Mandate should be conferred upon His Britannic Majesty to be exercised on his behalf by the Government of the Union of South Africa to administer the territory aforementioned, and have proposed that the Mandate should be formulated in the following terms; and

Whereas His Britannic Majesty, for and on behalf of the Government of the Union of South Africa, has agreed to accept the Mandate in respect of the said territory and has undertaken to exercise it on behalf of the League of Nations in accordance with the following provisions; and

Whereas by the aforementioned Article 22, paragraph 8, it is provided that the degree of authority, control or administration to be exercised by the Mandatory not having been previously agreed upon by the Members of the League, shall be explicitly defined by the Council of the League of Nations:

Confirming the said Mandate, defines its terms as follows:—

Article 1

The territory over which a Mandate is conferred upon His Britannic Majesty for and on behalf of the Government of the Union of South Africa (hereinafter called the Mandatory) comprises the territory which formerly constituted the German Protectorate of South-West Africa.

Article 2

The Mandatory shall have full power of administration and legislation over the territory subject to the present Mandate as an integral portion of the Union of South Africa, and may apply the laws of the Union of South Africa to the territory, subject to such local modifications as circumstances may require.

The Mandatory shall promote to the utmost the material and moral well-being and the social progress of the inhabitants of the territory subject to the present Mandate.

Article 3

The Mandatory shall see that the slave trade is prohibited, and that no forced labour is permitted, except for essential public works and services, and then only for adequate remuneration.

The Mandatory shall also see that the traffic in arms and ammunition is controlled in accordance with principles analogous to those laid down in the Convention relating to the control of the arms traffic, signed on September 10th, 1919, or in any convention amending the same.

The supply of intoxicating spirits and beverages to the natives shall be prohibited.

Article 4

The military training of the natives, otherwise than for purposes of internal police and the local defence of the territory, shall be prohibited. Furthermore, no military or naval bases shall be established or fortifications erected in the territory.

Article 5

Subject to the provisions of any local law for the maintenance of public order and public morals, the Mandatory shall ensure in the territory freedom of conscience and the free exercise of all forms of worship, and shall allow all missionaries, nationals of any State Member of the League of Nations, to enter into, travel and reside in the territory for the purpose of prosecuting their calling.

Article 6

The Mandatory shall make to the Council of the League of Nations an annual report to the satisfaction of the Council, containing full information with regard to the territory, and indicating the measures taken to carry out the obligations assumed under Articles 2, 3, 4 and 5.

Article 7

The consent of the Council of the League of Nations is required for any modification of the terms of the present Mandate.

The Mandatory agrees that, if any dispute whatever should arise between the Mandatory and another Member of the League of Nations relating to the interpretation or the application of the provisions of the Mandate, such dispute, if it cannot be settled by negotiation, shall be submitted to the Permanent Court of International Justice provided for by Article 14 of the Covenant of the League of Nations.

The present Declaration shall be deposited in the archives of the League of Nations. Certified copies shall be forwarded by the Secretary-General of the League of Nations to all Powers Signatories of the Treaty of Peace with Germany.